"In *The Majesty of the Law,* Justice Sandra Day O'Connor has blended personal reflections with key professional insights to give us a richly textured account of the fascinating history, current status, and hopeful future of the rule of law. The fact that the author is destined to take her place among the most influential Justices to serve on the modern U.S. Supreme Court makes this important book all the more significant."

—JAMES F. SIMON, Martin Professor of Law at New York School and author of *What Kind of Nation: Thomas Jefferson, John Marshall, and the Epic Struggle to Create a United States*

SANDRA DAY O'CONNOR was born in El Paso, Texas, raised on a ranch on the Arizona–New Mexico border, attended college and law school at Stanford University, and began her public service in Phoenix, Arizona. She has been married to John O'Connor since 1952, and they have three sons. Nominated by President Reagan as Associate Justice of the Supreme Court of the United States, she took the oath of office on September 25, 1981, the first woman to do so.

CRAIG JOYCE is a Law Foundation Professor and codirector of the Institute for Intellectual Property and Information Law at the University of Houston Law Center.

Author proceeds from the sale of this book will be received by the Arizona Community Foundation.

THE MAJESTY OF THE LAW

RANDOM HOUSE TRADE PAPERBACKS | NEW YORK

The MAJESTY
of the LAW

Reflections of a Supreme Court Justice

SANDRA DAY O'CONNOR

EDITED BY CRAIG JOYCE

2004 Random House Trade Paperback Edition

COPYRIGHT © 2003 BY ARIZONA COMMUNITY FOUNDATION

This work was originally published in hardcover by Random House,
an imprint of The Random House Publishing Group, a division
of Random House, Inc., in 2003.

A leatherbound, signed first edition of this book has been published by
The Easton Press.

LIBRARY OF CONGRESS CATALOGING-IN-PUBLICATION DATA

O'Connor, Sandra Day
The majesty of the law: reflections of a Supreme Court Justice / Sandra Day
O'Connor; edited by Craig Joyce
p. cm.
Includes bibliographical references. .
ISBN 0-8129-6747-x
1. United States. Supreme Court. 2. Judges—United States. 3. Rule of Law—
United States. 4. O'Connor, Sandra Day I. Joyce, Craig. II. Title.

KF8742 .O274 2003   347.73'26—dc21   2002068210

Random House website address: www.atrandom.com

Printed in the United States of America

8 9 7

Book design by Barbara M. Bachman

This book is dedicated

to my law clerks—past, present, and future

Preface

When my husband John and I packed up and moved from Arizona to Washington, D.C., in 1981 to begin my service on the nation's Court, we looked forward to the many new experiences—both professional and personal—we were sure to have: enjoying new and wonderful friends; meeting with Presidents, Vice Presidents, cabinet members, ambassadors, and other Justices and judges from around the world; travel to each of the fifty states and sometimes other countries for speeches or meetings; and, most important, I looked forward to the privilege of applying myself to work worth doing, addressing the toughest legal issues in our nation, helping shape the development and explanation of the principles of federal law required to resolve these issues.

I felt molded in large part by my life in the Southwest, where I had spent my earliest days on a cattle ranch in a dry and isolated part of the Arizona desert. My favorite author, Wallace Stegner, put it best when he said, "There is something about living in big empty space, where people are few and distant, under a great sky that is alternately serene and furious, exposed to sun from four in the morning till nine at night, and to a wind that never seems to rest—there is something about exposure to that big country that not only tells an individual how small he is, but steadily tells him *who* he is."[1]

This book is an attempt to speak about my exposure not only to the Arizona desert and sun but to the rest of our country as well—exposure to the richness of its history, to the Supreme Court and to some of its members, and to some of the legal issues I have confronted along the way.

When the Supreme Court sat on the bench again the first Monday of October 2001, it had its full complement of nine members—one appointed by President Ford (Justice John Paul Stevens), four by President Reagan (Chief Justice Rehnquist, myself, Justices Antonin Scalia and Anthony Kennedy), two by President Bush (Justices David Souter and Clarence Thomas), and two by President Clinton (Justices Ruth Bader Ginsburg and Stephen Breyer). The process of nominating a new Justice tends to receive a good deal of attention. In more than two hundred years, the Court has had only 108 Justices, which comes to about one appointment every two years. An appointment to the Court is, therefore, in terms of frequency, about half as special as a nomination to the presidency—and involves infinitely less public participation and releasing of balloons. Nonetheless, a Court appointment (which requires both nomination by the President and confirmation by the Senate) is an occasion for public interest, as we have been reminded graphically in the past twenty years.

The person making the nomination—the President—doubtless pays special attention to these appointments. From the President's point of view, I suppose it's a little like trying to rear children. The President only gets to control the process for a brief period—in choosing a particular nominee—and then the Justice, like an eighteen-year-old, is free to ignore the President's views. And Justices are usually walking around in their judicial chambers long after the President who appointed them has departed the Oval Office. Parenting and nominating Justices have both been common activities among Presidents: all of our Presidents except seven had children, and all except three—Harrison, Taylor, and Carter—nominated at least one Supreme Court Justice.[2] Like fathers in an earlier day, the President makes the proposal and escorts the new Justice down the aisle in the marriage between the Justice and the Court, which, barring impeachment, lasts until death does them part.

As I suspect has been the case with most Justices, my nomination

East courtroom frieze (Adolph Weinman, 1932–1934) in the Supreme Court building, titled *The Majesty of the Law and the Power of the Government.*

King John of England (1166–1216), holding the Magna Carta, in the north frieze of the Supreme Court courtroom (Adolph Weinman, 1932–1934).

to the Court was a great surprise to the nation but an even greater surprise to me. My former colleague Justice Lewis Powell once said that being appointed to the Court was a little like being struck by lightning in both the suddenness and the improbability of the event.[3] I certainly never expected to be on the Court. Rather, I looked forward to continuing my career as a state court judge, having served happily as a trial judge and then, with equal contentment, on the Arizona Court of Appeals, for whose members I had deep affection and great professional respect. I had anticipated that I would live the balance of my life in our adobe house in the desert, where John and I had many friends and a pleasant way of life, and where we expected our sons to settle.

My situation changed dramatically on June 25, 1981, when then–Attorney General William French Smith called my home and said he wanted to talk to me about the Potter Stewart vacancy on the Supreme Court. The metaphorical lightning bolt suddenly seemed as if it might head in my direction, and I was about as astonished, though slightly less frightened, as if I had seen a real bolt of lightning making its way straight for me.

The attorney general asked me to come to Washington to visit with him, with some of President Reagan's staff and close advisors, and with the President himself. I did so, and on July 6, twelve days after Attorney General Smith first phoned me, the President called to ask if he could announce his intention to nominate me to the Court. I said I would be honored if he did.

From my point of view, the nomination was traditional in at least some ways. Like many nominees, I went to Capitol Hill to pay my respects to the appropriate legislators. And as I imagine is the case for all nominees, I lay in bed the night before the confirmation hearings worrying about how I would be treated and how well I would be able to respond to the questions.

After sitting in the witness chair on national television answering endless questions about the Constitution, various cases, and my personal feelings on some of life's great issues, I began to think that the hearings would never end. Fortunately, however, Nancy Thurmond was giving a tea for me at four o'clock on the third day of the hearings.

Mr. Thurmond, otherwise known as Senator Strom Thurmond, was the chairman of the Judiciary Committee, and so, fortunately, he made sure that I got to his wife's tea on time.

I was sworn in on Friday, September 25, 1981. At the President's request, John and I rode with him and Mrs. Reagan from the White House to the Supreme Court. While I waited to take the oath of my new office, I was seated in the chair that John Marshall had once used. After my voice echoed the Chief Justice's administration of the oath, I was seated at the end of the bench in our beautiful courtroom, and I looked down at my parents, my husband, and our three children. I will never forget that moment.

Oscar Wilde said that the only thing worse than being talked about was not being talked about.[4] I will readily confess, however, that my first years on the Supreme Court sometimes made me yearn for obscurity. The press constantly accompanied me in huge flocks; everywhere that Sandra went, the press was sure to go.

With some exceptions, things have quieted down since. But amusing stories do still result from my former media exposure. John witnesses some of the incidents that I don't see and laughingly relates them to me. After being in Washington a few years, we went to a restaurant for dinner with one of my law clerks. On our way out, John heard someone say about me, "It doesn't look like her, but it's her." Others have asked me if I knew how much I looked like Sandra O'Connor. Some say, "Don't I know you?" And a few people, when they hear that Justice O'Connor is present, walk over to shake John's hand and tell him how proud they are to meet a Justice.

The appointment of a woman to the Supreme Court of the United States opened many doors to young women all across the country. The following letter that I received shortly after I was nominated sums up how a great many women in this country reacted to President Reagan's decision:

> I cannot begin to describe with what delight I viewed the surprising headlines in Chicago's newspapers the day of your nomination. I actually stood there with my mouth hanging

open and an idiotic grin on my face, feeling overwhelmingly euphoric and proud.

What [it] affirm[s] to this 27-year-old female [is] that determination, judiciousness, skill and professionalism are valued and rewarded in our society, that females certainly do possess these qualities, that people will find it increasingly difficult to deny and discourage these in females, and that there is absolutely no excuse not to get everything I want in life.

Some women even gave me advice about how to deal with my brethren. One wrote: "I am so proud of you as a woman. The old 'Supreme Court' will never be the same with a lady among those men. That should wake them up a little. Don't let them push you around."

While almost all of the mail was extremely upbeat, there were a few exceptions.

MRS. JOHN O'CONNOR
C/O THE WHITE HOUSE
WASHINGTON, D.C. 20500

Dear Mrs. O'Connor:

I am disgusted and disappointed that President Reagan has nominated a woman to the Supreme Court. A female justice, engaging in routine matters, would find herself asserting issues and arguing contentions, activities which more accurately become the Marxist-related feminists rather than a wife and a mother who respects the psychological components of a family. . . .

In view of these matters, I hope that you turn down President Reagan's nomination.

cc: President Ronald Reagan

I received a postcard addressed as follows:

Woman
Judge Elect O'Connor
c/o White House
Washington, D.C.

Back to your kitchen and home female! This is a job for a man
and only he can make the rough decisions. Take care of your
grandchildren and husband.

Senior Citizen

Hundreds of men have spoken to me throughout every part of this
country, in airports and all sorts of public places, saying things like "I
think it is absolutely wonderful that there's a woman on the Court. It's
about time. I'm happy for you, I'm happy for women, but most of all
I'm happy for the country."

Thank goodness for men. I am indebted to two of them for my appointment: the President and Potter Stewart, about whom the following little poem was written:

A toast to Potter Stewart,
   His chivalry can't be beat;
The first Supreme Court Justice
   To give a lady his seat.

I am still amazed that I am that lady.

One result of becoming a Supreme Court Justice is the steady and
frequent arrival in the mail of invitations to attend and speak at special
events across the country. They come from universities, colleges, and
high schools, from state and local bar associations, from women's
groups, religious organizations, and civic organizations, and from
fund-raisers of every kind and description. The last are easily declined
because federal law prohibits federal judges from speaking at fund-
raising events even for worthy causes. Some invitations are hard to
refuse because they come from my alma mater, or from organizations

that have been a part of my life or the lives of one of my children or grandchildren, or from a close friend.

I decided that one way I could select which invitations to accept was to speak at least once in each of our fifty states. By my nineteenth year on the Court, I had, indeed, spoken in each state at least once.

But that method of choosing still left open the question of what topic to address. Most audiences would be delighted to hear details of how the Court reached a consensus on some hot-button issue, or gossip about the Court or its members. But those topics are, of course, off limits.

Above the bench in the courtroom of the Supreme Court is a sculpted marble panel. In the center of this work is an allegorical figure depicting the Majesty of the Law. My seat in the courtroom is almost directly below this image. The panel itself suggests why we revere the Majesty of the Law. It is an essential safeguard of the liberties and rights of the people. It allows for the defense of human rights and the protection of innocence. It embodies the hope that impartial judges will impart wisdom and fairness when they decide the cases that come before them. In thinking about this book, I found myself drawn to the ideas represented by the panel above me. In the pages that follow, I explore themes such as the history of the Constitution, of the Court, and of some former members of the Court, of the expansion of roles for women, and of the Rule of Law worldwide. My own education was not specialized in constitutional or legal history, and the opportunity to learn more in these areas was welcome. In this effort, I was joined and assisted greatly by my law clerks, to whom this book is dedicated.

This book, then, is the result of more than twenty years of thinking about and speaking about some of the major themes in our national history and the principal challenges facing our world today. With the breakup of the Soviet Union and the development of many new nation-states around the world, and with the concerns we all have following the destruction at the World Trade Center on September 11, 2001, the articulation and consideration of our own history and our basic constitutional structure appear more important than ever before. My hope is that the historical themes explored in this book, and the reflections expressed here, will help the reader better understand our own system, and also why and how the Rule of Law offers the world its best hope for the future.

—*Sandra Day O'Connor*
June 2002

CONTENTS

PART ONE

———

Life on the Court

Despite all that is written about the nation's Court and all the television coverage of the Justices' speeches and public appearances, day-to-day life at the Court is something of a curiosity to the public. Each Justice is asked frequently what she or he does each day, how we work together with other members of the Court, and what it was like to be nominated and confirmed. In Part One I try to answer these questions.

The daily activities of the Court are not as well known as those of the President or of Congress. Some say that the Court operates behind closed doors, and thus out of public view. Most of our daily work does, in fact, occur in our chambers. But the fruits of that work—our decisions—are in writing and fully available to the public and the media to read, discuss, and critique.

Indeed, in that sense the Court is perhaps the most open of the three branches of government. We explain the reasons for our decisions in detail. If our opinion is not unanimous, the dissenting and concurring Justices likewise explain their views. All these explanations are distributed in print and on the Internet for the world to see. No such justification is routinely given for decisions of the executive branch or the legislative branch. The fact that the Court enforces on itself an obligation to explain what we do is one reason to have some confidence in our labors.

Still, the public interest in *how* we do our work remains. Here is one insider's look at "life on the Court."

CHAPTER ONE

What's It Like?

———

WHAT IS IT LIKE WORKING AT THE SUPREME COURT?
Because I never dreamed that I would end up where I am, I had no preconceived ideas about the job upon arriving for work the first day. I had not been admitted to practice before the Court. The first argument I ever witnessed in the Supreme Court was one that I considered as a member of the Court. My guess is that such experiences were not uncommon for new Justices, at least until more recent years.

All I knew was that the job would be a tremendous undertaking. I had no specific ideas about the mechanics of being a Justice, however, or what the decision-making process on the Court was really like. I hoped that I had the basic ability and could develop the skills not only to do the job but to do it well in order that not only women but most citizens would think that the President had made a good choice.

There is one custom we have on the Court that was a pleasant surprise to me and that I treasure. Each day when there is oral argument, just before we go out on the bench, and each day before we confer, every Justice shakes the hand of every other Justice. To an outsider, this may seem baroque and unnecessary, but you must realize we are a very small group. We see and interact with one another often, and we all know we will continue to do so for the rest of our professional lives. It is important that we *get* along together so we can *go* along together.

The one-page memo and the color-coded distribution sheet have yet to reach the Supreme Court. Indeed, the Court is a more reliable backstop for the health of the paper industry than any protectionist leg-

Chief Justice Warren Burger administers the Constitutional Oath of Office to Justice Sandra Day O'Connor as her husband, John, holds the Bibles, at the Supreme Court building, September 25, 1981.

Below: President Ronald Reagan, Chief Justice Warren Burger, and Justice designate Sandra Day O'Connor at the White House, September 22, 1981.

islation Congress might pass. A Justice is by protocol allowed to make a grocery list without making eight copies to distribute around the Court, but pretty much everything else is done not only on paper but with copies for every other Justice to read as well.

Petitions asking the Court to grant review of a case come to us throughout the year from both the federal and the state court systems. And they come in significant numbers. We now receive more than seven thousand applications a year. Many call but few are chosen; the Court accepts for full review with briefing and oral argument no more than one hundred or so cases for each year's term. In addition, the Court summarily decides up to another hundred or so cases without oral argument and full briefing. In making this drastic culling, the Court has relatively few hard-and-fast rules to guide or restrict its decisions.

We follow an unwritten policy that it takes the agreement of at least four Justices to accept a case. With each petition we consider the importance of the issue, how likely it is to recur in various courts around the country, and the extent to which other courts considering the issue have reached conflicting holdings on it.

My own evaluation of the applications is based on what I believe to be the primary role of the Court: with fifty separate state-court systems and thirteen federal circuits, our task is to try to develop a reasonably uniform and consistent body of federal law. Petitions seeking full-scale review in cases posing a genuine conflict among the lower courts on an important issue of federal law obviously are much more likely to garner the required number of votes to grant the petition than are petitions in cases where the lower courts are generally in agreement on the legal issue in the case.

Each year the members of the Court must read the briefs in the one hundred or so cases on which the Court hears oral arguments. After argument, each case has to be decided and explained in a published opinion.

During the weeks of oral arguments the Justices confer after the arguments are heard. This is where we learn how each Justice thinks the case should be resolved and why. Based on this discussion, writing assignments are made for the case. If the Chief Justice is in the majority on a case, he assigns the writing of the Court's opinion to one of the Justices in the majority or to himself. If not, the most senior Justice in the majority makes the assignment. Likewise, if a dissent is to be written and joined by more than one Justice, the most senior Justice planning to join that dissent assigns the writing.

The writer of the majority opinion must try to reconcile the views of those in the majority. When the opinion draft is circulated, each Justice reads it and decides whether to join it or to ask for revisions as a condition of joining. Sometimes a Justice will write a concurring opinion subscribing to the result in the majority opinion but based on different reasons, which it provides. If there is a dissenting view, that too is written up and circulated to all the Justices. In the end the opinion for the Court may be the result of many drafts and changes. Eventually, each participating Justice will have agreed to one or more of the opinions in the case. Each term produces something like twenty-five hundred pages' worth of opinions in the *United States Reports*. It all adds up to a lot of paper.

Serving on the Court has provided me with a number of pleasant surprises. Some people think that the Court is full of bitter battles, and it *is* true that the Court's opinions sometimes include strong language. But in fact one of my earliest and most rewarding experiences on the Court, and one that I did not fully anticipate, was of the warmth, kindness, and civility of my fellow Justices. Every one of my colleagues has been very thoughtful and considerate. There have been times with some previous Courts when some members did not get along and when some animosity persisted among certain Justices. Happily, that has not been the situation during my time here. It is a particular pleasure to be able to serve in an atmosphere of respect and affection for one's colleagues.

What is quite remarkable in my view is that each and every petition for review, whether produced by a sophisticated lawyer in a high-rise or handwritten by a prison inmate or a private citizen in her home, is reviewed with care by each Justice. And every written opinion of the Court is read with utmost care and attention by every other Justice, with an eye toward refinement or improvement. The process we follow, I think, provides some reason to have faith in the nation's judicial system.

Of course, not everyone is happy with the Court's decision in any given case. After all, you have two sides and only one can win. And often that unhappy party is the court below, because the Supreme Court reverses about two thirds of the lower-court decisions in those cases it reviews.

When I am not hearing oral arguments, researching and considering the law, or discussing the cases with my colleagues or my clerks, part of my time is spent dealing with a mass of correspondence. Some relates to pending cases. I ignore all such letters. Many letters are from schoolchildren who want information from me or about me. I do the best I can to process and answer these.

People often think of the Supreme Court as a remote Washington institution. State and local judges are forced by proximity to stay in touch with the concerns of those they serve. The Supreme Court, in contrast, serves a national purpose for a vast country. One might wonder, therefore, if the Court is simply a large, federal institution, distant and out of touch with the people. But in fact the Court is not a bad place from which to get some sense of the nation's concerns, or at least its national legal concerns. The more than seven thousand petitions for review each year come from all across the country and involve a very wide range of legal issues. The Court hears oral argument in cases that have their genesis in front-page actions by Congress as well as in the actions of police officers in tiny towns. The attorneys who appear before the Court, and the clients whose problems have brought them there, present a similarly broad geographical cross section.

Justices are drawn from all over the country and are a diverse group. This, in my view, is another reason to be optimistic about the Court. Diversity is its strength, just as it is the strength of America itself. In my twenty-plus years on the Court, I have learned at least one lesson very vividly. A Justice is constantly called upon to try to draw some harmony from that diversity—and even to reconcile the irreconcilable.

E. B. White said, "Democracy is based on the recurrent suspicion that more than half of the people are right more than half of the time."[1] In the narrow view, the Supreme Court is based on the suspicion that five Justices are similarly correct. In the broader view, I think that the Justices contribute to the wider democracy. We struggle with national issues and attempt to define from a national perspective what it is that the federal laws and the Constitution say. If you don't agree with all of the Court's holdings, you are certainly not alone. But you may be confident that we never stop trying in our writings on every case on our agenda to contribute appropriately to the fragile balances of our national democracy.

CHAPTER TWO

The Court's Agenda

---

*I*T IS SAID THAT DAVY CROCKETT ONCE HEARD DANIEL WEB-
ster speak, and that afterward he said to Webster: "I had heard that
you were a very great man, but I don't think so. I heard your speech
and understood every word you said."

Crockett probably would have thought the Supreme Court to be a
great court. Notwithstanding the public's interest in the Court, and despite the Court's voluminous output, opinion polls reveal that the public knows profoundly little about our legal system generally and even
less about what the Supreme Court does, where it is going, or what it
has held. For example, a recent poll told us that 37 percent of our citizens believe it is up to the criminal defendant to prove his innocence.[1]
One would suppose that viewers of *Perry Mason* or *Law & Order* would
have learned long ago that a criminal defendant is presumed innocent
until proven guilty beyond a reasonable doubt. Of those polled, 78 percent believe the Supreme Court can review and reverse *every* decision
made by a state court.[2] Yet certainly every high school government
class learns that federal courts, including the Supreme Court, have the
power to decide only issues of *federal*, not state, law.

One may gain considerable insight into where the Court has been
and where it is likely to go from a study of the Court's plenary docket—
the cases decided by the Court after full briefing and oral argument. To
put the numbers in context, the Court agrees to review only a small
percentage of the cases brought to its attention. When I arrived at the
Court in 1981 we received around 4,000 applications a year to review
particular lower-court decisions, but we accepted and decided with full

The west façade of
the Supreme
Court building,
c. 1992.

Sandra Day O'Connor,
Associate Justice,
Supreme Court of the
United States.

opinion only about 150 a year. Recently, the Court has been receiving over 7,000 petitions a year and has been accepting fewer than 100. The number of petitions granted declined after Congress in 1988 made the Court's appellate jurisdiction discretionary.

Although the spotlight of publicity on the Court has varied in intensity over the years, most of the subject areas of the Court's plenary docket throw off a steady glow from year to year. One especially noteworthy example is the Court's criminal-procedure docket. Criminal-procedure cases come from both the state and the federal court systems, although by far the greater number of criminal prosecutions are handled in the state courts. The number of criminal-procedure cases decided by the Court rose gradually from about twelve per term in the 1950s to around twenty-five per term in the mid-sixties, and has remained essentially constant since then.[3] Comprising about one sixth of our cases, the criminal-procedure docket is an important and constant presence.

What accounts for this striking stability in the number of criminal cases on our docket? My guess is that criminal procedure is simply not perfectible. The Court must constantly reexamine the way in which law enforcement agencies, legislatures, and the Court itself strike the balance between the rights of defendants and the interests of society at large. And I think this continuing process of reexamination is healthy. First, it helps to remind us all that important issues are at stake when the machinery of the state proceeds against the least favored members of our society. Second, it allows the law to be developed gradually and in small steps. Third, it enables the Court to correct or refine rules that prove ineffective or counterproductive. Correction of this nature is not only inevitable, it is an essential part of our legal system. It is, indeed, the possibility of later correction that allows many advances to be explored in the first place.

Like the Court's criminal-procedure docket, much of its civil docket also reflects a rather steady routine. About one third of our docket is in the area of general federal law–business regulation.[4] The rate at which we decide these cases has been quite steady over the last thirty years. This is not surprising, because most of the cases that we accept for review arise from conflicting interpretations of federal law reached in the different federal circuit courts of appeal. If there is one fixed and invariant rule of law, it is that so long as there is more than one circuit, there will be more than one view of what the law is. As the saying goes: two lawyers, three opinions.

Yet within the broad area of general federal law, we find some mature, aging subject areas and some new, more fertile ones. We have, for example, seen a persistent drop in federal tax cases, from an average of more than eight a term from 1953 to 1965 to about four a term since then.[5] Whether this reflects the Court's complete satisfaction with the current state of tax law or its utter despair, I cannot say. There has been a similar drop in the number of decisions reviewing action by the National Labor Relations Board.[6] In these areas the governing federal statutes are older, and their various provisions have been dissected and analyzed to the point where little further enlightenment seems possible. Unsurprisingly, the Court begins to see less of them.

Quite the opposite occurs when new legislation comes on the scene. Recent employment-related federal legislation—the Americans with Disabilities Act, the Employee Retirement Income Security Act, the Age Discrimination in Employment Act, and the Occupational Safety and Health Act—has spawned a significant amount of new litigation. All of the statutory environmental-law cases on the Court's books—more than sixty in all—were decided in the last thirty terms.[7]

In other areas, of course, a sudden burst of activity by the Court is triggered not by new legislation but by a decision of the Court itself. Our construction of the Eighth Amendment's prohibition of cruel and unusual punishment supplies one example. The Court decided no such cases between 1953 and 1970. Since the 1970 term and the death penalty decision in *Furman v. Georgia*,[8] however, the Court has decided eighty-three cases on capital punishment.

A broader area of even more striking growth is the Court's civil rights docket: cases touching on due process, freedom of expression, equal protection, and the like. These are the cases based on the Bill of Rights and the ones most often covered by the media. You will not be surprised to learn that the number of civil rights cases decided by the

Court underwent a quantum jump in the mid-1950s, following the decision in *Brown v. Board of Education*.[9] That landmark ruling was one of five separate school-desegregation cases that were consolidated for decision in *Brown* for a single opinion of the Court: *Brown* itself was from Kansas; the other four were from Delaware, Virginia, South Carolina, and the District of Columbia. The decision that resulted was certainly one of the most important in the Supreme Court's history, requiring as it did an end to racial segregation of students in the public schools of this nation.

The Court's civil rights docket, broadly defined to include judicial procedure, equal protection, voting rights, and other "freedoms," grew steadily longer through the 1960s, reaching a high of close to sixty cases per term at the beginning of the 1970s, probably as a result of the *Brown* case and its progeny. Since then there has been a steady decline.[10]

One final portion of the docket worth mentioning, in part because it has received much comment, is the Court's recent jurisprudence concerning issues of federalism and separation of powers. These issues concern the balance of power between the states and the federal government—a balance struck by the constitutional limits on state and federal power, the rules concerning preemption of state law by federal law, the doctrine of separation of powers, and the Eleventh Amendment, which addresses the states' immunity from lawsuits brought in federal court. The Court in recent terms has given a more expansive interpretation of the Eleventh Amendment, and that in turn has produced more cases in that area.

One generally doesn't have much appreciation for the delicate balance between the states and the federal government until adulthood, or at least until a high school civics class, but one federalism case from Florida involved something that every small child could tell a story about: sunken treasure. Some treasure seekers succeeded in finding many valuable items from a sunken seventeenth-century Spanish galleon—the *Atocha*—west of the Marquesas Islands. They claimed title to the artifacts, but the state of Florida, not content with golden sunshine, wanted the golden coins as well. Despite the fascinating facts, the outcome of the case hinged on a rather arcane question: how to apply the Eleventh Amendment to a case concerning admiralty jurisdiction filed against state officials in federal court for the recovery of property. As things turned out, the little guys beat the government—at least until they had to fill out their income tax reports.[11]

The trend in "federalism" cases is rather interesting. The number of such cases accepted by the Court averaged around fifteen per term through the 1950s and early 1960s, dropped substantially in the latter half of the 1960s (the same period in which the civil rights docket was expanding), and then rose steadily to an average of about twenty to twenty-five per term—a level that has been maintained up to now.[12] It has been suggested that "the continuing expansion of this segment of the docket leaves no doubt that the Justices of today have a strong interest in fine-tuning the federal system."[13] But it appears that, under the banner of "states' rights," issues affecting the federal/state balance have been shared by much of the nation since President Nixon's election in 1968. In that light, the Court's federalism "agenda," like the rest of its agenda, is largely a reflection of concerns that originate outside the Court.

This brief overview of argued cases indicates that the Court's business is of three types. First, there is the steady routine of resolving intercircuit federal-court conflicts and thereby overseeing the enforcement of complex federal statutes like antitrust law, labor law, and the internal revenue code. Similar, at least in its effect on our docket, is our responsibility to supervise the administration of criminal procedure. These two areas account for by far the largest part of our activity: about two thirds of our workload. And they probably receive the least publicity. I have noticed without surprise that there are few headline stories on our decisions concerning the power of the U.S. marshals to remove prisoners from state jails[14] or the rules on how to decide if a federal magistrate's report may be challenged in federal appeals court even if the losing party fails to object.[15]

Second, when our agenda does change, the change most frequently is a delayed response to changes in the nation's agenda. When Congress, the executive branch, or a state lights a new fire by passing significant new legislation or taking bold new action, we are inevitably summoned to attend to the blaze. Some litigants will ask us to fan the flames, others will demand their extinguishment, and still others will request only that the fire not be allowed to spread. Justice moves slowly (especially in a federal system where multiple courts may be entitled to review the issue before we do), so the Court usually arrives on the scene some years late. But once there, we must usually linger for a while. It often takes a series of decisions to flesh out a new statute or to draw new boundaries between state and federal authority, or to reconsider the limits on government intrusions on individual rights. Eventually, of course, most of what can be done in an appellate court is written and published, and thereafter we see little more of that particular conflagration.

Finally, I must concede, the Court occasionally starts a fire of its own. Or perhaps it would be more accurate to say that the Court occasionally supplies the crucial first spark. Perhaps *Brown v. Board of Education* was one such case. But cases of this type, despite the considerable publicity they receive, are rare. Generally, they represent an extremely minor, though disproportionately controversial, part of our docket.

Most of the Court's agenda is dictated by external forces: the actions of the other branches of the government, the decisions of the lower courts, and ultimately the concerns of the public. It is these forces, not secret ones within the Court, that frame the bulk of the issues we decide. The Court's role is uniquely reactive. It is the Constitution, after all, that limits our business to "Cases or Controversies."[16] The business of the Court is to resolve controversies, not to create them. That is how it should be. And, our docket reveals, that in fact is how it is.

I am sure we do not always succeed in striking precisely the right balance among the competing ideals of law, freedom, and justice. But we never stop trying. It is safe to say that at least one lawyer disagrees with almost every opinion we hand down; we don't take a case without two sides to it, and one side always must lose. Indeed, I have known judges whose natural temperament led them to endeavor to decide a case against the lawyers on *both* sides, but generally speaking, such efforts have not been crowned with success.

Despite the occasional obfuscation in its communications, the Court does its best to struggle with the difficulties it faces term after term. I think that Justice Rutledge spoke for every Justice when he said, "I believe in law. At the same time I believe in freedom. And I know that each of these things may destroy the other. But I know too that, without both, neither can long endure. . . . Law, freedom, and justice—this trinity is the object of my faith."[17]

CHAPTER THREE

Judicial Appointment
and Tenure: A History

———

*P*RESIDENT JOHN ADAMS ONCE SAID: "MY GIFT OF CHIEF Justice John Marshall to the people of the United States was the proudest act of my life."[1] Many students of American history have noted that, although Presidents change, the Supreme Court endures. A number of Justices have served on the Court for decades after the Presidents who appointed them have left office.

From 1790 until 2002, only 108 people have served as Justices of the Supreme Court of the United States. On the average, a new Justice is appointed every twenty-two months. Because of the significance of the Supreme Court in our government, the selection of its Justices garners intense interest.

The provisions of our Constitution relating to the Court are characteristically succinct. Article III, Sec. 1, provides that "the judicial Power of the United States shall be vested in one supreme Court, and in such inferior Courts as the Congress may from time to time ordain and establish. The Judges, both of the supreme and inferior Courts, shall hold their Offices during good Behaviour." Article II, Sec. 2, provides that "The President . . . shall nominate, and by and with the Advice and Consent of the Senate, shall appoint . . . Judges of the supreme Court."

The Constitution does not provide for the number of Supreme Court Justices. Congress originally fixed the number at six by the Judiciary Act of 1789. A month before President John Adams left office in

1801, Congress reduced the number to five in order to prevent the next President, Thomas Jefferson, from filling a vacancy. That plan failed, however, because Congress changed the law again in 1802 and restored the number to six. Jefferson made three appointments to the Court during his years as President. In 1807 Congress increased the number of Justices to seven. In 1827 it increased the Court's size again, to nine. The Judiciary Act of 1863 added a tenth Justice, but Congress reduced the Court back to seven in 1866 in an attempt to prevent President Andrew Johnson from filling vacancies with appointees who shared his views about the unconstitutionality of Reconstruction legislation. President Johnson did nominate one Justice, but the Senate took no action on the appointment. The last change in the Court's size occurred in 1869, when Congress increased it again to nine, where it has remained ever since.

Most of the increases in Court size were made to accommodate the duties of the Justices in "riding circuit" to hold court with district judges around the country and thus extend the law of the new federal government to the farthest reaches of the young nation. Although the Justices complained about their circuit-riding duties almost from the Court's inception, those duties were not ended by Congress until 1891. Because of circuit riding, it was common in the past to appoint to the Court a person from the circuit in which the vacancy occurred. This is no longer a consideration in the selection of Justices, as is apparent from the makeup of the present Court, with two Justices from Arizona: Chief Justice Rehnquist and myself.

The last effort to alter the size of the Court occurred in 1937 when President Franklin Roosevelt sought to increase it as a means of preventing the Court from declaring so much of his New Deal legislation unconstitutional. The President broadcast to the country his appeal to increase the size of the Court. He likened the three branches of government to plow horses and said that one of the horses—the Court—was not doing its share of the nation's work but instead was sitting as a superlegislature in declaring laws such as the Railroad Retirement Act and the Minimum Wage Law unconstitutional. President Roosevelt's plan was to obtain authority from Congress to appoint a new

Justice each time a Justice became seventy. This would have allowed him to increase the size of the Court immediately, unless those over seventy chose to resign or retire. Six members of the Court were over seventy when the proposal was made.

President Roosevelt's plan was opposed by Chief Justice Charles Evans Hughes and other members of the Court. It was opposed also by the Senate Judiciary Committee, to which the President's proposal had been assigned. After a bitter controversy, the plan failed to pass Congress. The Court has remained at nine members ever since.

The aftermath of President Roosevelt's Court-packing plan likewise was filled with controversy. Justice Van Devanter announced his decision to retire during the congressional battle over the Roosevelt plan. As a result, the forthcoming nomination of a successor by President Roosevelt was the subject of keen interest and much discussion nationwide. In August 1937 President Roosevelt sent to the Senate the name of his nominee: one of the Senate's own members, Senator Hugo Black from Alabama.

A great controversy erupted over the nomination. Senator Black lacked judicial experience, and he had been very active in partisan support of the President's programs, including the Court-packing proposal. The President realized, however, that the Senate would surely approve the nomination of one of its own members. Despite the misgivings of many conservatives, Black was confirmed.

Not long thereafter, news broke of Justice Black's membership some ten years earlier in the Ku Klux Klan. There were demands for his resignation from the Court, and he was literally besieged by the press for statements. The situation became so intense that Justice Black decided to make a public response on the radio. Speaking briefly on the broadcast, he admitted his former Klan membership but said he had resigned before entering the Senate, and he spoke with disapproval of any organization that "arrogates to itself the un-American power to interfere in the slightest degree with complete religious freedom."[2]

The controversy died down five days later when the President delivered his historic "quarantine" address concerning the prospects of a second world war. Justice Black served on the Court until he was eighty-five years old and will always be remembered as a great civil libertarian.

The language of the Constitution concerning appointments of "judges of the supreme Court" with the "advice and consent" of the Senate[3] was inserted during the closing days of the Constitutional Convention to replace the original language giving the Senate power to "reject and approve." In the intervening years the practice almost always has been that the President selects a nominee for the Court without any "advice" from the Senate, and merely forwards the nomination for the confirmation process.

In two instances, however, Congress actively attempted to influence the selection of a nominee. In 1869 both houses of Congress petitioned President Grant to nominate Edwin Stanton (discharged as secretary of war by Grant's predecessor, President Johnson, over congressional objections) to the Court. Grant made the nomination, but Stanton died unexpectedly a few days later.

In 1932 various senators advised President Hoover that they wanted a strong appointment to succeed Justice Oliver Wendell Holmes and specifically suggested Benjamin N. Cardozo, a distinguished New York jurist, who thereafter was nominated.

There is an often told story of President Hoover meeting with Senator Borah of Idaho about the Holmes vacancy. Borah staunchly supported Cardozo's nomination, although Hoover was hesitant about the appointment. The President, after discussing the vacancy generally, suddenly handed Borah a list on which he had ranked those individuals he was considering for the nomination in descending order of preference. The name at the bottom was that of Benjamin N. Cardozo. Borah glanced at it and replied: "Your list is all right, but you handed it to me upside down." Hoover protested at first, saying that there was the geographical question to be considered. Senator Borah retorted sharply that "Cardozo belongs as much to Idaho as to New York."[4]

What are the factors influencing the selection of a nominee to the Court? It is hard to generalize about this. Certainly, we know that all but twelve nominees have been of the same political party as the President making the nomination. We know also that all but 17 of the 108 Court Justices had some sort of political experience prior to their appointments: 27 as members of Congress, 6 as state governors, and 1 even as President (William Howard Taft). Over time, experience at the federal level has become more frequent than state service, although in the early years of the country, as might be expected, the reverse was true. Forty-one Justices had no prior judicial experience before going on the Supreme Court.[5] In fact, among them are some of the most respected Justices: the great Chief Justice John Marshall, Justice Louis Brandeis, Justice Felix Frankfurter, Justice Lewis Powell, and Chief Justice William Rehnquist.

There is no doubt that a President contemplating an appointment to the Court also considers the likelihood of Senate confirmation, geographical and religious balance, the person's reputation and ability, and any ideological beliefs and positions previously expressed by the nominee. As of 1981 it appears that another factor to be considered is the sex of the nominee.

In reference to geographical representation, some states have fared better than others. Before ascending to the high bench, the nation's Justices have resided in thirty-one different states, with fourteen from New York, ten from Ohio, eight from Massachusetts, and seven from Virginia; nine states have sent one; nineteen none at all.[6] That last fact of political life prompted Republican Senator William ("Wild Bill") Langer of North Dakota, then a senior member of the Senate's Committee on the Judiciary, to commence in 1953 a campaign of opposition to any and all presidential nominees to the Court until his home state received a Supreme Court nomination. He went to his grave in 1959 with his wish still unrealized—as it is to this day.

Since 1840 it appears to have been common practice for the names of possible nominees to be suggested to the President by the attorney general. In the past, some Chief Justices used their influence to urge particular nominations to the Court. Chief Justices Taft, Hughes, and Stone all expressed preferences for particular appointments.

Since World War II the American Bar Association also has played a role in passing on the legal and intellectual qualifications of those who are nominated to the Court. Recently, however, the administration of President George W. Bush decided that consultation with the American Bar Association would no longer be an official part of the nomination process.[7]

Because the nominee may well outlast the length of service of the President making the appointment, the President generally seeks to have a lasting effect on the Court and the nation through such appointments. It is also generally conceded, however, that Presidents frequently are disappointed because their appointees to the Court subsequently fail to follow the philosophy of their appointer when they arrive on the bench and start voting on the issues of the day. Even Presidents Jefferson and Madison were exceedingly disappointed at the failure of their appointees to resist the influence of Chief Justice John Marshall. Theodore Roosevelt was similarly chagrined by some of the rulings of Justice Oliver Wendell Holmes. President Truman remarked that "packing the Supreme Court simply can't be done . . . I've tried it and it won't work. . . . Whenever you put a man on the Supreme Court, he ceases to be your friend."[8]

Alexander Bickel said: "You shoot an arrow into a far-distant future when you appoint a Justice and not the man himself can tell you what he will think about some of the problems that he will face."[9]

Once a Supreme Court nomination is made, the Senate must give its "consent." There have been twenty-six instances altogether in which the nominations were not successful, whether because of rejection, withdrawal of the nomination, or postponement of any Senate action on the nomination.[10] There have been twelve appointments to the Court that were rejected by vote of the Senate, including President Nixon's nominations of Judge Haynsworth and Judge Carswell.[11]

Neither the Constitution nor the federal statutes set forth qualifications for a Supreme Court Justice. As a result, the Senate generally has limited its inquiry to the nominee's training, experience, and judicial temperament. By and large, senators expect and respect the right of a President to appoint to the Court people who share the President's political philosophy. There have been, however, instances when the Senate has exerted its undoubted right to make an independent evaluation of a nominee. Indeed, *The Federalist Papers* disclose that Alexander Hamilton anticipated that the Senate would explore the qualifications of the nominees fully but not reject them out of mere personal preference.[12] It is crystal clear that so far as our founders were concerned, "representativeness" was not even considered, let alone advocated. Merit was the sole criterion on the mind of the delegates to the Constitutional Convention, "representativeness" being reserved to the legislature.

The nomination of a Supreme Court Justice normally is referred to the Senate Judiciary Committee for public hearings, investigation, and a report and recommendation. If an appointment is controversial, the committee hearings and process take longer than otherwise. Only in approximately twenty-two nominations has more than one day of Senate hearings been conducted. The longest hearings were those on Justice Louis Brandeis, which lasted nineteen days, and on Justice Abe Fortas (in his unsuccessful bid to be Chief Justice), which lasted nine days.[13]

Usually, the entire confirmation process is completed in fewer than 60 days. There are, however, exceptions: 122 days for Justice Louis Brandeis, and 69 for Justice Thurgood Marshall. Often, a longer interval indicates larger controversy. There are those who say that the greater the controversy over the appointment, the greater have been the accomplishments of the nominee. One writer has said, in reference to Justice Brandeis, that "the great Justice has earned his appointment, but he has also earned his enemies."[14]

The Court, as an institution, generally is held in high regard by our citizens, and today its ultimate power remains unquestioned. The people with whom I share the Supreme Court bench represent a great cross section of our country. They are intelligent. They are experienced. They are knowledgeable and fair. They work very, very hard. They love and respect the Court and strive to preserve and protect it. These qualities, in large part, have made the Court what it is—and made it such an honor for me to serve on it.

CHAPTER FOUR

The Supreme Court Reports

———

*I*F YOU GO TO A LAW LIBRARY TO READ THE SUPREME COURT opinions written by my contemporaries, you will find them in volumes with labels such as "450 U.S."—that is, volume 450 of the *United States Reports*. Every opinion that is delivered by the Justices is put into these volumes by the Reporter's Office at the Court and published by the Court for the benefit of scholars, lawyers, and judges. The power of the Supreme Court flows not so much from its authority to make decisions in individual cases as from the fact that these decisions become binding law throughout the nation. That can happen only if they are published for everyone to see.

But if you look over to the previous bookshelf where the earlier volumes of the *United States Reports* stand, you will find slightly different notations on the spines: not just "5 U.S." or "17 U.S.," but labels like "1 Cranch" or "4 Wheaton." Many a lawyer who can't recall more than a few Justices of the current era remembers the names Dallas, Cranch, Wheaton, and Peters.

These were the early reporters of the Supreme Court: not, as they are today, employees of the institution but private entrepreneurs who hoped to make money selling their reports of Supreme Court opinions to the public. These businessmen—together with Justice Joseph Story, who saw the importance of fast, inexpensive, and accurate reporting of Supreme Court cases—did much to make the Supreme Court what it is; and two of them, perhaps unintentionally, also helped mold the shape of our copyright law.

The first of the reporters was a Philadelphia lawyer by the name of

Portrait of Reporter of Decisions Richard Peters, Jr. (served 1828–1843).

Portrait of Reporter of Decisions Henry Wheaton (served 1816–1827).

Alexander Dallas, who would later become the secretary of the trea-sury.[1] Dallas decided to publish the opinions of both the Pennsylvania state courts and the federal courts sitting in Pennsylvania. From 1790 to 1800 the latter included the Supreme Court of the United States, which sat in Philadelphia while the new capital city of Washington was being designed and built.[2]

Dallas was a pioneer of American case reporting and had much to learn about the enterprise. His volumes, while very useful to the bar, suffered from several important problems. The first was delay: the Supreme Court cases decided in 1793 weren't published by Dallas until 1798, and the cases decided in 1800 weren't put out until 1807.[3] There was also expense: the reports cost about five dollars a volume, a price well beyond the means of many lawyers of the time.[4] In addition, many cases were omitted, largely at Dallas's own discretion.[5]

Most surprising to modern lawyers, though, was the fact that Dal-las's reports were quite likely not very accurate. The Supreme Court did not at the time prepare written opinions for distribution. Rather, the Justices delivered the opinions orally from the bench. Dallas's re-ports generally were reconstructed from his notes, and sometimes from the notes of others when Dallas himself wasn't in the audience. Dallas seemed to have had few qualms about omitting material he thought irrelevant, or modifying that which he retained.[6]

All these problems led to much criticism of Dallas's work, and when the capital finally moved to Washington, Dallas abandoned the task.[7] Dallas's successor, William Cranch, who was a judge in the Dis-trict of Columbia, fared not much better. His reports, too, were slow, inaccurate, incomplete, and expensive.[8] Ultimately, they also proved unprofitable for Cranch himself, and in 1816 the baton passed to Henry Wheaton.[9]

Henry Wheaton was more than just a reporter of cases. He was also a scholar. And he was a protégé of another great scholar, Supreme Court Justice Joseph Story.

Justice Story was second only to Chief Justice Marshall as a force in American law of the first half of the nineteenth century. He was a lead-ing commentator on admiralty and commercial law,[10] but he was also, like Marshall, a great nationalist. He saw the importance of having the Supreme Court create a strong system of federal law that would bind the states into one nation; and he saw that this goal would not be realized unless the Court's opinions were efficiently and widely distributed.[11]

Justice Story took Wheaton, six years his junior,[12] under his wing. They were good friends and even roomed together.[13] Story helped Wheaton get appointed as reporter[14] and also wrote scholarly commentary for early volumes of Wheaton's reports.[15] Further, he helped Wheaton convince Congress to give him a salary of one thousand dollars per year, in addition to the money Wheaton would make from sales of his volumes.[16] And Story's confidence was not misplaced. Wheaton's reports of Supreme Court opinions were prompt, accurate, and complete.

But they were still very expensive, selling for $7.50 each, more than most lawyers could afford.[17] And as a result, they made Wheaton very little money. Over the twelve years in which he published his reports, Wheaton grossed only $10,000.[18] Though he seems to have enjoyed the scholarly side of the business, he found himself having to look for other, more profitable appointments. He was talked about as a possible nominee to the Supreme Court itself, and when that failed, he sought unsuccessfully an appointment to the federal district court in New York.[19] Ultimately, he had to content himself with a diplomatic mission to Denmark. This was so minor a post as to be almost an insult, but it paid $4,500 a year, and in 1827 Wheaton sailed for Europe, leaving the reportership behind him.[20]

Richard Peters, Wheaton's successor, was not a scholar. His volumes did not include the commentary that Wheaton's had,[21] and his summaries of the reported cases were often unhelpful or even misleading.[22] Peters was basically a businessman, seeing the reports as a profit-making effort first and an intellectual one last or not at all.

Ultimately, however, Peters's quest for profits proved to be a great boon to the Court and the legal profession, because he realized that the way to make money as a reporter was to make the reports cheap enough for the average lawyer to buy them. In first lobbying for the post, Peters undertook to sell the volumes for no more than $5 each, rather than the $7.50 that Wheaton's cost.[23] What's more, he proposed to republish—in a six-volume edition selling for only $36—all the cases decided by the Supreme Court in the first thirty-seven years of its existence. This was less than a third of the $130 that the original editions cost—and when successful lawyers were making only about $700 a year, that made a very big difference.[24]

But although this offer was a boon to American lawyers, to the authority of the federal courts, and to Peters himself, it was not so warmly received by two people: Peters's predecessors, Cranch and Wheaton, whose own editions it would make nearly obsolete.[25] Cranch and Wheaton claimed a copyright in the opinions themselves. And while Cranch ultimately made a deal with Peters, Wheaton sued.

Wheaton v. Peters—a decision handed down in 1834 and reported in our present-day volumes of *United States Supreme Court Reports* as "33 U.S. (8 Pet.) 591"—was only the third copyright case decided in America, and the first that has had lasting importance. It involved a number of issues, ranging from the technical requirements of copyright registration to the existence of state common-law remedies alongside federal statutory ones. But at its heart lay the key problem of copyright law: the tension between the public benefits that come from exclusive copyrights and the public benefits that come from a rich and freely copyable public domain.

The Constitution itself authorized Congress to pass a national copyright law "To promote the Progress of . . . useful Arts, by securing for limited Times to Authors . . . the exclusive Right to their . . . Writings."[26] Providing authors the exclusive right to their works (in effect, a monopoly subject to limitations that Congress might impose in the public interest), the theory went, would make writing more profitable and thereby lead to greater artistic and intellectual development.

Affording copyrights to authors could be a two-edged sword, however: incentives to write and publish new works might foster creativity, but taken too far, such rights might also injure the public interest. As the Court's experience with the early *Supreme Court Reports* showed, if books were too expensive, many people wouldn't be able to afford them. If Wheaton could claim an exclusive right to reprint the decisions that came down during his tenure, much of the bench, the bar, and the public might be deprived of access to vitally important information. And this was especially problematic because the opinions were, after all, handed down by federal judges—government employees who were paid salaries from the public fisc. Why shouldn't the opinions, paid for with public funds, be equally owned by the entire public?

This, ultimately, is the way the Court decided the matter. No copyright could attach to the opinions of a court. Though a reporter may have a copyright in his annotations or his summaries of the cases, the Justices' opinions are not his, no matter how much effort he may have exerted in recording them. And the Justices themselves, being government employees, can have no rights in the opinions, either.[27]

Today this doctrine—that no work prepared by a federal official in the performance of his or her public duties is subject to copyright—is a cornerstone of the copyright law. At the time, though, it was hotly disputed. Justices Thompson and Baldwin dissented from the Court's judgment, concluding that Wheaton did have a copyright in his reports under state law, and that this state law should control.[28] Remarkably, when the opinions were read from the bench, tempers rose so high that the Justices almost came to fisticuffs. Only the intercession of Chief Justice Marshall managed to restore calm.[29]

Wheaton was, of course, bitterly disappointed, not the least because of what he saw as the betrayal by his former patron, Justice Story, in voting that the opinions were not copyrighted. The day before the opinion was handed down, Story had invited Wheaton and Peters to his office for a last chance at some sort of conciliation. The Court, Justice Story told the two reporters, had decided the case largely in Peters's favor. The points on which Wheaton might prevail—the relatively minor matters of Wheaton's own annotations and indices—should, Story suggested, be turned over to arbitration. Wheaton was deeply unhappy about this and, realizing that he had little to gain from the arbitration, rejected the suggestion.

Wheaton saw himself as entirely in the right: he had expended his efforts on a massive but ultimately unprofitable endeavor, and here his work was to be snatched away from him by Peters. Justice Story, though he was unhappy to decide against his old friend Wheaton, viewed the case as much more than a personal matter. He saw that, for the Supreme Court's decisions to be truly influential, they had to reach the broadest possible audience. His main sympathies lay with the Supreme Court, its institutional interest, and the interests of the nation as a whole. Justice Story was correct, and today the opinions of the Court, including dissents and concurring opinions, are published in the *U.S. Reports*, on the Internet, and by various legal publishing services. For better or worse, the work of every member of the Court is available for examination worldwide.

PART TWO

—

A Bit of History

To understand the Court, one must know a bit of the history of our Constitution: how it came to be written, some of the major controversies about its design, the battles over its ratification, and the writing and adoption of the Bill of Rights.

The Framers decided to leave in place the court systems that had existed in each state before the Constitution, and to create a Supreme Court for the new United States. They left it to Congress to decide whether to establish, in addition, a system of federal trial and appellate courts. The First Congress created a federal court system. We have continued to this day with parallel systems of state and federal courts, in which each court—in either system—is empowered to decide issues of federal law in cases within its jurisdiction. The main function of the Supreme Court of the United States is to help develop a uniform and consistent body of federal law by resolving conflicting holdings by the lower federal courts and the state courts.

Part Two addresses some of this history, as well as the concept of judicial independence and impeachment.

CHAPTER FIVE

Magna Carta and the Rule of Law

———

*T*HE GREATEST CONTRIBUTION FROM THE LEGAL SYSTEMS OF Great Britain and the United States toward peace in the world has been the principle that all nations should live under the Rule of Law. The concept of the Rule of Law—that laws should be enacted by democratically elected legislative bodies and enforced by independent judiciaries—is fundamental to a free society. The knowledge that there are certain basic rights of the individual that are enforceable even against the state has been the hallmark of our system of governance.

Our constitutional heritage has been influenced significantly by Magna Carta, the document signed by King John of England in 1215 limiting his own monarchical powers as a settlement with his own warring barons. Its importance is acknowledged in the Supreme Court building itself, where the two bronze doors through which most people enter the Court depict a scene of King John sealing Magna Carta. In the courtroom itself, as I sit on the bench, I can see a marble frieze portraying the great lawgivers of history. There, among Chief Justice John Marshall, Napoleon, and Justinian, stands King John—clothed in chain-mail armor and clutching a copy of Magna Carta.

We might wonder that a treaty extracted "at the point of the sword" from a feudal king would have such a powerful and enduring influence on constitutional development in England, the United States, and other nations. Magna Carta, however, expresses an idea that retains vitality today, more than 750 years after King John met the barons at Runnymede. That idea, as described by Sir Winston Churchill, is the "sovereignty of the law" as protection against at-

tempts by governments "to ride roughshod over the rights or liberties" of the governed.[1]

The origins of Magna Carta gave little hint of its subsequent importance. King John acceded to the demands of the barons in an unsuccessful effort to ward off a civil war. Some of the specific clauses of
Magna Carta, it is fair to say, reflected a self-interested effort by rebel-
lious barons to restore feudal custom and to protect themselves from
the king. The charter was annulled only two months after King John af-
fixed his seal. In the next two centuries Magna Carta was repeatedly issued, withdrawn, reissued, and confirmed. The 1297 confirmation
provided that the king's "Justices, Sheriffs, Mayors, and other Ministers shall allow . . . the Great Charter as the Common Law" and "that if
any Judgment be given from henceforth contrary to . . . the Charter . . . shall be undone, and holden for nought."[2] Magna Carta was of
great political importance in the struggles between the English Crown
and Parliament. It was cited as embodying the fundamental law of the
realm, binding on all persons—including the king.

The first colonists brought with them to America the perception of
Magna Carta as the written embodiment of fundamental law protecting the rights and liberties of all Englishmen everywhere. This view
was expressed in various colonial charters, including the Virginia
Charter of 1606 written in part by Sir Edward Coke, one of Magna
Carta's greatest exponents. The Massachusetts General Court resolved
in 1635 that "some men should be appointed to frame a body of
grounds of laws, in resemblance to a Magna Carta, which . . . should
be received for fundamental laws."[3]

During the American Revolution, Magna Carta again served as a
rallying point for those seeking protection against arbitrary government. As John Adams observed in 1778, "Where the public interest
governs, it is a government of laws and not of men. . . . If, in England,
there has ever been such a thing as a government of laws, was it not
Magna Carta?"[4]

When it came time to draft our own Constitution and Bill of
Rights, the founders adopted both certain concepts found in Magna
Carta and the more general notion of a written statement of funda-

mental law binding upon the sovereign state. Examples of important provisions of our Constitution that draw from Magna Carta are the requirement of legislative approval of taxation,[5] the guarantee of freedom of religion,[6] the requirement of speedy trials in criminal cases,[7] and the establishment of an independent judiciary.[8] Especially significant, of course, is the due process clause of the Fifth Amendment.

To appreciate the relation between Magna Carta and our constitutional right to due process, we need only recall the language of chapter 39 of Magna Carta: "No free man shall be taken or imprisoned or disseized or outlawed or exiled or in any way ruined nor will we go and send against him, except by the lawful judgment of his peers or by the law of the land."[9]

This language was echoed in our own Constitution nearly six centuries later in the Fifth Amendment, which declares: "No person shall be held to answer for a capital, or otherwise infamous crime, unless on a presentment or indictment by a Grand Jury . . . ; nor shall any person . . . be deprived of life, liberty, or property, without due process of law."[10]

The impact of Magna Carta on our constitutional development is not merely a historical one. The Supreme Court continues to refer to Magna Carta for inspiration and guidance in identifying those rights that are fundamental. Indeed, in the last forty years the Court has cited Magna Carta in more than fifty written opinions. These references, moreover, are not merely the sentimental acknowledgment of a fondly but dimly remembered ancestor. Instead, our Court has looked to concepts embodied in Magna Carta in important decisions that concern, for example, the Eighth Amendment prohibition of cruel and unusual punishment,[11] the requirement that trial by jury be afforded in state criminal prosecutions,[12] and the access of indigents to review of criminal convictions.[13]

Magna Carta relied on "the law of the land" to secure the citizen against the arbitrary action of the Crown.[14] The underlying idea of written fundamental law that protects the people from excesses by their government profoundly influenced and still continues to guide our constitutional development.

The bronze doors of the Court, depicting King John of England
at the signing of Magna Carta.

CHAPTER SIX

The Constitution

—

O N MAY 25, 1787, A QUORUM OF DELEGATES FROM SEVEN states met in Philadelphia, in answer to the call from the Annapolis Convention to draft what became the Constitution of the United States. The delegates unanimously selected George Washington as president of the convention. William Jackson was chosen as secretary, and the convention was adjourned over the weekend while additional delegates arrived in Philadelphia. Eventually, fifty-five participants assembled there from twelve of the thirteen states then in existence. They met throughout the sweltering summer, behind closed doors, to offer, consider, and debate the provisions of a new national charter. Their efforts culminated on September 17, 1787, when all twelve state delegations voted approval of the draft of our Constitution.

The bicentennial birthday of that effort produced significant changes for those of us sitting on the Supreme Court. In order to better prepare for the two hundredth birthday of our national charter, Chief Justice Warren Burger announced his retirement from the Court. One of my colleagues and a former Arizonan, William Rehnquist, became our sixteenth Chief Justice, and Antonin Scalia, a superb legal scholar and former Court of Appeals judge, joined us on the Court.

It seems natural for Supreme Court Justices to be vitally interested in the document we spend so many of our waking hours thinking and arguing about, and so many pages of the *United States Reports* writing about. But it is perhaps not so natural, in the twenty-first century, for most other Americans to spend much time thinking about or discussing our Constitution. Although more than two hundred years ago most Americans hotly debated the merits of the proposed Constitution, recent polls indicate that today almost half of our citizens do not know that there are three branches of government.[1] Thirty-five percent believe the Constitution establishes English as our national language.[2] Seventeen percent believe that the Constitution establishes America as a Christian nation.[3]

With such widespread lack of understanding about our nation's charter, the bicentennial celebration was welcome indeed. It provided an opportunity for each of us to learn more about the ideas embodied in the Constitution and the ways in which it shapes our lives. Such knowledge is not passed down from generation to generation through the gene pool; it must be learned anew by each generation. It is not enough simply to read or memorize the Constitution. Rather, we should try to understand the ideas that gave it life and that give it strength still today. Alexander Hamilton, one of the Framers, wrote in the first of *The Federalist Papers* in support of ratification of the Constitution that it was "reserved to the people of this country . . . to decide . . . whether [we] are . . . capable . . . of establishing good government from reflection and choice, or whether [we] are forever destined to depend for [our] political constitutions on accident and force."[4] Our citizens did reflect and make that choice, but we look around the world today and see that a great many other people have been dependent instead on "accident and force."

Our Constitution has lasted longer than any other among the world of nations today. Many of the early settlers were from England— a nation without a written constitution. But the pilgrims who landed on these shores at Cape Cod in 1620 drafted and signed a written agreement—the Mayflower Compact—even before setting foot in America. In 1639 the colonists in Connecticut also determined that a written charter was necessary to "mayntayne and presearve the liberty and purity of the gospell."[5] When the colonists began the Revolution in 1776, they expressed their reasons in a written document: the Declaration of Independence. Our ancestors firmly believed that to secure the "Blessings of Liberty to ourselves and our Posterity," a written constitution was a necessity.[6]

HISTORY

of the

UNITED STATES.

CONVENTION AT PHILADELPHIA.

1787.

HARTFORD.

PUBLISHED BY HUNTINGTON & HOPKINS.

1823.

Broadside of Constitutional Convention.

Portion of the
Constitution, including the
Three-Fifths Compromise.

Portrait of
President James Madison.

Much as it sometimes seems otherwise, however, the Constitution was not written as a full employment plan for the judiciary. On the contrary: the Constitution is interpreted first and last by people other than judges. The judicial branch is only an intermediate step in the continuing process of making our Constitution work.

The power of judicial review has been said by some to be the "cornerstone" of our constitutional law.[7] Certainly an independent judiciary as provided by the Constitution has assured that the governed as well as the government are bound by the Rule of Law. But a federal court is almost never the first to ponder the constitutional questions that come before it. Article III of the Constitution commands federal courts to decide only genuine cases or controversies. We cannot pluck interesting legal questions out of the air and decide them for the benefit of future generations. We need a concrete, real-life dispute. If the question is whether a particular government act violates individual rights, for example, a federal court has nothing to say until the action is taken or is about to be taken.

This means that, in the first instance, it is up to state and federal legislators and executives to decide that the laws they enact, or the actions they are about to take, are constitutional. This decision is as much their responsibility as it is the Court's. Thus, the Constitution requires all officials—legislative and executive, federal and state—to swear, upon taking office, that they will "support this Constitution."[8] Provisions of the Constitution are addressed directly to legislators and executive officials. The First Amendment says that "Congress shall make no law" abridging the freedom of speech,[9] and the Fourteenth Amendment provides that "no State shall make or enforce any law which shall abridge the privileges or immunities of citizens of the United States."[10]

The historical development of the Constitution supports the view that legislatures have an obligation to debate and consider the constitutionality of the laws they enact. George Washington, for example, thought that legislators should have supreme authority in constitutional as well as political decision making, and he believed that only legislatures could make constitutional decisions—that only legislatures could engage the public in an intelligent constitutional dialogue. Washington was confident that conscientious legislators would assure that national policy reflected what he called "the pure and immutable principles of private morality."[11]

Chief Justice John Marshall unequivocally declared in *Marbury v. Madison* that "it is emphatically the province and duty of the judicial department to say what the law is,"[12] but even he perceived a role for the legislature and the executive in constitutional interpretation. Marshall's later opinions acknowledge that even where questions are properly in the sphere of judicial review, Congress, the President, and all state officials have parallel, if not equal, responsibility for interpreting and enforcing the Constitution.

The *Congressional Record* is full of examples of legislators taking this responsibility very seriously. Questions of federalism worried both the proponents and opponents of the Sherman Antitrust Act; the checks and balances that the Constitution imposes on the different branches of government provoked heated debate at the time of the New Deal; and questions concerning the First Amendment and individual rights were raised continually during the McCarthy hearings.

These debates are not mere dress rehearsals for the inevitable judicial review. Many times, the legislature's or executive's decision will be final. This certainly is true when the legislative body decides not to enact a constitutionally questionable bill. Even when the government acts, the judiciary is not drawn into play until someone with a personal stake in the matter challenges the government practice in court.

As anyone who has had any dealings with the judicial system can tell you, this is no easy task. Yet without people willing to argue their interpretation of the Constitution "all the way to the Supreme Court," we would have little to do. Preparation for presenting cases to the Supreme Court often requires the expenditure of considerable time, money, and effort. For example, the argument in *Brown v. Board of Education*,[13] challenging racially segregated public schools in four states and the District of Columbia, was the culmination of years of work by hundreds of lawyers and researchers, costing thousands of dollars.

For another petitioner before the Court, Clarence Earl Gideon, it was not a question of time or money. He had plenty of time—he had been sentenced to five years in Florida state prison—and he had so little money that he was allowed to petition the Supreme Court without paying the usual fees and printing costs. What he needed was hope. It is perhaps a wonder that he had any left, after being tried and convicted without the assistance of a lawyer, and after his conviction was upheld on appeal. Somehow, Gideon still did have hope that the Supreme Court would consider his petition, handwritten on prison stationery, arguing that he had a constitutional right to the assistance of a lawyer when he was tried by the state. Of course, Gideon's hope turned out to have substance. The Court took his case and, after hearing full argument by appointed counsel, held that the Fourteenth Amendment guarantees state criminal defendants a right to counsel.[14]

Although the Supreme Court almost never has the first word in interpreting the Constitution, many believe that it usually has the last. The Supreme Court's interpretation of the Constitution is considered binding on the states and on the other branches of the federal government. But when it comes to putting the interpretation of the Constitution into practice, ultimately the Court must rely on the other branches of government.

There is a story, almost certainly apocryphal, that when the great Chief Justice John Marshall decided a very controversial case against the state of Georgia, President Andrew Jackson commented: "John Marshall has made his decision, now let him enforce it."[15] I think the story has survived despite numerous efforts by historians to discredit it because it reminds us of the remarkable nature of something that we Americans usually take for granted: the willingness of the other branches of government to enforce the Court's rulings, even those with which they disagree.

Certainly, one of the most dramatic examples of the executive branch enforcing a Supreme Court decision occurred on September 24, 1957, when President Eisenhower ordered federal troops to Little Rock, Arkansas, to ensure that, pursuant to the Court's decision in *Brown v. Board of Education* striking down racially segregated public schools, nine black children would enter Little Rock's Central High

School. On that day, President Eisenhower addressed the nation and explained that his duty to uphold the ruling of the Supreme Court was "inescapable."[16]

But far more remarkable and inspiring are the many more times state or federal officials conform their operations to Court decisions with little delay or dispute. For example, it was reported that the states' response to the Court's decision in *Gideon* was "swift and constructive,"[17] with the most dramatic response coming from Florida, the state that had tried Gideon without a defense lawyer. Barely two months after the Supreme Court issued its decision in *Gideon,* the Florida legislature approved a statute creating a public defender in each of the state's sixteen judicial circuits.

These examples illustrate this country's devotion to the Rule of Law—a devotion without which the protection of liberty would be impossible.

Because of the Court's crucial role as the protector of individual rights against majority rule, at times the Court's decisions will prevail over the strong disagreement of a great many Americans. If, however, one looks at the history of the Court, the country, and the Constitution over a very long period, the relationship appears to be more of a dialogue than a series of commands. Some Supreme Court decisions, controversial when they were issued, later have been strongly affirmed by the majority of Americans. *Brown v. Board of Education* is one of those decisions. Today the fundamental injustice of racially segregated public schools is beyond mainstream political debate. No one who rejects the basic premise of *Brown* could run for an elected office in this country and hope to win.

Gideon v. Wainwright is another example. Only months after the Court issued its decision, governors and legislators of states that had previously tried poor defendants without the benefit of counsel wholeheartedly embraced the Court's decision.

The history books also provide very clear examples of Supreme Court decisions that were completely rethought after vehement criticism by the nation. The infamous *Dred Scott* decision is the example that first comes to mind.[18] But it does not always take a civil war to reverse a Supreme Court decision. The Eleventh Amendment, which prohibits federal courts from hearing cases brought against a state by citizens of another state, passed swiftly after a Supreme Court decision allowed such suits.[19] The amendment was intended specifically to overrule the decision.

The vast majority of reversals of Supreme Court decisions, however, have not required amendments to the Constitution. Often the changes occur when the composition of the Court changes. When the Court in the 1930s struck down as unconstitutional much of the New Deal legislation that President Franklin Roosevelt offered as a way to deal with a severely depressed economy,[20] it met with a storm of criticism. After Justice Van Devanter's retirement in 1937 and the death of some of the Court's most conservative members, President Roosevelt appointed new Justices and the Court shifted its view of the constitutionality of some of the New Deal legislation.

There are more recent Supreme Court decisions on which dynamic dialogue between the Court and the American public continues. Since the Court struck down as unconstitutional limitations by states on abortions in the first three months of pregnancy,[21] large numbers of people have taken regularly to the streets to demonstrate either their support of or their opposition to the decision. Abortion is still hotly debated in all political arenas. No one, it seems, considers the Supreme Court decision in *Roe v. Wade* to have settled the issue for all time. Such intense debate by citizens is as it should be. A nation that docilely and unthinkingly approved every Supreme Court decision as infallible and immutable would, I believe, have severely disappointed our founders.

Finally, there are times when the Supreme Court does not act at all and it is left entirely up to the citizens to judge the constitutionality of the government's acts. Such a situation occurred in 1798, only seven years after the Bill of Rights was ratified by the states. The period was one of deep divisiveness in the nation. Some Americans believed that the country would go to war with France and accused other Americans of being too sympathetic to that country. The United States was a young, weak nation, and the party in power, the Federalists, believed that harsh criticism of the government during a time of crisis would lead to the country's downfall. So Congress, with the approval of President John Adams, passed the Sedition Act, which basically made it a crime to criticize the government.

The Supreme Court never ruled on the constitutionality of the Sedition Act. But the American people did—loudly and strongly. One of the first people tried under the Sedition Act was a member of Congress from Vermont named Matthew Lyon. An outspoken and rather rambunctious Jeffersonian, Lyon published a newspaper that included harsh criticisms of John Adams. He was convicted of sedition and spent the end of that congressional term in prison. The Federalists thought they had silenced a nuisance; instead they had created a hero. Lyon continued to publish severe criticisms of the Federalists, written from his prison cell. He ran for reelection from prison and won. When he completed his prison term, crowds turned out to greet him and cheer him on his return to Congress. Soon afterward, the Federalists were voted out of power and the party became extinct.

About 160 years later, in 1964, the Supreme Court, in *New York Times v. Sullivan*, found the people's judgment of the Sedition Act a powerful precedent on the meaning of the First Amendment guarantee of free speech. "Although the Sedition Act was never tested in this Court," the opinion said, "the attack upon its validity has carried the day in the court of history."[22]

Some might find it a bit frightening to consider that the responsibility for protecting our Constitution rests not just on judges but on a host of others as well. The responsibility is shared by state and federal legislators considering the constitutionality of proposed laws; by litigants who must marshal the time, money, and hope to take cases to court; by political officeholders (including the President himself)[23] who must see that the Court's rulings are put into practice; and by citizens, who ultimately must determine the nation's response to each major issue. I find the system quite comforting. By spreading the responsibility to uphold the Constitution among so many, the Framers enlisted a legion of defenders for their new charter.

President Franklin Roosevelt called the Constitution a "layman's document,"[24] and certainly it was not intended solely, or even primarily, for judges. While James Madison hoped that the courts would be an "impenetrable bulwark" against assumptions of power by the other branches, he also believed that state legislatures would be "sure guardians of the people's liberty."[25]

And when Madison argued for a bill of rights, he knew that the strength of these freedoms would depend on how firmly they stood in the hearts of citizens. He hoped that whatever the majority might want at any given moment, they would want to uphold the Constitution more. We honor the Constitution and its Framers when we run for legislative or executive office, write a letter to the President, our governor, or our legislator, take a constitutional case to court, or teach our children the meaning of the document—and when we argue among our friends and neighbors over the application of constitutional commands to modern life.

Our Constitution is not—and could never be—defended only by a group of judges. One of our greatest judges, Learned Hand, understood this very well. He explained: "Liberty lies in the hearts of men and women; when it dies there, no constitution, no law, no court can save it; no constitution, no court, no law can even do much to help it. While it lies there it needs no constitution, no law, no court to save it."[26]

Surely these are the words of truth. But our understanding today must go beyond the recognition that "liberty lies in [our] hearts" to the further recognition that only citizens with knowledge about the content and meaning of our constitutional guarantees of liberty are likely to cherish those concepts.

CHAPTER SEVEN

The Ratification

———

THE CONSTITUTION WAS APPROVED BY THE TWELVE STATE delegations to the Philadelphia Convention in 1787. But it did not become the Constitution of the United States until June 21, 1788, when New Hampshire became the ninth state to ratify the new plan of government.

The year 1788 also saw the formation of the first two national political parties in American life: the Federalists and the Anti-Federalists. These two groups had very different visions of America's future. The Federalists generally drew their ranks from the eastern shores of the thirteen states and from the merchants and business interests. They favored a strong central government able to regulate interstate and foreign commerce and to provide the naval power necessary to make America a great commercial and military power. The Anti-Federalists generally were farmers from the western portions of the young republic. They were suspicious of national government, preferring the grassroots democracy of the state assembly house to the grandiose dreams of a vast new nation entertained by the Federalists.[1]

We do not know whether a majority of the voters in 1788 supported ratification. Mr. Gallup and his pollsters were not there. But it is very likely the Anti-Federalists predominated.[2] We do know that, in a legal sense, the Anti-Federalists lost the great debate of 1788; after all, they opposed adoption of the Constitution. But on a deeper level, they were part of a remarkable dialogue about the ends of democratic government.[3] Both the Federalists and the Anti-Federalists represented values deeply ingrained in the American spirit. Many of the issues that di-

vided these two groups are still the source of lively debate in our courtrooms and our living rooms today. This is what makes the debate over
the ratification of the Constitution worth remembering and thinking
about.

Probably it is difficult for Americans today to conceive of the controversy that surrounded the proposal of the Constitution to the thirteen states for ratification. Have you ever tried to imagine how you
would have viewed the document produced behind closed doors in
Philadelphia had you lived in those days? What we regard today as a
stable and enlightened governmental structure was, in 1788, a radical
experiment in political theory.

The government proposed by the new Constitution was, of course,
not a pure democracy, although it had democratic elements. It was not
a confederation of states, but neither was it a centrist government on
the model of France or England. The three branches of the national
government were separated, but they each had a hand in the exercise
of the others' powers. The Anti-Federalists branded the proposed Constitution "a spurious brat," "a thirteen-horned monster," and "a het-
erogeneous phantom."[4] In contrast, the Federalists often referred to
the new Constitution as "our New Roof," thus downplaying its innova-
tive elements and giving the impression that the Philadelphia convention had made merely a few spring-housekeeping repairs to the
Articles of Confederation.[5]

That the Philadelphia Convention had done much more than
merely refurbish the old confederation between the states was readily
apparent to the Anti-Federalists. At the close of the Constitutional Convention, Edmund Randolph and George Mason of Virginia and El-
bridge Gerry of Massachusetts refused to put their names to the
document. They saw in the great powers given to the national government the end of the independence of the states and their legislatures.
They complained about the lack of a bill of rights, securing to the people the rights of free speech and press and the right to be free from the
kind of roving house-to-house searches carried on by the king's officers under the hated "writs of assistance."[6] Mason also decried the re-
fusal of the convention to provide for an end to the slave trade.[7]

Some of these concerns were to be among the main themes of the opposition in the state ratifying conventions. Underlying the concerns was a belief that "every man has a natural propensity to power."[8] Power given is likely to be exercised, and the proposed Constitution, in the view of the Anti-Federalists, gave too much unrestrained power to the new national government.

After the close of the Philadelphia Convention, the Constitution was sent to the Continental Congress of the old Articles of Confederation, which would decide whether or not the document should be submitted to the states for ratification. The Anti-Federalists were quick to point out that, by offering the Constitution to the states for ratification, the Continental Congress would essentially be "signing its own death warrant."[9] They even moved to censure the delegates to the Philadelphia Convention for exceeding their mandate from Congress, which was merely to *reform* the Articles of Confederation.

These efforts failed, and on September 28, 1787, Congress formally submitted the proposed Constitution to the states for their approval[10]—probably the only time in our history that politicians have literally voted themselves out of office.

By early January 1788, five states—Delaware, Pennsylvania, New Jersey, Connecticut, and Georgia—had ratified the Constitution, three of them unanimously. It was clear that the small states were satisfied with the convention's so-called Connecticut Compromise, which had guaranteed them equal representation in the Senate.[11] What was not so clear, given the strong difference of opinions, was how the Constitution would fare in the larger states, such as Massachusetts, Virginia, and New York. A national union was unthinkable without any one of these three states, the largest and most populous of the Confederation.

The Massachusetts ratifying convention opened on January 9, 1788, and the outlook for the new Constitution was not good. There were 355 delegates present, and the common estimate was that the Anti-Federalists held a thirty-vote advantage.[12] If Massachusetts failed to ratify the Constitution, it was unlikely that Virginia or New York would do so, and the work of the Philadelphia Convention would become just another failed political reform.

The convention opened with a debate concerning Article I, Sec. 2, of the proposed Constitution, which provided for two-year terms for members of the House of Representatives. Massachusetts was the birthplace of the town meeting and had a long history of annual elections to the state legislature. The Anti-Federalists, who were strong partisans of direct democracy, thought that a two-year term was a prescription for a standing aristocracy and would loosen the ties of political responsibility between the people and their representatives. The Federalists, many of whom had favored a longer term of office at the Constitutional Convention, saw representation not as a defect but as an opportunity. It would act as a filter, allowing less sectarian, more nationally minded politicians to find their way into Congress. As the Federalist Fisher Ames put it to his fellow delegates: "Much has been said about the people divesting themselves of power, when they delegate it to representatives; and that all representation is to their disadvantage. . . . I cannot agree to either of these opinions. The representation of the people is something *more* than the people."[13]

The debate between the Federalists and the Anti-Federalists over the ends of representative government remains with us today. Should our representatives be simple mirrors for the will of their constituents, as the Anti-Federalists thought, or should they be, in the words of Fisher Ames, "something more"? Should a representative be prepared to sacrifice the interests of his or her constituents in the name of the national interest? Should the terms of members of Congress be longer to reduce their ties to local interests and give them a more nationalist perspective?

The Federalists and the Anti-Federalists offered different answers to these questions, based on their divergent views about the ends of representative government. That many Americans would answer these questions differently today is an indication that the Federalists and the Anti-Federalists are in a sense still competing for control of American political culture.

Perhaps the chief objection of the Massachusetts Anti-Federalists was the absence of a bill of rights. As George Nassom, a leading Anti-Federalist at the Massachusetts convention, put it: "When I give up my natural rights it is for the security of the rest; but here is not *one* right secured, although many are neglected."[14] A more colorful complaint was made by Amos Singletary, who said that "lawyers, and men of learning and moneyed men" planned to control the government and would "secure all the power and all the money [and] swallow up all us little folks."[15] The people of Massachusetts were proud of their own Bill of Rights, drafted in 1780, largely by the pen of John Adams.[16] Throughout the convention, there were frequent references to the protections of the Massachusetts Constitution and their absence in the proposed federal Constitution. As the convention entered its third week, it became apparent that the new Constitution would be defeated unless some accommodation was reached with those who desired a bill of rights.

John Hancock, governor of Massachusetts and president of the ratifying convention, proposed just such an accommodation. He had remained scrupulously neutral up to this point. Now he came out in favor of ratification, but proposed that the convention adopt several amendments to be referred to the first Congress. These included a reservation to the states of all powers not expressly delegated to the federal government, the right to a jury trial in civil cases, and the right to an indictment by a grand jury in criminal cases.[17] Hancock's maneuver swung Samuel Adams, and with him about thirty Anti-Federalist votes, to the side of the new Constitution. On February 6, 1788, Massachusetts became the sixth state to ratify the Constitution, by a vote of 187 to 168. The convention also ratified nine amendments to be presented to the first Congress.[18] Both the new Constitution and the movement for a bill of rights had received a significant boost from the Massachusetts convention.

The call for a bill of rights was taken up in Maryland, where the ratifying convention met at Annapolis on April 21, 1788. As the *Maryland Farmer,* a widely read Anti-Federalist tract, put it: "Often the natural rights of the individual are opposed to the presumed interests or heated passions of a large majority of democratic government[.] [I]f these rights are not clearly and expressly ascertained, the individual must be lost."[19] Generally, the Federalists replied, as Hamilton did in

The Federalist Papers, that a bill of rights was unnecessary because the federal government was accorded only limited and expressly enumerated powers. In the *Federalist* (no. 84), Hamilton asked: "Why declare that things shall not be done which there is no power to do? Why, for instance, should it be said that the liberty of the press shall not be restrained, when no power is given by which restrictions shall be imposed?"[20] The Anti-Federalists responded that Congress's power to levy taxes or to regulate commerce could be used to stifle a free press.[21]

On April 28, 1788, Maryland became the seventh state to ratify the Constitution. The state convention proposed thirteen amendments, including one providing that "the freedom of the press shall be inviolably preserved."[22]

On May 23, 1788, South Carolina became the eighth state to approve the new Constitution.

All eyes now turned to Virginia, where the ratifying convention opened on the second of June. Patrick Henry, whose eloquence had helped fan the flames of revolution against the British Crown, was the leader of the Anti-Federalist forces. On the side of the new Constitution were James Madison—and a young lawyer named John Marshall, who would go on to become a great Chief Justice of the Supreme Court.

The principal concern of the Virginia Anti-Federalists was that the states would lose their political independence to the new national government. Patrick Henry opened his attack by challenging the very first words the Constitutional Convention had written. "Who authorized them to speak the language of, *We, the people,* instead of, *We, the states?*" Henry asked.[23] In the national government's power to lay taxes, to regulate commerce, and to control the armed forces, Henry saw the seeds of tyranny and the end of state government. "What shall the states have to do?" he asked. "Abolish the state legislatures at once," he cried; "[for] what purposes should they be continued?"[24]

For the Anti-Federalists, only one government could be truly sovereign, and in their eyes the Constitution left no doubt that the national government would call the dance and the states would merely follow. Others, in other states, agreed with Henry. For example, Thomas Wait of Maine wrote: "The vast Continent of America cannot be long subjected to a Democracy if consolidated into one government. You might as well attempt to rule Hell by Prayer."[25]

In Virginia James Madison made the Federalist reply. The national government was given the great powers of taxation and control of commerce and the military because these were exactly the areas where Americans had found the Articles of Confederation wanting. If these powers were necessary to efficient national government, what was the sense of withholding them? Madison asked. The powers of the national government were in any case expressly enumerated, and the states by implication retained the power to legislate on all other subjects. Madison feared not the annihilation of the states but rather "that the powerful and prevailing influence of the states will produce such attentions to local considerations as will be inconsistent with the advancement of the Union."[26]

On June 25, 1788, the Virginia convention ratified the Constitution by a vote of only 89 to 79. The delegates' concern that the powers of the state legislatures be preserved was reflected in the first among twenty amendments that the Virginia convention proposed to Congress. It provided "that each state in the Union shall respectively retain every power, jurisdiction, and right, which is not by this Constitution delegated to the Congress of the United States, or to the departments of the federal government."[27] Eight other states made similar proposals, and this express guarantee of state sovereignty and autonomy became the Tenth Amendment to our Constitution.[28]

Issues of state sovereignty in the face of a national government have been with us ever since 1788. For example, the fears of the Anti-Federalists about a dilution of the power of the people to elect their representatives were addressed eventually, at least in part, by the Seventeenth Amendment, providing for direct election of senators, and by the gradual removal of various barriers to the exercise of the franchise by women, by people of all races, and by nonproperty-owners.

But in our nation's worst failure, for almost a century after the ratification of the Constitution the state sovereignty so dear to the hearts of the Anti-Federalists was used by some to shield the evil of racial discrimination and the institution of slavery. It took a tragic civil war and adoption of the Thirteenth, Fourteenth, and Fifteenth Amendments to begin the process of assuring equal justice under the Constitution for *all* our citizens, black as well as white.

The remaining autonomy of the states, however, has been a force for good in some other areas. In the early 1900s, states such as New York and Wisconsin enacted minimum-wage and maximum-hours laws to deal with the terrible working conditions in urban factories. Not until the Great Depression did the federal government abandon its laissez-faire attitude toward business and undertake many reforms borrowed from the example of a few pioneering states.[29] More recently, a number of states have taken the lead in developing "workfare," re-training programs for displaced workers, new forms of health and medical insurance, and a variety of laws to protect the environment. And in another exercise of state sovereignty, states have sometimes provided greater state constitutional guarantees of individual liberty than are provided in the Bill of Rights.

Questions of state autonomy also have been a source of contro-versy for legal scholars and the Supreme Court itself. In the late 1930s, with the advent of significant federal intervention into economic af-fairs, the Court began to treat the Tenth Amendment as "but a truism that all is retained that has not been surrendered."[30] As a constitutional matter, congressional power under the commerce clause seemed to be limitless. In the 1970s the Court shifted its position and found in the Tenth Amendment "the constitutional policy that Congress may not exercise power in a fashion that impairs the States' integrity or their ability to function effectively in a federal system."[31] In the 1980s a closely divided Court reversed itself again in *Garcia v. San Antonio Metro Transit Authority*, embracing the view that the Tenth Amend-ment was merely declaratory, and that the states could protect their au-tonomy without judicial intervention through their influence in the national political processes.[32]

In the 1990s the debate continued, as the Court limited its reliance on the "federal legislative process model." In 1992, in *New York v. United States,* we stated: "The Constitution . . . 'leaves to the several States a residuary and inviolable sovereignty.' . . . Whatever the outer limits of that sovereignty may be, one thing is clear: *The Federal Government may not compel the States to enact or administer a federal regulatory program.*"³³ We reiterated the point in *Printz v. United States* with forceful language: "Congress cannot circumvent [the constitutional] prohibition by conscripting the States' officers directly. The Federal Government may neither issue directives requiring the States to address political problems, nor command the States' officers . . . to administer or enforce a federal regulatory program."³⁴

Our decisions in *New York v. United States* and *Printz v. United States* thus confirm that the judicial branch still does have an important role to play in articulating affirmative restrictions on the extent to which Congress may directly regulate the states or their officers.

Whatever the next chapter of the Court's Tenth Amendment jurisprudence holds, we cannot afford to forget the Anti-Federalists' concern: the state legislatures *are* closest to the people and reflect their will in the most direct manner. As Justice Holmes once warned, we must never allow the use of federal power "to prevent the making of social experiments that an important part of the community desires, in the insulated chambers afforded by the several States."³⁵

For the Anti-Federalists, the autonomy of the states and the rights of the individual were part and parcel of the same program of democratic freedom. They saw in the state legislatures democracy close to the source, the expression of the people themselves. One of the important lessons of 1788 is that the independence of the states helps to protect one of our most cherished liberties: the right to govern ourselves.

Like all truly great debates over first principles, the ratification debates of 1788 have never really ended. Compromises were reached over the autonomy of the states in the face of a national union, but such compromises are not self-effectuating. In a real sense, the Federalists and the Anti-Federalists bequeathed to us the principles themselves, not the answers. We are called upon to balance those principles again and again in the circumstances of our age.

The "dual sovereignty" of our national and state governments is a novel experiment. But like many ingenious and complex innovations, it is a fragile one. Today the forces of economic and technological modernization, as well as the international climate, often suggest the expediency of the Federalist vision of a powerful national government. In the face of daunting economic and social problems, the sweep of federal power is sometimes alluring.

We must never forget, however, that the answers to many of our deepest national dilemmas may lie not in Washington, D.C., but in the American spirit of ingenuity embodied in lawmaking authority closest to the people themselves: our state and local legislatures. In 1788 Americans faced the challenge of adopting a radically new system of government. One of the *most* important challenges facing Americans today is preserving the role that independent state governments must play in ensuring the success of that system of government in the new century and beyond.

CHAPTER EIGHT

The Evolution of the Bill of Rights

———

*A*S THE PREVIOUS CHAPTER ILLUSTRATES, THE BATTLE OVER the Bill of Rights was hard fought. Both sides were armed with strong arguments to support their positions. These arguments were repeated over and over again as the Constitution was sent to the various state assemblies for ratification. As it turned out, the Anti-Federalists were not without influence. In some state legislatures they held a majority of the votes. Thus, key states such as Massachusetts and Virginia refused to ratify the Constitution unless a bill of rights was added.

Their argument was simple and eminently logical: many state constitutions already contained a bill of rights, and they saw no good reason why the federal Constitution should not contain one as well. It did not have to be a lengthy document. All that was required was a short, plain statement that powers not expressly conveyed to the new government were reserved to the states. As Patrick Henry put it, "Why not say so? Is it because it will consume too much paper?"[1]

The bottom line was this: the Constitution was not going to be ratified unless the Federalists compromised by agreeing to add a bill of rights. And that is precisely what they did. To overcome the objections of the Anti-Federalists, the Federalists promised that, soon after the Constitution became effective, amendments would be added to expressly limit certain actions by the federal government and to protect the autonomy of the states. Thus, the Bill of Rights recognized the proposition that the states are powerful sovereigns, nearly equal to the national government.

This is the great irony of the Bill of Rights. Most Americans think of the Constitution and the Bill of Rights as going hand in hand. But the more appropriate analogy is ball and chain. The Bill of Rights was a restraint imposed on the new federal government to keep it from running out of control. It was put there in response to concerns by people who would have been quite happy had the Constitution never been ratified. Adding to the irony is this fact: while the Constitution is the cornerstone of our nation's commitment to principles of representative government and majority rule, the Bill of Rights is a decidedly anti-majoritarian document. In the Bill of Rights, the Framers built a wall around certain fundamental individual freedoms, forever limiting the majority's ability to intrude upon them.

As originally adopted, of course, the Bill of Rights was directed only at abuses of power by the *federal* government. Since then, however, the protection it affords to individual rights and liberties has expanded. This is a result of the Fourteenth Amendment, added in the wake of the Civil War. That amendment requires *states* to accord all citizens due process and equal protection of the laws. In a series of landmark decisions, the Supreme Court has interpreted the Fourteenth Amendment to incorporate most of the other detailed provisions of the Bill of Rights—such as freedom of the press,[2] and the right not to be tried twice for the same crime.[3] Thus, the fundamental liberties guaranteed in the Bill of Rights now are protected against encroachment by the states as well as by the federal government.

The Bill of Rights is truly a remarkable document. Upon reading it, one cannot help but be struck by how concise it is. Countless thousands of pages have been written about it, but the Bill of Rights itself sums up our most precious freedoms—more than two dozen fundamental rights—in fewer than five hundred words. And its brevity is not accidental. Before James Madison rose in Congress to read his first draft, he pored over hundreds of provisions suggested by various state ratifying conventions. He could have compiled them all into a lengthy document, but chose not to. He decided, quite deliberately, to single out only a handful of fundamental principles. His view was that enumerating additional rights of less significance would risk diminishing the document's importance. After all, a laundry list of lesser rights, such as the right to wear powdered wigs in public, would sit uneasily beside such fundamental liberties as freedom of speech and religion.

Madison was keenly conscious of the language he used in framing the Bill of Rights. The proposals offered by the various state conventions used tentative terms. An earlier state version of what became our Eighth Amendment provided that "excessive bail *ought not* to be required." Madison replaced the tentative terms with stronger ones, transforming suggestions into bold declarations. Thus, the Eighth Amendment declares in no uncertain terms that "excessive bail *shall not* be required. . . ." This kind of language does not *request* that the government afford the people certain freedoms; it *demands* it. It declares that they exist as a matter of natural law, and that the government has no authority to interfere with their exercise.

Likewise, the First Amendment does not *ask* the government to refrain from intervening in religious matters. It declares unflinchingly that "Congress *shall make no law* respecting an establishment of religion, or prohibiting the free exercise thereof." This strong language serves two purposes. It inspires and reassures those of us who hold the rights, and it warns any who would dare violate these rights that they may not do so.

The Bill of Rights is both simple and eloquent. The ten amendments are written in language that any literate American can understand and many can recite from memory. And at the same time that they are forcefully written, they are neither rigid nor inflexible. The Bill of Rights was drafted intentionally in broad, sweeping terms, allowing meaning to be developed in response to changing times and current problems. In many ways, the Bill of Rights is like a novel by Faulkner or a painting by Monet: it does not change, but our understanding and perception of it may. Had the Bill of Rights been written in less broad terms, it might not have withstood the passage of time. The world today is a much different place than it was two centuries ago. We have different problems, different priorities, and different technologies than our ancestors had.

As a result, several of the amendments are as vital today—or more so—than when they were adopted. Consider the First Amendment's declaration that "Congress shall make no law . . . abridging the freedom of speech." In drafting this provision, the primary concern was to protect political speech: specifically, criticism of the government. In England, outspoken critics of the king had sometimes been labeled traitors and severely punished. It was thus of immense importance to the early Americans, in setting up their own government, to permit all kinds of political speech. More than two hundred years later, we continue to value the importance of speech on political topics and afford it constitutional protection, no matter how controversial or despised its substance may be. Indeed, the First Amendment has been relied on to permit even neo-Nazis to march and speak in a city that included Holocaust survivors.[4]

At the same time, the First Amendment has been invoked to protect speech on all sorts of topics far removed from politics—topics that its drafters could never have imagined. This has required the Supreme Court to grapple with a host of difficult issues. One case, for instance, questioned whether the First Amendment prohibits a high school principal from keeping stories about pregnancy and birth control out of the school paper.[5] Another asked whether pharmacies must be permitted to advertise their prices for over-the-counter drugs.[6] We have even had to decide whether New Hampshire residents who disagree with the state motto, "Live Free or Die," can use tape to cover that part of their license plates.[7]

Nevertheless, the guarantee of "the freedom of speech" contained in the Bill of Rights is not absolute. The Court has held, for example, that obscene speech is not protected.[8]

Further removed from the drafters' vision of the First Amendment are cases holding that the First Amendment protects conduct that conveys a particular message. Thus, the Court has ruled that a junior high school could not prohibit its students from wearing black armbands to protest the nation's involvement in the Vietnam War.[9] And, more recently, the Court held that the First Amendment invalidates a statute criminalizing the burning of an American flag as a form of protest,[10] although it does not invalidate a prohibition on nude dancing in public places.[11]

Another constant and inexhaustible source of litigation has been the Fourth Amendment, which protects Americans against "unreasonable searches and seizures." This amendment was included in the Bill of Rights to outlaw in this country the much despised British practice of conducting unannounced house-to-house searches, pursuant to so-called writs of assistance.

But the Fourth Amendment has come to stand for much more. Technological advancements that Madison and his contemporaries could never have foreseen have made it possible for the government to conduct a search without ever entering a person's home. For example, wiretaps allow people's conversations to be monitored and recorded without their knowledge. The Court has held that to be a search.[12] It has also determined that a search occurs when police officers use thermal-imaging devices to "see" through walls.[13] But this leads to further questions. Does it matter whether the technology is generally available to the public? How available is generally available? Do Fourth Amendment protections decrease as technology becomes even more advanced?

Questions like these are difficult, and no amount of study of James Madison's private notes will yield a conclusive answer.

Just as technology has made the Fourth Amendment a murkier area than our forebears could have suspected, biological science has complicated application of the Fifth Amendment. The Fifth Amendment guarantees that no one "shall be compelled in any criminal case to be a witness against himself." We all know from watching TV police shows what the Fifth Amendment means: "You have the right to remain silent." The government cannot force you to testify against yourself if you are accused of a crime. The inspiration for this amendment can be traced all the way back to the Inquisition, where heretics were routinely tortured until they confessed their sins.

But today the government can often tell whether someone is guilty without an oral confession. It can test drivers' blood to see if they have been driving while intoxicated. Or it can analyze defendants' DNA structure to determine conclusively whether a single hair or body-fluid sample found at the scene of a crime belongs to them. The question for the Court has become whether the Fifth Amendment allows the government to compel the extraction and use of such evidence.

These amendments—the First, Fourth, and Fifth—were adopted in the infancy of our republic, but they remain a constant source of litigation, controversy—and inspiration—even in a new millennium. Time and technology have advanced, yet these provisions remain vital because our ancestors recognized the importance of framing our most basic rights in broad terms.

On the other hand, other of the amendments are little remembered today. Cited very rarely is the Third Amendment, which declares: "No Soldier shall, in time of peace be quartered in any house, without the consent of the Owner, nor in time of war, but in a manner to be prescribed by law." This had been a very real problem in eighteenth-century England. Soldiers were put in people's homes, and the homeowner was made responsible for providing room and board. But this has never been a policy in our country. While the government may, in times of war, take young people out of their homes and draft them into the military, it rarely tries to put soldiers *into* people's houses.

There are two other amendments that do not enumerate any specific freedoms, but which were nonetheless of vital significance to those who drafted the Bill of Rights. They are the Ninth and Tenth Amendments.

The Ninth Amendment provides that the rights enumerated in the Bill of Rights are not the *only* rights possessed by the people. Probably the most famous example of an unenumerated right is the right to privacy. In *Griswold v. Connecticut,*[14] the Court held that the Constitution protects a right of privacy, including the right of married couples to use contraceptives. The nature and description of unenumerated rights, and the extent to which they are subject to the highest level of judicial scrutiny, is hotly debated. But there is little doubt that some such rights do exist. And there is little doubt that we will see more litigation to test and define them.

The Tenth Amendment sets out in a single sentence the Anti-Federalists' main concern about the Constitution: that the new government not be permitted to usurp the sovereign authority of state governments: "The powers not delegated to the United States by the Constitution, nor prohibited by it to the States, are reserved to the States respectively, or to the people." The amendment makes clear that the power of the federal government is derived from the states, and that the Constitution is not to be construed to convey any more power to the government than is absolutely necessary to carry out its enumerated functions. All other power belongs to the states.

This understanding is consistent with the sentiments of the Anti-Federalists, who recognized that state legislatures were closer to the people than the new national government and more accurately reflected the people's wishes. It is also consistent with the sentiments of the Federalists, who, while desiring a strong central government, wanted to preserve strong state governments to prevent the federal government from abusing its power.

Of course, the Ninth and Tenth Amendments are not often relied upon by litigants. Like the Third Amendment, they have been largely ignored, at least for the time being. But this does not mean that they will not become more vital in the future. One would think that, after two centuries, we would have figured it all out. But we have not. More than two hundred years after the Bill of Rights was adopted, courts still grapple with many of the same questions. Thus, even though the First Amendment's freedom of speech clause and the Fourth Amendment's prohibition of unlawful searches have been subjects of litigation since the Framers' days, we their descendants are still working out the details.

And new questions are always being raised—questions that no one could have foreseen in our nation's earliest years. That is the beauty of the Bill of Rights. Along with the new questions come new understandings of what the amendments mean. For while the text of the Bill of Rights does not change, our perspective on it has evolved with the passage of time. The adoption of the Bill of Rights deserves our praise and thanksgiving. It is part of our American contribution to the notion of justice and freedom.

CHAPTER NINE

The Judiciary Act of 1789 and the American Judicial Tradition

---

HE JUDICIARY ACT WAS PASSED BY THE FIRST CONGRESS OF the United States on September 24, 1789. The act stands at the beginning of a tradition that has well served the entire nation—and should continue to be viewed with pride by all Americans. For us the legal system plays a special role in how we preserve what we most value as a nation and in how we strive to become the nation that we aspire to be. The Judiciary Act was a crucial, foundational part of that American tradition of seeking to perfect the nation through considered change in accord with the Rule of Law. This impulse underlies many of the nation's greatest successes and remains as important today as it was more than two hundred years ago. In celebrating the Judiciary Act, we celebrate those people who have sacrificed to protect that legal system.

The Judiciary Act established many of the nation's fundamental legal institutions. As mandated by the Constitution, it established the Supreme Court of the United States and set the number of Justices—originally, at six. The Office of the Attorney General arose from the Judiciary Act. And the First Congress, exercising the discretion explicitly vested in it by the Constitution, chose to create a system of subsidiary federal courts, in addition to the Supreme Court. Because this decision was essential to the creation of an independent federal judiciary, Justice Felix Frankfurter deemed it the act's "transcendent achievement."[1] The nationwide network of federal, "district" trial courts exists to this day. Thankfully, a group of permanent circuit court judges has replaced the circuit court system originally established by the act, a system that, until 1891, employed local district court judges and visiting Supreme Court Justices, who literally "rode the circuit" of the intermediate courts scattered throughout the country.

While providing for an independent federal judiciary, the act recognized the competence and vital role of the states and their judicial systems. Congress vested exclusively in the federal courts only a small portion of the jurisdiction permitted by Article III, leaving the rest to be exercised either by the state and federal courts concurrently, or by the state courts alone, in the first instance. Though it gave state courts the power to rule on federal law, the act's Section 25 preserved the independence of that body of law by giving the Supreme Court the authority to review state-court judgments. This provision was vital to the nation's development. Justice Oliver Wendell Holmes claimed that, notwithstanding the undoubted importance of the judicial power to declare acts of Congress unconstitutional, the union itself "would be imperiled if we could not make that declaration as to the laws of the several States."[2]

Because this one act of Congress established so many lasting, fundamental elements of the nation's judicial system, it has deservedly won much praise. Justice Henry Brown in 1911 deemed the Judiciary Act "probably the most important and the most satisfactory Act ever passed by Congress."[3] A more recent commentator, the late Professor Paul Bator, noted that, since its passage, the act "has ever since been celebrated as 'a great law.'"[4]

The Judiciary Act stands as the single most important legislative enactment of the nation's founding years. The Declaration of Independence made clear that the American Revolution sought to defend our people's most basic liberties and cherished values. The Constitution, together with the Bill of Rights, gave form to the government that would protect those liberties and secure the common good. That government would succeed, and the liberties and values of our founding generation would be protected, only through the nation's commitment to the legal process and the Rule of Law. The Judiciary Act of 1789 gave concrete, practical form to that commitment and provided the means for our nation's continuing constitutional revolution.

For more than two centuries we have remained committed to the Rule of Law—to respect for the legal process that protects what our nation most values while allowing debate on what most needs change. The federal judiciary has often been the focus and defender of that tradition, which has served us admirably from the eighteenth century to now, the twenty-first. The judges who have so well performed the duties prescribed for them through all those years deserve our continued gratitude.

A comparison of the two profoundly important revolutions that occurred nearly simultaneously in 1789—the legal revolution in the United States initiated by passage of our Judiciary Act, and the much more visible revolution across the ocean in France—illustrates this nation's distinctive commitment and approach. The French revolutionaries valued reason and assumed that pure acts of will, guided by reason, would allow them to construct the ideal society. That revolution was one of transformation, seeking to uproot that which had gone before. Our nation's revolution was, by contrast, essentially one of conservation: conflict and institutional change appeared necessary to protect traditional liberties, community structures, and personal rights.

The two revolutionary traditions contained distinctly different conceptions of the legal process. The French revolutionaries, on balance, perceived law as an instrument of power. Law to them appeared at first to be merely the bulwark of the old order, and thus the legal system was an oppression that had to be overthrown. Once in power, the revolutionaries used the law to reconstruct their world. Law became an instrument to eradicate "undesirable" social orders, to ensure state control over the economy, and even to transform time and space. The revolutionaries redivided the calendar and gave each portion a new name. More familiar to us is the system of measurement they crafted: the metric system.

By contrast, the American revolutionaries embraced the legal process as their chosen means of protecting the values that their revolution had vindicated, and of providing for the community's peaceful, continuous evolution. In this sense, the Judiciary Act created the vehicle for this ongoing process of measured, considered change. Yet that act created only the mechanism of that change. In the end the nation's hope rested with those who safeguarded the legal process and with those who believed that law should govern all citizens impartially, that citizens must resolve their differences through the democratic process as provided by law, and that the legal process must be valued as the means of preserving that which is most fundamental to the nation.

The course of France and the United States in the years following their respective revolutions of 1789 illustrates their differing approaches. The French Revolution did, at least for a brief period, transform society. Successive cadres of revolutionaries stripped away the institutions and customs that stood between the centralized state and the most intimate details of each citizen's life. Various factions declared various rights and each time set the French nation upon a new course. Violence tore at the country: the civil war and executions that took hundreds of thousands of lives in the Vendée; the near anarchy of the September 1792 Massacre of the Innocents; the organized political violence of the Terror; and, finally, the foreign wars that led to the rise of Napoleon and the end of revolution.

During the same period, the United States was, in comparison, a tranquil place, in which the only war was a war of words. We often overlook how much, at least in domestic affairs, the disagreements of that time were cast in legal terms, and how often they were resolved in debates about or through the legal process. Many of the great conflicts of the day possessed this character. The debate over Alexander Hamilton's financial plans for the new nation often was framed in terms of the constitutionality of the first Bank of the United States. So, too, debate over the Alien and Sedition Acts became a struggle over the powers granted by law to the national government. The trial of Aaron Burr, the attempted impeachment of Justice Chase, the debate over the scope of the common law of crime, and the conflicts surrounding President Adams's midnight appointments (culminating in the case of *Marbury v. Madison*[5]) suggested that the nation would define itself

Justice John Marshall, Chief Justice of the United States (1801–35).

through debate within and concerning the legal system and the distribution of powers allowed by law.

⟁ This commitment to change in accord with the Rule of Law has
continued and increasingly has required that questions of fundamental concern to our citizens be resolved through the legal system. In the
early nineteenth century Alexis de Tocqueville, who wrote extensively
about his travels across the then-new nation of the United States, remarked upon this development: "There is hardly a political question in
the United States which does not sooner or later turn into a judicial
one."[6] This conclusion may overstate the matter, but it points to the enduring pattern of how our nation's commitment to the Rule of Law underlies and channels political change.

Judges may not usually be cast as revolutionaries. But our American reliance upon considered change to preserve enduring values ac-
cords a special role to the legal process. To be sure, the legal system
addresses only those issues thrust upon it and in this manner only
marks the shadows cast by more important institutions and social
forces—especially the legislative process and ongoing debate among
citizens about the nation's future. Even so, those who serve the legal
process have played a crucial role in protecting and shaping the varied
aspects of our constitutional system, as well as our nation's devotion to
change and continuity balanced through commitment to the Rule of
Law.

A brief mention of the contributions of some of the nation's great
judges illustrates three aspects of that commitment: the importance of
a strong and independent federal judiciary; due accord by that judiciary for the legislative process; and adherence to the Rule of Law, even
in the face of considerable popular opposition.

The fourth Chief Justice of the United States, John Marshall, contributed as much as any other person to that first element of our judicial tradition: ensuring that a strong and independent judiciary serves
the nation. It is no overstatement to claim that Chief Justice Marshall
fulfilled the Constitution's promise of an independent federal judiciary. While the Judiciary Act provided the foundation for the eventual

development of our judicial tradition, much of what is distinctive and praiseworthy in the subsequent development of the federal bench can be traced to Marshall's efforts.

Although it may be difficult to imagine our nation without an independent and vigorous federal judiciary, that fortunate result was hardly foreordained. The Supreme Court considered very few cases during its first years, and produced opinions that were marked by division. All but one of the original Justices left the Court after a relatively brief period of service. While on the Court, several Justices vigorously participated in partisan political activities—leading in one case to a nearly successful impeachment effort.

Unsurprisingly, the Supreme Court possessed neither public trust nor a particularly prominent national role. Congress suspended the Court's term so that it would not be able to consider certain cases, and many of the most prominent statesmen—Thomas Jefferson and James Madison included—argued that the states, rather than the Court, should finally determine certain constitutional issues. When President John Adams offered to reappoint former Chief Justice John Jay to the Court, Jay declined, replying that the Court could not "obtain the energy, weight, and dignity which were essential to its affording due support to the National government, nor acquire the public confidence and respect which, as the last resort of the justice of the nation, it should possess."[7]

Chief Justice Marshall's great achievement was to rescue the Court, and by extension the federal judiciary, from this dire state, and to fashion a role not unlike that which exists today. As one legal historian has concluded: "The genesis of the American judicial tradition was the transformation of the office of appellate judge under Chief Justice John Marshall."[8] Marshall unified the Court, which began to issue single, unanimous opinions in most cases. The Court became more independent. With Marshall as their Chief, members of the Court largely ceased participation in partisan activities. While the Court's efforts continued to engender criticism, as they inevitably do, those criticisms were based upon differences regarding fundamental legal principles rather than upon the personal behavior of individual Justices.

Largely through Chief Justice Marshall's efforts, the Court also assumed a role commensurate with its status under the Constitution as one of the three branches of national government. In the case of *Marbury v. Madison*, Chief Justice Marshall established the Court's ability—even responsibility—to judge the constitutionality of statutes passed by Congress when judges are called upon to apply them. Indeed, it was a section of the Judiciary Act that the Court, in an opinion by the Chief Justice himself, declared unconstitutional in *Marbury*. The Marshall Court also asserted the federal judiciary's responsibility to pursue its interpretation of the Constitution in the face of contrary assertions by state legislatures, state judges, or officials of the executive branch.

Beyond establishing the judiciary's unique and coequal constitutional role, the Court under Chief Justice Marshall's leadership interpreted the broad provisions of the Constitution to allocate power among the other, often competing, institutions in the federal union. Through a series of landmark cases, Marshall carved out a broad role for Congress in the exercise of its limited powers. At a time (quite unlike the present) when the power of the states threatened to engulf the still undefined powers of the new national legislature, his opinions ensured that the states could not frustrate the legitimate efforts of Congress—especially efforts to regulate the national economy. And in other cases, Marshall pioneered the Court's role in protecting individual rights against unconstitutional intrusions by state or national government.

By the time of Chief Justice Marshall's death in 1835, the Supreme Court was a respected institution, sufficiently powerful and independent to fulfill the role provided for it by the Constitution.

Another Chief Justice, William Howard Taft, succeeded brilliantly in continuing and building upon Chief Justice Marshall's efforts to strengthen the federal judiciary—not to mention being almost single-handedly responsible for the construction of its present building, in which all of his successors have presided.

As Chief Justice, Taft was responsible for many of the institutional changes that allowed the federal judiciary to adapt and respond to the great demands of twentieth-century America. He was instrumental in creating the institutions needed to manage and coordinate a federal judicial system, instead of the previous, loose amalgamation of individual judicial districts. He crafted and lobbied for legislation that gave the Supreme Court itself a great deal of control over its own docket.

Chief Justice Taft envisioned a judicial system that would be a more efficient and effective instrument of justice, open to all citizens with worthy claims, and able to respond to the legal demands of modern times. To fulfill this vision, he sought to unify and simplify the federal rules of procedure, combining the disparate practices existing in law and equity and placing them under the supervision of the Supreme Court. This goal was not fulfilled until after Taft's death, but it could not have been brought to fruition without his efforts.

Reflecting upon Chief Justice Taft's efforts to transform the federal judiciary, Justice Felix Frankfurter concluded that "Taft's great claim . . . in history will be as a law reformer."[9] Justice Frankfurter ranked Chief Justice Taft's accomplishments next to those of Chief Justice Oliver Ellsworth, the principal drafter of the Judiciary Act of 1789. While Chief Justice Ellsworth devised the judicial system, "Chief Justice Taft adapted it to the needs of a country that had grown from three million to 140 million."[10] Indeed, the judicial system so largely shaped by Taft now accommodates the needs of a nation of nearly 300 million.

A later group of judges built upon Chief Justice Marshall's and Chief Justice Taft's successes by accommodating the power of the federal judiciary to the values of democracy and to the demands of change in early-twentieth-century America. These judges brilliantly displayed the second characteristic of our nation's legal tradition: that the judiciary, though powerful, must not trammel the legitimate operation of the legislative process. This group included many of the giants of the field—Justice Oliver Wendell Holmes, Judge Learned Hand, and Justice Felix Frankfurter—and taught us that one value an independent judiciary must strive to protect is the ability of the community to define its future in accord with the Rule of Law.

Chief Justice Marshall had been, in a sense, nearly too successful in establishing an independent and strong federal judiciary. By the end of the nineteenth century, the federal judiciary was so powerful that certain judges' view of broad provisions of the Constitution led the courts to invalidate a range of congressional, and especially state, legislation. The stricken measures often attempted to confront the problems associated with an expanding national economy, increasing industrialization, and often-violent labor strife. The great contribution of Justices Holmes and Frankfurter and of Judge Hand is their reminder that judges cannot, ultimately, presume to direct the nation's ongoing process of change accomplished through the legislative process. Their work helps us remember that judges are citizens like others in the republic and not, in Judge Hand's phrase, Platonic Guardians.

All three judges drew their theories of judicial restraint from their skepticism that those in power possess some ultimate truth. As Justice Holmes wrote: "When men have realized that time has upset many fighting faiths, they may come to believe even more than they believe the very foundations of their own conduct that the ultimate good desired is better reached by free trade in ideas."[11] These judges doubted claims of superior knowledge or wisdom put forth by jurists who would displace legislators' considered judgment in assessing the meaning or constitutionality of a statute. In terms that bear repeating, Judge Hand laid out the task of a judge who must interpret a statute:

> The judge must always remember that he should go no further than he is sure the government would have gone, had it been faced with the case before him. If he is in doubt, he must stop, for he cannot tell that the conflicting interests in the society for which he speaks would have come to a just result, even though he is sure that he knows what the just result should be. He is not to substitute even his juster will for theirs; otherwise it would not be the common will which prevails, and to that extent the people would not govern.[12]

Similar regard for the democratic mandate given to legislators required a degree of restraint in deciding constitutional issues, too.

Judge Hand praised Justice Holmes for his caution in applying the theory of the day to place constitutional barriers before the legislatures: "That caution in the end must rest upon a counsel of skepticism or at least upon a recognition that there is but one test for divergent popular convictions, experiment, and that almost any experiment is in the end less dangerous than its suppression."[13]

In a few quarters, this theory of judicial restraint lies in some disrepute. But judicial restraint is not, as critics may argue, to be confused with an absence of belief or with opposition to "progress." In his youth Justice Holmes was a fervid abolitionist and nearly died as he lay wounded in the midst of a Civil War battle. Even as a judge, Learned Hand participated in the Progressive reform movement led by President Theodore Roosevelt. Before donning his robes, Justice Frankfurter involved himself in a range of social causes: investigating labor unrest, defending Sacco and Vanzetti, and advising President Franklin Roosevelt during the New Deal period, to name a few.

Yet all three recognized that, as judges, they were not charged with crafting the ideal world. They all touted Professor James B. Thayer's observation that excessive judicial interference dulls citizens' attention to, and responsibility for, first principles, and that "under no system can the power of courts go far to save a people from ruin; our chief protection lies elsewhere."[14]

Only the nation's commitment to its fundamental beliefs and to the legal process will preserve the country and its citizens' liberties. Judges alone cannot forestall considered and needed change, nor should they follow the model of the French revolutionaries and attempt to replace their inheritance with one particular version of the ideal society.

On the whole, this view of the judicial role triumphed and became an essential element of our nation's legal tradition. In the twentieth century the states and Congress increasingly were able to confront a broad range of social problems. Their constant experimentation led to labor legislation, environmental laws, regulation of many aspects of the economy, and a vast array of social programs. While many in our society may disagree with particular measures, a broad consensus has formed that judges will not pass upon the wisdom of these measures. Judges will uphold the great *commands* of the Constitution but will also recognize that one of the Constitution's great *lessons* is that "We the People" ultimately govern the nation, protect our liberties, and are responsible for the nation's success or failure.

There is a third central feature to consider in understanding our nation's judicial tradition: adherence to the Rule of Law, even when that adherence draws widespread popular opposition. Just as Justices Holmes and Frankfurter and Judge Hand teach us that judges should not interfere unduly with the democratic process, the federal judges of the old Fifth Circuit in the 1950s and 1960s, through their record in valiantly enforcing the Supreme Court's decisions in *Brown v. Board of Education*[15] and related cases, demonstrate the true meaning of courage and commitment to the Rule of Law.

The jurisdiction of the old Fifth Circuit included many of the Southern states. In that region of the nation in particular, the 1950s and early 1960s presented unusual tension between the clear law of the land and traditions of manifest inequality. The Constitution declares that "no State shall . . . deny to any person within its jurisdiction the equal protection of the laws."[16] In parts of the South, however, the widespread system of segregated schools, and the entire set of practices that denied citizens opportunities and civil rights on account of their race, conflicted with this constitutional command. In a series of famous cases, most prominently *Brown* but also other decisions before and after *Brown*, the Supreme Court made clear the meaning of that command in midcentury America.

The Court can decide matters for the nation as a whole. But it cannot enforce its decisions across a country as vast as ours. Thus, in the Fifth Circuit, it fell largely to a small group of federal judges to ensure that the Constitution and the Supreme Court's teaching would endure in the face of often great, often widespread, and occasionally violent resistance.

As we know now, the Rule of Law prevailed. But that conclusion was for many years less than certain, and much that prevented bloodshed, established and protected civil rights, and maintained respect for

The Fifth Circuit Court of Appeals, May 9, 1959. Top row: Judges Jones, Cameron, Brown, and Wisdom. Bottom row: Judges Rives, Hutcheson, and Tuttle.

an independent legal system can be traced to the courage and dedication of that small band of judges. Many have singled out for praise a group of leaders on the Fifth Circuit during that period, known colloquially as "the Four": John Minor Wisdom of Louisiana, Elbert Tuttle of Georgia, Richard Rives of Alabama, and John Brown of Texas. Professor Burke Marshall, a former assistant attorney general, has concluded: "Those four judges have made as much of an imprint on American society and American law as any four judges below the Supreme Court have ever done on any court. . . . If it hadn't been for judges like that on the Fifth Circuit, I think *Brown* would have failed in the end."[17] The dedication of these judges to the Constitution shaped nearly every significant event in the struggle for civil rights: the battles over desegregation of the state universities and local school systems, the efforts to give effect to the right to vote, and the conflicts over dismantling the Jim Crow system of public segregation.

It is cause for both celebration and shame that Judges Wisdom, Tuttle, Rives, and Brown—and other federal judges like them—had to sacrifice so much, personally and professionally, merely to perform their duty. After Judge Frank Johnson had affirmed equal protection principles in the Montgomery bus boycott case, for example, a bomb exploded at the home of his mother, listed in the telephone directory as Mrs. Frank M. Johnson, Sr. Vandals desecrated the grave of the son of Judge Rives, who also participated in the decision of that case.[18] Judge J. Skelly Wright, in the midst of a multiyear struggle between his court and local officials over the desegregation of New Orleans's schools, required shifts of federal marshals to protect his home and escort him to and from work.[19] Many of the judges received death threats and suffered ongoing harassment. In perhaps the greatest hardship, many of them also were ostracized by former friends and associates, made outcasts in their own communities, and condemned for understanding and upholding the Constitution.

We can now celebrate the courage of these judges, yet still feel shame that simple principles of equality were so steadfastly resisted. Through the years, many others—lawyers and nonlawyers alike—have sacrificed to preserve this nation's commitment to the Rule of Law.

Only at our peril do we ignore that sacrifice—or forget that we, too, are called upon to uphold that ultimate tradition and value.

In the end, the examples of the three groups of judges recognized above inspire and instruct us. In addition, their sacrifice and service illustrates the most important aspects of the Judiciary Act of 1789. For the act initiated and made possible the American judicial tradition, with its judicial independence, commitment to considered democratic governance, and adherence to the Rule of Law.

The Judiciary Act was enacted, literally, in another millennium. Yet it endures today as the font of continuing constitutional revolution, preserving—even as it enables us as a people to enhance—our most cherished values and freedoms. Much has changed since the days when Justices of the Supreme Court rode circuit throughout a nation that was then as much a confederation as a union, with an economy that was overwhelmingly rural, a "peculiar institution" (slavery) of incalculable evil—and a future that was, at best, uncertain.

We should be proud of our successes during the two centuries–plus that have passed since 1789. The nation has established its place in the world as a land of freedom and opportunity. We have righted some injustices, and we strive to right others. We owe much of that success to the men and women who have shaped and maintained our nation's judicial tradition. We have succeeded in large part because we have remained committed to considered change through adherence to the Rule of Law. The Judiciary Act did not, of course, create that tradition, yet it was an important part of its beginning.

CHAPTER TEN

Impeachment and Judicial Independence

———

EDERAL JUDGES, INCLUDING JUSTICES OF THE SUPREME Court, are appointed not for life but for "good behavior."[1] That language means that judges can be removed from office by impeachment. There has been only one impeachment trial of a Supreme Court Justice in our nation's history: the 1805 trial of Justice Samuel Chase.

Justice Chase was a colorful figure. A bright and accomplished man, he was one of the signers of the Declaration of Independence and had served as chief judge of the highest court of Maryland for five years before being appointed to the Supreme Court by President Washington. But he was not easy to get along with. He would often speak rudely and intemperately, and he had an authoritarian manner more suited to an aristocratic regime than to our budding democratic one.

During the early years of the Court, there were too few Supreme Court cases to keep the Justices occupied year-round. In the first ten years of the Court's history, for instance, it heard only about one hundred cases,[2] and for much of the year the Justices rode circuit, going to various parts of the country to play the role of trial judges. It was this duty that got Justice Chase into hot water.

There were several things of which Chase was accused, but three in particular deserve note. First, it was alleged that at the treason trial of John Fries (the leader of an early tax rebellion), Chase had made up his mind on a point of law without giving the lawyers a chance to argue it first. Second, a few years later at the sedition trial of James Callender, Chase had supposedly allowed a biased juror to be seated, refused to let in the testimony of a certain witness, and interrupted and harassed defense lawyers in the presentation of their case. And third, a few years after that, while presiding over a grand jury, he had allegedly urged the jurors to investigate some supposedly seditious publishers—and had criticized as politically motivated the recent abolition of several federal judgeships, which Chase believed had violated constitutional guarantees of an independent judiciary.

These three charges had a few important things in common. First, they were not remarkably serious allegations. Justice Chase wasn't being accused of any crime, or of any serious judicial misconduct such as bribery. Some of the things he was alleged to have done were more legal errors than anything else. They, perhaps, reflected more partisanship than is quite right in a judge, but that's very much a matter of degree, and also something we wouldn't today consider grounds for impeachment.

The other important point about these charges is that they all came in highly political contexts. The 1790s and early 1800s saw the birthing pains of our modern two-party system, and the parties—the Federalists and the Republicans—were very much at each other's throats. In 1805 Thomas Jefferson, a Republican, was the President, and the Republicans also controlled Congress. But the judiciary was filled mostly with Federalists appointed by John Adams.

Many Republicans, including those who were behind Justice Chase's impeachment, resented the Federalists' continuing control of the judiciary through Adams's appointments, fearing that it might last decades into the future. Impeachment was the chief device available to them to wrest the lifetime judiciary out of the Federalists' hands. By his remarks concerning several hot-button issues of the day—including the Sedition Act, a notorious piece of legislation enacted earlier by the Federalists but quickly condemned by others as an attempt to stifle political opposition and a violation of the First Amendment—Chase had provided his party's political opponents an opening they could not resist.

Today, of course, most people would roundly condemn political impeachments of federal judges. Everybody knows—or thinks they know—that federal judges are appointed for life and are meant in part to act as a check on the political branches. But the Constitution does not actually say this. Rather, it says that federal judges "shall hold their Offices during good Behaviour" and can be removed from office for "Treason, Bribery, or other high Crimes and Misdemeanors."[3]

"Good Behaviour" and "high Crimes and Misdemeanors," however, are flexible terms. Does frustrating the will of the democratically elected branches of government qualify as "bad behavior" or a "high misdemeanor"? Is letting one's political biases affect one's decisions, or conducting oneself intemperately and imperiously on the bench, impeachable?

Today we would probably say no. But at the time Justice Chase was on the bench, some said yes. In the words of one senator of the day, "Removal by impeachment was nothing more than a declaration by Congress to this effect: you hold dangerous opinions, and if you are suffered to carry them into effect, you will work the destruction of the Union. We want your offices for the purpose of giving them to men who will fill them better."[4]

So the stage was set. The impeachment trial took place in the Senate chamber, before the then thirty-four senators. The Vice President, Aaron Burr, was the presiding officer. In a somewhat macabre twist, Burr, who had killed Alexander Hamilton in a duel, was at the time under indictment for Hamilton's murder in New Jersey and New York. Wags remarked that, while in most courts the murderer was tried before the judge, in this court the judge was being tried before the murderer![5] The trial was also pretty much the only form of entertainment in Washington, then a new city with nothing else interesting going on.[6]

The trial itself appears to have been rather humdrum. History records no *Perry Mason*–like twists or surprises. The evidence was not remarkably contested, and the lawyers' arguments, while learned, were rather long and at times quite dull.[7]

But the ultimate result of the trial may well have been a surprise to many. Though twenty-five of the thirty-four senators were Republicans—more than the two thirds that the Constitution requires for conviction of impeachment—a majority voted for acquittal on most charges. The highest vote for conviction was on the charge relating to the grand-jury harangue, but even there only nineteen of the senators voted for conviction, four short of the number needed. Samuel Chase walked out of the Senate chamber still a Justice of the Supreme Court and remained in that office until his death six years later.[8]

Why the six Republicans broke party ranks and voted not guilty on all counts is not completely clear. Most believe that a good part of their reluctance to convict was a recognition that a healthy nation required a truly independent judiciary—a judiciary whose members could make decisions, sometimes even politicized decisions that could later be assailed as legally erroneous, without fear of reprisal. Perhaps some of the senators did what is often so hard but so important for politicians to do: they saw beyond the political imperatives of the moment, and beyond their desire to cast out a partisan and disliked opponent.[9]

In any case, regardless of the motivations of the individual senators—and regardless of the fact that the great majority of Republican senators voted to convict Chase on at least one count—the judgment of history has been clear. Since 1805, no Supreme Court Justice has ever again been impeached, and the only lower-court judges who were impeached were accused either of criminal misconduct or, in one Civil War case, of accepting a commission from the Confederacy.[10] Whether or not the senators expected it at the time, the legacy of the Chase impeachment has been the independent judiciary we know today.

CHAPTER ELEVEN

A President, a Chief Justice, and the Writ of Habeas Corpus

N̸O SPEAKER CAN FIND WORDS TO COMPETE WITH THOSE spoken at Gettysburg by Abraham Lincoln in 1863. That is surely true for Edward Everett, perhaps the greatest orator of the nineteenth century. He was commissioned to be the keynote speaker at the dedication of the cemetery at Gettysburg. Everett's oration was a two-hour affair, filled with rhetorical flourishes, peppered with allusions to Greek antiquity, and ending with a recitation of every hill and gully where men had fought and fallen at Gettysburg. The speech was considered the masterpiece of Everett's career.

But it was quickly overshadowed when Lincoln rose from his chair and gave, as his secretary modestly described it, a "half dozen words of consecration." Lincoln was, indeed, a poor prophet when he predicted that "the world will little note nor long remember what we say here."[1]

Lincoln's "few appropriate remarks"[2] began this way: "Fourscore and seven years ago our fathers brought forth upon this continent, a new nation, conceived in Liberty, and dedicated to the proposition that all men are created equal. Now we are engaged in a great civil war, testing whether that nation—or any nation, so conceived and so dedicated—can long endure."[3]

In the early days of the Civil War, it looked as though the young American nation, "conceived in Liberty," might *not* "long endure." It faced so many threats. The Southern states had broken away. European powers were poised to intervene, to divide the young nation permanently into Union and Confederacy.

The war posed another sort of danger as well—a danger less obvious, perhaps, than columns of soldiers marching through the countryside but far more insidious to a nation "conceived in Liberty." It was the danger that a government at war might use its extraordinary powers to stamp out political opposition. And when President Lincoln suspended the writ of habeas corpus during the Civil War, there appeared to be a good chance of that happening.

First, a bit of background is in order. Nonlawyers may recognize the term "habeas corpus" as a sort of criminal appeal. In our day there has been ongoing debate about how to regulate habeas corpus proceedings brought by prisoners, particularly those on death row. In 1996 Congress passed a new law making it more difficult for prisoners to challenge their convictions or sentences by invoking the writ of habeas corpus. This new law—the Antiterrorism and Effective Death Penalty Act—has prompted quite a bit of activity in the courts and has had a far-reaching effect. But history shows that constant change is part and parcel of the remedy of habeas corpus.

We can trace the writ of habeas corpus as far back as the Norman Conquest of England. Back then, William the Conqueror sent royal judges to ride throughout the countryside of his new kingdom dispensing justice. These itinerant judges would, on occasion, order local sheriffs to "have the bodies" of accused criminals brought before their courts. That's where we get the Latin phrase "habeas corpus." It means, literally, "have the body." And we call it a "writ" because these traveling judges would put their orders into a "written" document.

So habeas corpus began as a way of dragging an unwilling suspect into court. But eventually people who were *unlawfully imprisoned*—say, by a corrupt mayor, or even the king—began asking royal judges to bring them out of jail and into court, where their jailers would have to justify why they were in custody. This explains why today, when a prisoner seeks a writ of habeas corpus, technically the prison warden is the proper defendant to name.

England grew to regard the writ of habeas corpus as a beacon of individual liberty against the gloom of tyrannical government. It was not a "Get Out of Jail Free" card, mind you—but it at least ensured that a prisoner could have his day in court. If you were to ask an Englishman to name the greatest legal documents in English history, right alongside Magna Carta would be the Habeas Corpus Acts passed by Parliament in the 1600s, guaranteeing this remedy to all English subjects.

When English settlers moved to the New World, they brought with them more than hammers and saws to build new homes, plows and shovels to till new fields. They also brought with them the English common law to build their new legal system. That included habeas corpus. When tensions mounted between the colonies and the Crown, royal governors were known to lock up "troublemakers." And local courts were known to issue writs of habeas corpus to release those troublemakers.

One of the guiding principles of the American Revolution was that governments should not be able to lock up citizens arbitrarily, or simply because they raised their voices against the government. The founders took this concern to heart at the Constitutional Convention. Like their ancestors, they saw the writ of habeas corpus as a bulwark against tyranny. So, to safeguard the writ, our new Constitution provided that "the Privilege of the Writ of Habeas Corpus shall not be suspended, unless when in Cases of Rebellion or Invasion the public Safety may require it."[4]

There was only one brief incident during the early days of the republic when "public Safety" led to suspension of the writ. During the War of 1812, General Andrew Jackson imposed martial law in New Orleans. At one point he locked up a newspaper editor who had been fiercely critical of him. When a judge issued a writ of habeas corpus to free the editor, Jackson not only ignored the writ—he arrested the judge, too. Only a few days later, when a peace treaty had been signed and the British fleet sailed away from the coast, did Jackson release both editor and jurist.

This proved to be an isolated incident. After that brief wartime interlude, courts went on issuing the writ as justice demanded.

As time went on, the writ of habeas corpus took on new dimensions. For a time, the writ became a lightning rod for people on both sides of the slavery issue. When runaway slaves were apprehended by slave catchers in Northern states, abolitionist lawyers helped them secure their freedom with writs of habeas corpus from sympathetic courts. Perhaps the most successful lawyer in this regard was Salmon P. Chase, secretary of the treasury under Lincoln and later Chief Justice of the Supreme Court. Chase extracted so many slaves from jail that he earned the moniker "Attorney General for Fugitive Slaves."[5]

While abolitionists interposed the writ as a shield to protect freed slaves, some proslavery forces tried to use it as a sword. Some Northern states let slave masters use the writ of habeas corpus to force local sheriffs to bring back runaway slaves.[6] But this fight over the soul of habeas corpus—a long-standing instrument of freedom—was interrupted by the Civil War.

The year 1861 was a difficult time, to say the least. Barely a month after Lincoln became President, Washington was abuzz with rumors that Confederate soldiers, gathering at Harpers Ferry in Virginia, might move against the capital. The Southern states had been seceding, one by one, and it looked as though Maryland—south of the Mason-Dixon Line and still a slave state—might be next. Lincoln himself had traveled incognito through Baltimore, at night, to avoid assassination plots on his way to his own inauguration.

In April, in the midst of all this confusion, a trainload full of Union soldiers passed through Baltimore en route to Washington. They were fresh recruits from Massachusetts, outfitted with polished boots and belt buckles, satin-trimmed coats and hats. They had been summoned to man the defensive fortifications around the capital.[7]

These soldiers were greeted not by brass bands and waving flags but by an angry mob of Southern sympathizers who were spoiling for a fight. The soldiers literally had to fight their way across the town of Baltimore to reach another station, where their train to Washington waited. Four of them did not make it out of town alive. Later that night local authorities—whose sympathies clearly ran in a southerly direction—burned the bridges and cut the telegraph lines[8] between Baltimore and Washington, claiming that Union soldiers might come back, looking for revenge after the riot. But as one commentator has put it, "Bridge-burning looked like plain treason to the government in Washington, which was now defenseless and cut off from the rest of the North."9

Washington had a rebel army to its south and a secession-minded mob to its north. Congress was out of session. Lincoln felt the need to take things into his own hands. Invoking his power as commander in chief, he authorized local military commanders to suspend habeas corpus along the railroad line from Washington to Philadelphia. Essentially, this meant that the army could arrest civilians without getting a warrant from a court or without probable cause to believe a crime had been committed by the person arrested, and without providing the speedy jury trial that the Constitution guarantees in times of peace.

Enter Mr. John Merryman, a member of the Maryland legislature. Merryman had been recruiting local men to march south and join the rebel army. When a Union general found out, he ordered Merryman's arrest and packed him off to Fort McHenry in Baltimore Harbor (of "Star-Spangled Banner" fame) for the rest of the war. Merryman, in turn, applied for a writ of habeas corpus from his local federal circuit judge.

This was when Supreme Court Justices still rode the circuit,10 hopping onto their horses to serve as federal circuit judges around the country. When Merryman filed his request with his local circuit judge, he went to none other than Roger Taney, Chief Justice of the Supreme Court of the United States.

The Chief Justice was no friend of the Republican administration, having written the *Dred Scott* decision only four years before. When he received Merryman's petition, Taney ordered the commander of Fort McHenry to bring Merryman to his court in Baltimore.11 Instead of sending Merryman, the colonel sent back an aide bearing a polite message. The President had authorized the colonel, in this time of war, to suspend the writ of habeas corpus. Merryman would stay at Fort McHenry. This, as you can imagine, incensed the Chief Justice. He wrote a fiery opinion arguing that only Congress had the power to suspend habeas corpus. The President's job, he said, was merely to see that the laws be, as the Constitution says, "faithfully executed."[12]

Lincoln did not publicly respond to Taney's opinion until Congress met a month later, on July 4. Lincoln said that, had he not suspended habeas corpus immediately, Washington itself might now be in Southern hands. That, of course, would have prevented Congress from meeting, let alone from responding to the rebellion. Lincoln then took aim at Taney's claim that the President's job was to sit back and ensure that the laws be faithfully executed, even in the face of Merryman's efforts to recruit soldiers for the Confederate cause. In the Confederacy, constituting fully one third of the country, the Constitution itself was being ignored. Should Lincoln's hands be tied by the writ of habeas corpus in such a national emergency? He asked: "Are all the laws, *but one,* to go unexecuted, and the government itself go to pieces, lest that one be violated?"[13]

Merryman stayed in jail. Now, Merryman was only one of many people arrested in the early days of the war and held, without benefit of habeas corpus relief, for providing military aid to the young Confederacy. Lincoln later said that he regretted not arresting even *more* traitors to the Northern cause—particularly those who, like Robert E. Lee, had abandoned the Union army to lead its Southern enemy to victory after victory.[14]

Scholars still debate whether Lincoln had authority to invoke the constitutional provision suspending habeas corpus during the early days of the war. I will not wade into the muddy waters of that debate. I am more interested in what Lincoln *did* after March 1863—for that is when Congress gave him legislative authority to suspend the writ. From that point forward, Lincoln faced no constitutional obstacles. He could arrest whomever he chose, without courts interfering with writs of habeas corpus. What did Lincoln do at this point? Did he attempt to stifle political debate by imprisoning his opponents? Put another way, did he trample on the civil liberties that the writ of habeas corpus was meant to protect?

A recent historical study, entitled *The Fate of Liberty,* says no. The author, Mark Neely, combed through the musty boxes of arrest records from the Civil War "to find out who was arrested when the writ of habeas corpus was suspended and why."[15] Neely concludes that, throughout the war, Lincoln was guided by a "steady desire to avoid political abuse under the habeas-corpus policy."[16]

According to the best estimates, about thirty-eight thousand civilians were arrested by the military during the Civil War. Who were they? Almost all fell within a few categories: "draft dodgers, suspected deserters, defrauders of the government, swindlers of recruits, ex–Confederate soldiers, and smugglers."[17] And strikingly, most of these were Confederate citizens, caught behind Northern lines. The numbers show that very few civilians were taken from their homes and arrested. And of those few arrests, only a handful were colored by political considerations.[18]

Indeed, Lincoln issued his most sweeping proclamation suspending habeas corpus not to silence political dissent, but to stop judicial interference in the draft. Early in the war, patriotic zeal was so strong that volunteers flooded into the army. But as the war dragged on, public enthusiasm ebbed. Eventually, the government was reduced to instituting a draft. Conscription was rather unpopular, to say the least. Imagine the unrest that accompanied the burning of draft cards during the Vietnam War multiplied several times over in the New York City draft riots in 1863. The problem was especially bad in Pennsylvania. Coal miners attacked men thought to be "in sympathy with the draft."[19] State and federal courts added to the problem. They were churning out writs of habeas corpus, freeing soldiers as soon as they were drafted. Lincoln observed that "the course pursued by certain judges is defeating the draft."[20]

Lincoln's response was to suspend the writ throughout the North in any case that involved military arrest of deserters or draft dodgers. And for good measure, he threw in prisoners of war, spies, and those giving assistance to the enemy[21]—say, by smuggling goods to the Confederate government.

But his focus was always on military necessity. Lincoln never tried to suppress political dissent. He understood that a democracy only grows stronger by allowing people to voice their opposition to the gov-

Clement L. Vallandigham.

ernment, even in the midst of war. He understood that the strength of the Union lay not only in force of arms but in the liberties that were guaranteed by the open, and sometimes heated, exchange of ideas. And as one historian has put it, "the opposition press in the North was vibrant, vigorous, and often vicious."[22]

This point is illustrated by the most sensational arrest of the Civil War: that of Clement Vallandigham, a former Democratic congressman from Ohio. Vallandigham was an outspoken Confederate sympathizer, a man who minced no words expressing his contempt for the Lincoln administration. He was one of the "Peace Democrats" or "Copperheads," who originally earned their name from "the poisonous snake that attacks without notice." The Copperheads co-opted the title, broadcasting their opposition to the war by wearing the head of the goddess Liberty cut from copper pennies as lapel pins.[23] It is a nice irony, I think, to remember whose head appears on the penny today! The Copperheads must be turning in their graves.

In May 1863 General Ambrose Burnside was in charge of the Department of the Ohio. Burnside, it turned out, is a man better remembered for his long whiskers—or "sideburns"—than for his political acuity. The general announced that anyone within his jurisdiction who was in the "habit of declaring sympathies for the enemy" would be arrested as a traitor.[24]

Vallandigham took Burnside's proclamation as a challenge. At a public rally opening his campaign for governor of Ohio, Vallandigham gave a vitriolic speech, denouncing the President as "King Lincoln," accusing Burnside of being a heavy-handed tyrant, and calling for a negotiated peace with the South.[25] Burnside read the speech, arrested Vallandigham, and shipped him off to a jail in Boston.

This, of course, was exactly what Vallandigham wanted. Overnight he became a martyr for the Copperhead cause. The papers called him "Valiant Val."[26] Democrats triumphantly announced that Lincoln had finally shown his true colors: he was nothing more than a petty tyrant.

Lincoln, for his part, was not pleased by the general's actions. To be sure, he was not *fond* of Vallandigham. The former congressman had been constantly stirring up sentiments against the war, and Lincoln suspected that he was purposely fanning the flames of street violence in opposition to the draft.[27] But Lincoln realized that the arrest was valuable ammunition for his political opponents.

Burnside, ever the zealous soldier, had one more blunder to make. Turning his attention to Illinois, the general decided that the *Chicago Times* was getting too loud in criticizing the war effort. It was time to shut that paper down. So he sent out two companies of infantry, and they stopped the presses.

This was too much. Lincoln had to engage in what today might be called "damage control." Burnside had proclaimed that traitors would be either put on trial or sent "into the lines of their friends."[28] Lincoln decided to take the second option. Early one morning, Union troops escorted a bewildered Vallandigham to the Confederate lines in Tennessee and set him free.[29] After some confusion, he made his way to Charleston, South Carolina, where he exchanged some awkward pleasantries with his Confederate hosts and eventually caught a slow boat to Canada.

The next order of business was to get the *Chicago Times* back in circulation. Lincoln rescinded Burnside's order, called back the troops guarding the presses, and warned his overzealous general not to arrest any more civilians or shut down any more newspapers without express approval from Washington.[30]

Although Lincoln had undone most of the damage, he still wanted to make a point. He explained to a group of New York Democrats that he would not allow civilians to be arrested merely for "damaging the political prospects of the administration or the personal interests of the commanding general."[31] Arrests would be made only to protect national security. Now, national security is always a difficult line to draw, especially during a civil war. But the line had to be drawn somewhere, if the Union was to be preserved. That line was at agitation. Lincoln asked:

"Must I shoot a simple-minded soldier boy who deserts, while I must not touch a hair of a wily agitator who induces him to desert? . . . I think that, in such a case, to silence the agitator and save the boy is not only constitutional, but withal a great mercy."[32]

The Vallandigham episode is emblematic of Lincoln's approach to political liberties during the Civil War. The President was not out to trample on the First Amendment. He was not intent on crushing his political opposition. He suspended the writ of habeas corpus in response to perceived military threats to the Union. After he, and later Congress, removed that constitutional safeguard, the Lincoln administration did not use its power selfishly or arbitrarily. It arrested only those people who actively supported the Confederate war machine—people like Merryman, who recruited troops to march south. And when people walked the fine line between political dissent and treason, as Vallandigham did, Lincoln tried to err on the side of free speech.

Midway through the war, Lincoln predicted that habeas corpus would quickly be reinstituted after the war was over. He could not bring himself to believe that Americans would allow the wartime suspension of habeas corpus to extend into peacetime, he said, "any more than I am able to believe that a man could contract so strong an appetite for emetics during temporary illness as to persist in feeding upon them during the remainder of his healthful life."[33] Lincoln died before he could see the writ of habeas corpus restored.

In one of his famous debates with Stephen Douglas, Lincoln spoke about how a society that tolerates slavery corrodes the very foundations of its own liberty. These words, I think, reveal Lincoln's awareness that he was not battling just for territory on a map. He was battling to preserve a nation "conceived in Liberty."

Lincoln asked:

What constitutes the bulwark of our own liberty and independence? It is not our frowning battlements, our bristling sea coasts, the guns of our war steamers, or the strength of our gallant and disciplined army. These are not our reliance against a resumption of tyranny in our fair land. All of them may be turned against our liberties, without making us stronger or weaker for the struggle. Our reliance is in *the love of liberty* which God has planted in our bosoms. Our defense is in the preservation of the spirit which prizes liberty as the heritage of all men, in all lands, everywhere. Destroy this spirit, and you have planted the seeds of despotism around your own doors. Familiarize yourselves with the chains of bondage, and you are preparing your own limbs to wear them. Accustomed to trample on the rights of those around you, you have lost the genius of your own independence, and become the fit subjects of the first cunning tyrant who rises.[34]

Still today we should heed the wisdom of a man who led our nation to a "new birth of freedom." We must always be, first and foremost, lovers of liberty.

PART THREE

People Who Have Helped
Shape the Court

Of the 108 Associate Justices and 16 Chief Justices who have served on the Supreme Court, most are not remembered by the public today, although all have contributed in some way to the body of law recorded in our opinions since the Court first sat in 1790.

Many of the most notable Justices of the nineteenth century, including John Marshall, Joseph Story, and Roger Taney, already have appeared in the preceding pages.

In Part Three I have included commentary on only a few of their fellow Justices who have served on the Court, all of them from the twentieth century. My selections here do not reflect any view of the value of the subjects' historical contributions relative to those of other Justices. Rather, the Justices remembered here were chosen because each of them made some important contributions to the law or to the judicial system.

The lives of all the Justices, and their contributions to the fabric of the Court's history, no doubt will continue to provide interesting opportunities for research, by legal historians and ordinary citizens alike, for years to come.

CHAPTER TWELVE

The Rights of the Individual
and the Legacy of Holmes

———

IN 1901, A YEAR BEFORE OLIVER WENDELL HOLMES, JR., TOOK his seat on the Supreme Court of the United States, he wrote: "The men whom I should be tempted to commemorate would be the originators of transforming thought. They often are half obscure, because what the world pays for is judgment, not the original mind."[1]

Holmes was writing in halfhearted praise of Chief Justice John Marshall; he thought Marshall lacked an original mind. But insofar as he was praising Marshall for his judgment, he may well have been giving some thought to himself, and to how he would be remembered when the time came to commemorate *his* life and *his* work.

It would be hard to come up with a more accurate prediction of how Holmes would in fact be remembered nearly a century later. The world does pay for judgment, and the world got fifty years' worth from Holmes: twenty on the Massachusetts Supreme Judicial Court, from 1882 to 1902, and then thirty on the Supreme Court of the United States, from 1902 to 1932. But that is not the whole story. Other Justices have served comparable tenures and are barely remembered today. Few commemorate the career of Samuel Miller, who spent twenty-eight years on the Court, or William Johnson, who was a Justice for thirty years, or even Bushrod Washington, who had a thirty-one-year Court career. These Justices have been forgotten by everyone except legal antiquarians. Even Edward White, who spent the last nineteen of his twenty-seven years on the Court as Holmes's colleague

This informal photograph of Oliver Wendell Holmes
was made when Holmes was a comparative newcomer
in Washington. He was Associate Justice from 1902–1932.

and the last eleven of those nineteen as the Chief Justice, is largely lost to history.

Instead, Holmes is remembered exactly as he would have liked, as an "originator of transforming thought." And his description of such people, that they "often are half obscure," fits our memory of Holmes perfectly. It may sound a little odd to refer to Holmes as half obscure. After all, there is no figure in American legal thought whose life and writings have been more frequently examined.

But when it comes to the influence of Holmes on our notions of the individual's rights against the state, Holmes remains half obscure in a double sense. First, while his contributions to our understanding of the Bill of Rights are unmistakable and were enough to move Justice Robert Jackson to refer to Holmes as one of the two "most liberty-alert Justices of all times,"[2] they coexist uneasily with a full picture of Holmes the man and Holmes the Justice. If much of Holmes's thought is in full view today, because it continues to influence the way we conceive of the balance between the individual and the state, there is another portion—a less familiar part—that no longer exerts such an influence. Second, even within the sphere in which Holmes continues to inform our understanding of the proper balance between the government and its citizens, his influence is only half perceived by most. Certain of his contributions receive the entire spotlight, while others remain neglected.

The first area of the law in which Holmes's thought remains with us is well known to most American lawyers, if not necessarily to citizens generally: Holmes's contribution to our understanding of the First Amendment's guarantee of the freedom of speech. But little commentary has been directed toward the second area of Holmes's work, that involving the right of an accused criminal to a fair trial, and the power of the federal courts to step in when the local state courts have not fulfilled their constitutional obligations. The influence of Holmes is felt as strongly here as anywhere.

At the beginning, however, his influence would have been nearly impossible to predict. When Holmes was appointed to the Court in 1902, he was an unlikely person to develop a jurisprudence of individual liberties. He was already sixty-one years old, already well known as a writer and a state-court judge. He had published his most celebrated work, *The Common Law,* more than twenty years before. He was the author of innumerable articles and opinions. None of this work gave any indication that Holmes would have any particular interest in the rights of the individual.

Of course, Holmes can hardly be faulted for this. As a scholar, his interests ran to common-law subjects like torts or contracts. As a state-court judge, Holmes had little occasion to consider the Bill of Rights, which at the time was understood to limit the power only of the federal government, not of the states. Most of his caseload concerned the same common-law fields he had explored as a scholar.

In the legal climate of the late nineteenth century, Holmes's lack of interest in the Bill of Rights was the norm. Even in the federal courts the Bill of Rights was rarely at issue. The Fourth Amendment, for example, which prohibits "unreasonable searches and seizures," and which in the last three decades has accounted for a relatively large share of the Supreme Court's caseload, was the subject of almost no litigation. As late as 1927, Felix Frankfurter could confidently assert (in an article about Holmes) that whether the police had violated the Fourth Amendment was one of a group of mundane questions that "are neither frequent nor fighting issues before the [Supreme] Court."[3] That Holmes took no interest in the Bill of Rights before he took his seat on the Court thus makes him no more or less than a person of his times.

Much of Holmes's scholarly work had been devoted to debunking the widespread idea that human beings were born with "natural rights" that were conferred by God and could be derived from broad moral principles. This idea was basic to the jurisprudence of the time. In fact, it was an important element of the political philosophy underlying the formation of the nation itself. The Declaration of Independence, for example, speaks of inalienable God-given rights, the abridgment of which permits revolution. Yet Holmes disagreed quite strongly. He wrote: "The law talks about rights, and duties, . . . and nothing is . . . more common in legal reasoning, than to take these words in their moral sense, . . . and so to drop into fallacy. . . . Nothing but confusion of thought can result from assuming that the rights of man in a moral sense are equally rights in the sense of the Constitution and the law."[4]

These are not the words of a scholar (or judge) prone to an expansive reading of the Bill of Rights. Holmes continued to observe a rigid distinction between law and morality while on the Court. In 1918 he explained that "the jurists who believe in natural law seem to me to be in that naive state of mind that accepts what has been familiar and accepted by them and their neighbors as something that must be accepted by all men everywhere." He found such a view preposterous, observing: "The most fundamental of the supposed preexisting rights—the right to life—is sacrificed without a scruple not only in war, but whenever the interest of a society, that is, of the predominant power in the community, is thought to demand it."[5]

That there were no natural rights did not mean that there were no rights at all, of course; it meant only that the rights had to be embodied in a man-made law before they could be enforced. Holmes made this distinction clear in one of the first of his many letters to Harold Laski, in which he admitted: "All my life I have sneered at the natural rights of man—and at times I have thought that the bills of rights in Constitutions were overworked—but . . . they embody principles that men have died for."[6]

Holmes's initial distinguishing mark on the Court was his series of dissents from opinions striking down social welfare legislation, and his view of the Court's limited role with respect to economic regulation may be his strongest legacy to current American jurisprudence. These dissents provided an occasion for Holmes to set out a theory of the Constitution that would enable the government to prevail over the individual most of the time.

The best known of these cases was the first, *Lochner v. New York*, decided in 1905, in which the Supreme Court of the United States struck down a state health measure limiting the working hours of bakers. Holmes's dissent includes these ringing words that have been studied by generations of American law students: "This case is decided upon an economic theory which a large part of the country does not entertain. . . . But a constitution is not intended to embody a particular economic theory, whether of paternalism and the organic relation of the citizen to the State or of *laissez faire*. It is made for people of fundamentally differing views, and the accident of our finding certain opinions natural and familiar or novel and even shocking ought not to conclude our judgment upon the question whether statutes embodying them conflict with the Constitution of the United States."[7]

Holmes would repeat this theme in countless similar cases throughout his career. He dissented, for example, when the Court struck down a federal statute establishing a minimum wage for women,[8] and when the Court invalidated a state law forbidding employers from requiring their employees not to join labor unions.[9] But his disagreement with his colleagues was not based on any concern for the health of bakers, or for the ability of women to earn a decent wage, or for the rights of workers to join unions. In each of these cases, other Justices had written dissenting opinions voicing such concerns. But Holmes intentionally chose *not* to join them.

Holmes's point was a different one: it was not that the law was properly aimed, but that the state had the power to pass the law regardless of its aim. "State laws may regulate life in many ways," Holmes wrote, "which we . . . might think as injudicious or if you like as tyrannical as this."[10] As Holmes put it, the supposed "liberty of the citizen to do as he likes so long as he does not interfere with the liberty of others to do the same, which has been a shibboleth for some well-known writers," was no more than a romantic ideal with no place in the rough-and-tumble world.

Holmes's often rigid majoritarianism shows up much more clearly in a group of cases we hear little about these days, because in these cases Holmes's majoritarianism coincides with an outcome modern minds generally find repugnant.[11]

In *Bailey v. Alabama*, the Court considered a state law that criminalized an employee's breach of an employment contract. This was an era when agricultural employees in the South often had to borrow money from landowners and agree to work off the debt with their labor. The Court found that the law's effect was to create a form of slavery, in violation of the Thirteenth Amendment to the Constitution. Holmes dissented, on the ground that the abolition of slavery did not limit the power of the government to compel an employee to continue working until he had paid off his debts.[12]

In *Meyer v. Nebraska*, the Court refused to permit Nebraska to criminalize the teaching of languages other than English. Holmes again dissented. As he explained, "no one would doubt that a teacher might be forbidden to teach many things."[13] A prohibition on the teaching of foreign languages was simply one aspect of the state's power to dictate what an individual might or might not learn.

Finally, in *Buck v. Bell*, the 1927 case that still serves as one of our most startling reminders of how quickly things change, Holmes wrote for a unanimous Court in upholding the power of the state to sterilize the mentally retarded. In words that sound chilling to the modern ear, Holmes explained: "We have seen more than once that the public welfare may call upon the best citizens for their lives. It would be strange if it could not call upon those who already sap the strength of the State for these lesser sacrifices, often not felt to be such by those concerned, in order to prevent our being swamped with incompetence. . . . Society can prevent those who are manifestly unfit from continuing their kind. The principle that sustains compulsory vaccination is broad enough to cover cutting the Fallopian tubes. Three generations of imbeciles are enough."[14]

Throughout much of his tenure on the Court and in much of his scholarly work, Holmes took a strong view of the power of the state with respect to the individual. Holmes's faith in eugenics and his affirmation of governmental power have been frequently criticized, beginning in Holmes's own day.[15] But this is the part of Holmes's jurisprudence that exerts the least influence today. The Court has never cited *Buck v. Bell*, for instance, as support for any important proposition. In this sense, then, this part of Holmes's jurisprudence has indeed become "obscure"; it may still be recalled, but it no longer possesses any vitality.

Putting aside his dissents of the *Lochner* era, Holmes's strongest influence on current constitutional interpretation may reside in his rein-terpretation of the First Amendment's guarantee of freedom of speech. In the last few years, the Court has heard literally dozens of cases that call upon it to interpret the First Amendment's speech clause. Until World War I, however, the First Amendment was an extremely rare sub-ject of litigation before the Court. Holmes wrote an opinion for the Court in one of these unusual prewar cases, *Patterson v. Colorado,* decided in 1907. One would hardly suspect that, a decade later, the author would become the Court's leading exponent of the freedom of speech.

Mr. Patterson was the publisher of articles and a cartoon that ac-cused the Colorado Supreme Court of having decided some recent cases in a corrupt manner. The Colorado court itself fined Patterson for contempt. Holmes had no difficulty dismissing Patterson's argument that the First Amendment gave him a right to express his opinion of the judges. Holmes explained that "the main purpose" of the First Amendment is only "to prevent . . . *previous restraints* upon publica-tions": it was not, however, intended to "prevent the subsequent pun-ishment of such [publications] as may be deemed contrary to the public welfare."[16]

This view of the First Amendment—that it prevented the govern-ment from suppressing speech in advance but permitted the prosecu-tion of offending speech afterward—was widely but not universally held at the time. Justice Harlan dissented in *Patterson,* and expressed the now orthodox opinion that the First Amendment carries force both before and after publication. Initially, however, Holmes himself took the narrower position.

By 1919, Holmes had changed his views.[17]

Schenck v. United States involved the prosecution of a man who, during World War I, had printed and circulated leaflets arguing that the government lacked the power to conscript soldiers to fight in Eu-rope.[18] In an opinion written by Holmes, the Court affirmed Schenck's conviction but in a manner that revealed a broader understanding of the First Amendment than had ever been expressed by the Court. "It well may be," said Holmes, "that the prohibition of laws abridging the freedom of speech is not confined to previous restraints."[19] Here Holmes expounded a view of the First Amendment that was revolutionary for the Court. "We admit," he wrote, "that in many places and in ordinary times the defendants in saying all that was said in the circular would have been within their constitutional rights."[20] The government could prosecute Mr. Schenck only because he expressed his opposition to the draft in wartime, when his words posed "a clear and present danger" to the war effort.[21]

For the first time, the Supreme Court held that the First Amendment protects the right of citizens, in peacetime, to criticize the government and to express their opinions on controversial public issues. *Schenck* was a landmark in this regard.

Later that year, in another case involving criticism of the government's conduct of the war, Holmes had further opportunity to express his views of the First Amendment. The defendants in *Abrams v. United States* had published articles asserting that the war was being fought for the benefit of the rich but was not in the interest of workers. Despite pressure from some of the other Justices, who thought that a separate opinion by Holmes would lend support to a radical cause,[22] Holmes dissented in language that remains the classic exposition of the rationale for a right to freedom of speech. He wrote:

> Persecution for the expression of opinions seems to me perfectly logical. If you have no doubt of your premises or your power and want a certain result with all your heart you naturally express your wishes in law and sweep away all opposition. . . . But when men have realized that time has upset many fighting faiths, they may come to believe even more than they believe the very foundations of their own conduct that the ultimate good desired is better reached by free trade in ideas— that the best test of truth is the power of the thought to get itself accepted in the competition of the market, and that truth is the only ground upon which their wishes safely can be carried out. That at any rate is the theory of our Constitution.[23]

In the end, it has been Holmes's view of the freedom of speech that has prevailed.[24] It took some time. In the 1920s, although the Court silently adopted Holmes's view that the First Amendment protects the right to express unpopular opinions, Holmes was still disagreeing with fellow Justices in cases involving criticism of the government right up until he retired.[25] Even in the aftermath of the Second World War, when the Court finally explicitly adopted Holmes's view that the government could not punish spoken beliefs that did not pose a "clear and present danger," the Court continued to permit the government to prosecute those who advocated support for communism or for the Soviet Union.[26]

It was not until 1969, in *Brandenburg v. Ohio*, that Holmes's broad view of a constitutional right to express even the most noxious opinions finally took hold. In that case the Court drew a firm distinction between advocacy of beliefs, which receives constitutional protection regardless of the content of those beliefs, and "incitement to imminent lawless action," which can be prosecuted as a crime.[27] Even where speech is repugnant, and even where it might well lead to violence somewhere down the road, our Constitution protects the right of the speaker to be free from the government's interference.

This is a legacy of Holmes that should not be underestimated. That anyone should be able to say whatever he likes, no matter how unsettling it may be to the people in power, is hardly an obvious proposition and is hardly universally accepted even today. There are many places where people are still thrown in prison for expressing views critical of the authorities. There were many more such places—and the United States was one of them—when, in 1919, Holmes wrote his opinions in *Schenck* and *Abrams*. The freedom to express unpopular or controversial ideas is a concept far too large to attribute to any one person. But its timing in the history of American jurisprudence can be traced directly to Holmes.

There is another of Holmes's contributions in the realm of individual rights—and one significantly less celebrated—that bears noting. In our criminal justice system, the local state courts handle most of the ordinary criminal cases. Where a state prisoner has been denied his rights under the Constitution, however, the prisoner may seek a writ of habeas corpus in a federal court. This has been true for most of our history.[28] But our current understanding of the scope of the writ—that is, the scope of the power of federal courts to intervene in state criminal prosecutions—derives substantially from Holmes. His influence can be seen quite starkly by comparing two cases handed down eight years apart.

The first is *Frank v. Mangum*,[29] decided in 1915. Leo Frank was sentenced to death in the state of Georgia after having been convicted of a highly publicized murder. He may well have been innocent.[30] Throughout his trial the courtroom was packed with spectators inflamed by anti-Semitism, and an angry mob waited just outside the courtroom door. The danger to Frank and to the jurors, should Frank not have been convicted, was so apparent that at one point the judge and the jurors had to meet with the chief of police and the local militia colonel to secure everyone's safety. Unsurprisingly, the jury found Frank guilty.

Frank sought a writ of habeas corpus in the federal courts, on the ground that he had been denied his constitutional right to due process of law. The Supreme Court, however, held that he could not obtain one. The Court reasoned that Georgia provided an appeal from a conviction alleged to be the result of an unfair trial. Frank had in fact appealed, but the Georgia courts had found that his trial was fair. The majority concluded that the federal courts lacked the authority to upset this finding. Once the state courts had determined that Frank's trial was not unfair, that was the end of the matter.

Holmes dissented. As for Frank's right to due process, Holmes explained that "whatever disagreement there may be as to the scope of the phrase 'due process of law,' there can be no doubt that it embraces the fundamental conception of a fair trial, with opportunity to be heard. Mob law does not become due process of law by securing the assent of a terrorized jury."[31] And as for the more technical but equally important question of a federal court's power to intervene where due process was lacking, Holmes chided his colleagues for their undue deference to the local courts. In his view, the federal courts' "power to secure fundamental rights . . . becomes a duty and must be put forth."[32] As Holmes put it, "The supremacy of the law and of the Federal Constitution should be vindicated in a case like this."[33]

Eight years later the composition of the Court had changed somewhat and a similar case came up to be decided. This time Holmes's broader view of the power of federal courts to enforce the constitutional rights of criminal defendants commanded a majority. *Moore v. Dempsey* involved the trial of a group of black men accused of killing a white man, a trial similar to Leo Frank's a few years earlier. A mob surrounded the courtroom and threatened to lynch the defendants and the jurors if the latter did not find the former guilty. The entire trial lasted only forty-five minutes, and the jury took only five minutes to reach a guilty verdict. As in *Frank* eight years before, the state courts permitted an appeal but found that the trial had not been unfair. This time, however, Holmes had the support of his colleagues in refusing to defer to the state courts. Where "the State Courts failed to correct the wrong," he observed, nothing "can prevent this Court from securing to the petitioners their constitutional rights."[34]

This was a fundamental shift in the Court's understanding of the power of federal courts to enforce the constitutional rights of accused criminals. Holmes's broader view has stayed with us. While the Court has tinkered continuously with the finer points of the scope of habeas corpus, the fundamental point that Holmes expressed in the *Frank* dissent and the *Moore* majority opinion has been reaffirmed repeatedly ever since.[35]

Holmes's influence in this area is not nearly as well known as his influence with respect to the freedom of speech, but it may be equally important.[36] We have seen quite dramatic changes in criminal procedure in the United States over the last two generations. Many of these changes could not have taken place without a broad conception of the power of federal courts to ensure that individuals are treated fairly in the state courts. Without Holmes's broad view, the federal courts (including the Supreme Court) would simply have had no occasion to define the constitutional rights possessed by defendants in local prosecutions.

On Holmes's ninetieth birthday, the year before Benjamin Cardozo would replace him on the Court, Cardozo had this to say about Holmes: "Men speak of him as a great Liberal, a lover of Freedom and its apostle. All this in truth he is, yet in his devotion to Freedom he has not been willing to make himself the slave of a mere slogan. No one has labored more incessantly to demonstrate the truth that rights are never absolute, though they are ever struggling and tending to declare themselves as such."[37]

Cardozo may have captured the paradox embedded in Justice Holmes's views of the Bill of Rights. As we have seen, Holmes's pronouncements of the values underlying the freedom of speech and the right to a fair trial marked him as the great liberal Justice of his era. This side of Holmes's jurisprudence possesses even more vitality today than it did in his own times, as his dissenting opinions have come to define our jurisprudence in these areas.

At the same time, as Cardozo noted, Holmes did not always conceive of individual rights as absolutes, particularly when substantive due process was involved. Where such rights conflicted with the rational preferences of the majority, it was the majority's will that prevailed. This side of Holmes's thought, the often rigid positivism that would have permitted the state to sterilize the mentally retarded or prohibit the teaching of foreign languages, exerts no similar influence. It is a matter of historical interest only. In terms of the current understanding of the relationship between the individual and the state, this side of Holmes's jurisprudence has slipped into obscurity.

Professor Thomas Grey has written that "while [Holmes] conceived of law as a tool for the achievement of the good," his view of "what the good was" tended toward no more than the will of the majority at any given time.[38] This observation goes a long way toward explaining Holmes's double-edged dissents of the *Lochner* era, in which he often voted to uphold statutes while lamenting their stupidity. But at least in the two areas considered here—the freedom of speech and the right to a fair criminal trial—I suspect that Holmes had a more personal conception of the good, one that did not depend on the views of the community. Holmes's strongest legacies may represent exceptions rather than the rule, in that they may involve the relatively unusual legal questions as to which Holmes had a passion for ends as well as means, for outcome as well as process.

If so, then our celebration of Holmes's influence today pays the highest tribute to the breadth of his thought. Judges and scholars come and go, and the main body of their work may have an influence after they have gone. But Holmes's thought and writing were so broad that even a small portion of it can cast the largest shadow.

CHAPTER THIRTEEN

William Howard Taft and the
Importance of Unanimity

———

JOHN MARSHALL IS WIDELY, AND RIGHTLY, CONSIDERED THE greatest Chief Justice the Court has ever had. Through his recognition of the right of judicial review, he secured for this Court a role in shaping the nation's most important principles: racial equality, individual liberty, the meaning of democracy, and so many others.

There is, however, another great Chief Justice, one who perhaps deserves almost as much credit as Marshall for the Court's modern-day role but who does not often receive the recognition: William Howard Taft. Taft, of course, was remarkable even before he became Chief Justice—but even the presidency did not hold as much charm for him as his eventual position on the Court. Mrs. Taft noted in her memoirs that "never did he cease to regard a Supreme Court appointment as vastly more desirable than the Presidency."[1]

Mrs. Taft, however, disagreed. She loved being First Lady and was a good one at that. She was responsible for bringing the cherry blossoms to Washington, a feat for which I am particularly grateful. While she was First Lady, she also became the first woman to sit within the bar of the Court. She had come to see the new Justices sworn in and demanded to be seated there.[2] She was a difficult woman to refuse.

Taft, on the other hand, was an unpopular President. His bid for reelection was so unsuccessful that he himself described his defeat as "not only a landslide but a tidal wave and holocaust all rolled into one general cataclysm."[3]

William Howard Taft, President of the United States, 1909–1913;
Chief Justice of the United States, 1921–1930.

Despite his failures as President, however, as "chief executive" of the Supreme Court, Taft could only be considered a success. When he took over the job, he found a federal system overwhelmed with cases, putting the Supreme Court's docket as much as five years behind and placing the other federal courts in similarly dire straits.[4] Taft, with his experience as an executive and his connections on Capitol Hill, succeeded in securing twenty-four additional federal judgeships.[5] He also founded the predecessor to the Judicial Conference of the United States, whose job it became to keep statistics on the work of federal courts and to suggest reforms to keep the federal system functioning smoothly.[6]

Taft lessened the load on the Supreme Court by successfully lobbying Congress to pass a statute that gave the Court greater control over its own docket by substituting discretionary certiorari review—review that allows the Court to choose which cases come before it—for much of what had previously been mandatory appellate jurisdiction.[7]

But Taft's concern for the Court went beyond simple efficiency; he saw it as something much grander than a court of error securing justice for individual litigants. In his view, individual litigants received all the justice they required through the federal district courts and courts of appeals. The Supreme Court's role was only "to maintain uniformity of decision for the various courts of appeal, [and] to pass on constitutional and other important questions."[8] Control over its own docket allowed the Court to pass over ordinary lawsuits and to spend more time on these sorts of questions.

In keeping with his vision of the Court as a "player" on issues of national importance, Taft also lobbied Congress to appropriate funds to build the present Supreme Court building, an edifice whose grandeur matched Taft's sense of the significance of the business conducted there.[9]

Chief Justices Taft and Marshall both placed great value on keeping the courts over which they presided unanimous. John Marshall began his chief justiceship by putting to an end the English practice of seriatim opinions, where each Justice wrote separately to give his own view of the case.[10] Marshall accomplished this by writing the opinions of the Court himself; in his first four years on the bench, he wrote in all of the cases not decided per curiam, save the two in which he did not participate. In these four years there were no dissents and only one separate concurring opinion.[11]

Marshall explained his Court's ability to achieve unanimity thus: "The course of every tribunal must necessarily be, that the opinion which is to be delivered as the opinion of the court, is previously submitted to the consideration of all the judges; and, if any part of the reasoning must be disapproved, it must be so modified as to receive the approbation of all, before it can be delivered as the opinion of all."[12] Certainly, Marshall's description of a Court striving for genuine consensus did not present the complete picture. In order to maintain agreement, Justices on the Marshall Court also acquiesced in opinions with which they did not agree. Marshall began one of his rare dissents with a disclaimer: "I should now, as is my custom, when I have the misfortune to differ from this Court, acquiesce silently in its opinion . . ."[13]

Thomas Jefferson, who was not always pleased at the outcomes reached by the unanimous Court, had another explanation for the Marshall Court's unanimity. He attributed the Court's level of agreement not to Marshall's willingness to modify opinions to reach consensus but rather to the Chief's overwhelming influence on the other Justices. When the time came for President Madison to fill a vacancy on the Court, Jefferson lamented: "It will be difficult to find a character of firmness enough to preserve his independence on the same bench with Marshall."[14]

The Court led by Chief Justice Taft was also remarkably cohesive: 84 percent of its opinions were unanimous.[15] Taft did not approve of dissents, believing that "it is more important to stand by the Court and give its judgment weight than merely to record my individual dissent where it is better to have the law certain than to have it settled either way."[16] Taft's concern with the certainty of the law had to do not only with the need for people to plan their lives and business transactions around it, but also with the legitimacy of the institution itself. According to Taft, "most dissents . . . are a form of egotism. They don't do any good, and only weaken the prestige of the Court."[17] Accordingly, he asserted that he "would not think of opposing the views of my brethren if there was a majority against my own."[18] In general, he kept to this view, writing only twenty dissents during his nearly ten years on the Court.[19] On the rare occasion when he did dissent, he was clearly troubled by it. He began his dissent in *Adkins v. Children's Hospital* with a disclaimer: "I regret much to differ from the Court in these cases."[20]

Taft's goal of achieving unanimity on the Court was no doubt helped by judicial norms of the day, which generally disfavored dissent.[21] Canon 19 of the code of judicial ethics then in place stated the principle this way: "It is of high importance that judges constituting a court of last resort should use effort and self-restraint to promote solidarity of conclusion and the consequent influence of judicial decision. A judge should not yield to pride of opinion or value more highly individual reputation than that of the court to which he should be loyal. Except in case of conscientious difference of opinion on fundamental principle, dissenting opinions should be discouraged in courts of last resort."[22]

These norms affected even Justices Holmes and Brandeis, who, along with Justice Stone, vexed Taft with their vigorous dissenting opinions, most famously in cases involving the freedom of speech.[23] Taft's frustration with the three was great enough to declare them all "of course hopeless" when they would not join the other six Justices in a case "to steady the Court."[24] But remarkably, even the "Great Dissenter" Holmes thought it was "useless and undesirable, as a rule, to express dissent."[25] Brandeis, too, recognized that he could not "always dissent," and kept his disagreement to himself when he felt he had been out of line with his fellow Justices on too many recent occasions.[26]

At least some of the Taft Court's agreement, however, was due to the Chief Justice's efforts to keep it together. First, Taft himself played some role in the perpetuation of the general judicial norm against dissent; he was the chair of the committee that drafted Canon 19.[27] But he also made many more efforts directly targeted at his Court. One estimate has it that Taft was personally responsible for suppressing at least two hundred dissenting votes.[28]

How did he do it? Taft, who did not have the jurisprudential talent of Marshall, surely was not able to keep the Court together simply by the force of his legal reasoning. Instead, he used his influence over appointments to the Court to block those, like Learned Hand, whom he thought would "almost certainly" be dissenters.[29] Taft made every effort to maintain a personal relationship with all of his colleagues, so much so that Justice Holmes in 1925 reported that "never before . . . have we gotten along with so little jangling and dissension."[30] Taft also used his assignment power to ensure that the opinion writer would garner as many votes as possible for his view.[31]

But achieving unanimity did not end with opinion assignment; it was an ongoing struggle. Professor Robert Post, who is currently writing the Holmes Devise history of the Taft Court, has uncovered the Court's original conference books. He has found that 30 percent of the Taft Court's unanimous opinions required a Justice to change his conference vote in order to achieve unanimity, and a further 12 percent required a Justice to side with the majority after originally passing or registering a tentative vote.[32]

In part, these switches occurred because the Justices of the Taft Court did what Marshall had aspired to do: achieve unanimity by carefully crafting opinions to meet the concerns of all of the Justices.[33] Taft led this practice by example, holding up voting on a complicated utility-valuation case to allow Justice Brandeis to work through his concerns, and then scheduling an entire day of discussion on the matter.[34] Taft also encouraged the Justices to keep their opinions to bare essentials, avoiding controversial discussions unnecessary to the result. Taft himself omitted a lengthy discussion of Congress's commerce-clause power from one opinion at the request of Justice Butler, commenting that although the removal meant a "real sacrifice of personal preference, . . . it is the duty of us all to control our personal preferences to the main object of the Court, which is to do effective justice."[35]

When methods of accommodation failed, however, the Justices of the Taft Court were willing to sign on to unanimous opinions that contained statements of the law with which they did not agree. Correspondence between the Justices shows that many of their votes were changed only under protest. Justice Butler responded to a Holmes opinion thus: "I voted the other way and remain unconvinced, but dissenting clamor does not often appeal to me as useful. I shall acquiesce." Other Justices were more blunt. Justice Brandeis concurred in an opinion of Justice Stone, commenting: "I think this is woefully wrong, but do not expect to dissent." Justice Sutherland ultimately joined an opinion to which he had originally responded: "Sorry, I cannot agree."[36]

Times have changed. In the 1991–2000 terms, only 44 percent of the Court's opinions were unanimous, with 19 percent decided by only one vote. While these numbers do not indicate the sort of political divisions of which we are sometimes accused, the current Court certainly has not achieved anywhere near the level of consensus enjoyed by the Taft Court. In fact, that level of agreement did not last long even back then. In the 1940s, only a decade after Taft left the bench, the statistics looked more modern: only 39 percent of the decisions were unanimous, and 14 percent were decided by a margin of one. The numbers have remained relatively stable since.

Despite the statistical difference, in some ways the Taft Court sounds a lot like the Court on which I sit. We all strive to write opinions that will satisfy the concerns of as many of our colleagues as possible. We all greatly prefer the Court to be unanimous or almost so whenever possible, and we work to make that happen. I have never heard any of my colleagues express in seriousness the view about which Justice Brennan used to joke: the most important skill for a Supreme Court Justice to have is the ability to "count to five."[37]

The statistical differences between the Taft Court and the present Court probably reflect the lengths to which we are willing to go to achieve unanimity. The agreement we do achieve is almost exclusively accomplished by the extensive revision of opinions in response to comments by other Justices. Unlike the Justices of the Taft Court, neither my colleagues nor I make a practice of joining opinions with which we do not agree. While unanimity is most certainly a goal of the present-day Court, it does not overwhelm our other goals. When agreement cannot be reached, each one of us takes the opportunity to make our disagreement known, often quite forcefully. Rather than following Taft's Canon 19, we generally follow the practice recommended by a later Chief Justice, Charles Evans Hughes: "When unanimity can be obtained without sacrifice of conviction, it strongly commends the decision to public confidence. But unanimity which is merely formal, which is recorded at the expense of strong, conflicting views, is not desirable in a court of last resort, whatever may be the effect upon public opinion at the time."[38]

Perhaps ironically, we owe our ability to dissent in such cases in part to Chief Justice Taft. Taft's focus on unanimity was motivated largely by a concern for the institutional integrity of the Court[39] and was consistent with his attempts to transform the Court from simply a higher appellate body to an expounder of national principle. Taft was as concerned that the Court be a grand presence in the public mind as he was that it be a grand presence on Capitol Hill. He recognized, rightly, that too much fragmentation among the Justices would undermine the public's confidence in the institution and its decisions.

No doubt, the same can be said of John Marshall, who was dedicated to establishing the Court as a body justified in exercising its newly recognized power of judicial review. It is the success of Taft and Marshall in bolstering the Court's integrity that allows us the luxury of expressing our individual views today.

Although I believe that the Court ought to be careful not to squander the nest egg our predecessors have left us, I am thankful that it is there to use when needed. Dissents can play an important role in the future course of the law. One need look no further than Justice Holmes's dissent in *Lochner*,[40] or Justice Harlan's in *Plessy v. Ferguson*,[41] to see the good that can ultimately come from the expression of a minority view. Harlan's view in *Plessy* was in fact so worth expressing that when the Court finally came around to it in *Brown v. Board of Education*,[42] Chief Justice Warren went to great efforts to do so unanimously. *Plessy* and *Lochner* show us that what was once simply a powerful disagreement by one individual may eventually become the law of the land.

There is value to dissent even if it does not eventually carry the day. Dissenting opinions can force the Justices in the majority to respond to criticisms, honing the Court's opinion. Karl Llewellyn referred to this function of dissent with an idiom that particularly appeals to the cowgirl in me: "riding herd on the majority."[43] Dissents also can serve to limit the holding of the majority opinion—what Justice Brennan called "damage control"[44]—and to alert future litigants, and all those who must be governed by the law, of the precise scope of the Court's opinion.

Perhaps most important, the dissent plays a role in showing those members of the public who disagree with the Court's opinion that their views, while they did not prevail, were at least understood and taken seriously. The citizens of this nation are educated and aware enough to understand that the questions that come before the Court rarely have easy answers. The existence of dissent demonstrates, indeed embodies, the struggles we undergo in reaching our decisions. Only a very unsophisticated public could be duped into thinking the law on such controversial issues as abortion rights, immigration, and the rights of criminal defendants could be resolved so simply as to engender no disagreement whatsoever.

This function of dissent demonstrates one thing that Chief Justice Taft may have missed: at times the existence of dissent can bolster, rather than undermine, the Court's legitimacy. Again, a quote from Chief Justice Hughes is useful: "What must ultimately sustain the Court in public confidence is the character and independence of the judges. They are not there simply to decide cases, but to decide them as they think they should be decided, and while it may be regrettable that they cannot always agree, it is better that their independence should be maintained and recognized than that unanimity should be secured through its sacrifice."[45]

We should never lose sight of how regrettable it is when the Court cannot find its way to agreement. The Court must always try through all available means to find grounds on which there can be genuine agreement. I feel such pride in the Court when we are able to issue unanimous opinions in controversial cases, as we have done recently in a difficult case or two. But when agreement is not possible, I also feel pride when my colleagues and I are able to disagree honestly and respectfully.

I admire Chief Justice Taft for his heroic efforts to keep his Court together—for his flexibility and his willingness to discuss cases repeatedly and at length until that Court could find agreement. These efforts have contributed perhaps more to the Court than the other things Taft gave us: more than our building, grand as it may be, and more even than the greater degree of control over our docket. I appreciate Taft the most for setting an example for future Courts of the importance of reaching agreement when possible, and for helping secure for today's Court the respect required to enable us to depart from unanimity when disagreement is necessary.

CHAPTER FOURTEEN

Charles Evans Hughes and President Roosevelt's Court-Expansion Plan

———

THE PAST THREE QUARTERS OF A CENTURY HAS SEEN MANY changes in the legal world. In considering the new difficulties faced by modern judges, one President remarked: "The duty of a judge involves more than presiding or listening to testimony or arguments. It is well to remember that the mass of details involved in the average law case today is vastly greater and more complicated than even twenty years ago. Records and briefs must be read; statutes, decisions, and extensive material of a technical, scientific, statistical, and economic nature must be searched and studied; opinions must be formulated and written. The modern tasks of judges call for the use of full energies."[1]

Of course, these were the words of President Franklin Roosevelt in 1937. Yes, though much has changed in the years since, one thing has remained constant: judges are perennially overworked, understaffed, and (some of us occasionally are tempted to think) underappreciated. Although many fine minds have been brought to bear on the question of how we can solve some of these problems, not all solutions have been equally welcome. President Roosevelt's plan to help the judges whose plight he so feelingly described fell into this latter category. In fact, his plan—the effect of which would have been to add six Justices to the Supreme Court—precipitated what has been called "the fiercest

Justice Charles Evans Hughes, Associate Justice of the
U.S. Supreme Court (1910–16), U.S. Secretary of State (1921–25),
Chief Justice of the United States (1930–41).

battle in American History between two branches of our government over a third."[2]

The current head count of Justices on the Court is engraved neither in stone nor in the Constitution. Indeed, there have been so many fluctuations in the number of Justices that the history of these changes has been put into verse to help jog the memory.

> Congress decided at first to fix
>   the number of Justices at six.
> Congress planned on a change to five,
>   but the six remained very much alive.
> Six high judges, supreme as heaven—
>   and Jefferson added number seven.
> Seven high judges, all in a line—
>   two more added, and that made nine.
> Nine high judges were sitting when
>   Lincoln made them an even ten.
> Ten high judges, very sedate;
>   when Congress got through, there were only eight.
> Eight high judges who wouldn't resign;
>   President Grant brought the figure back to nine.
> Would a Justice feel like a packed sardine
>   if the number was raised to—say—15?[3]

Historians have always focused on what is widely believed to be the *real* reason for President Roosevelt's plan to raise the number of Justices to fifteen. According to accepted wisdom, President Roosevelt was more than a little annoyed that the Justices were giving a thumbs-down to so much of his New Deal legislation. And he wasn't just imagining things. For in the 140 years between 1790 and 1930, the Court had overruled only sixty acts of Congress—barely half an act per year. But during President Roosevelt's first term, the Court overruled twelve acts—and some of those were President Roosevelt's favorites! In fact, on so-called Black Monday (May 27, 1935), the Court struck down three pieces of legislation at once. At that pace, President Roosevelt feared the Court would soon dismantle his New Deal completely.

So he came up with what he thought was a clever proposal. He would get Congress to pass a bill that would let him appoint a new Justice every time a Justice turned seventy years old. Coincidentally, six members of the Court were over seventy then. A cartoon published at the time revealed what people thought the President was after: it shows the nine then-current Justices on the bench—along with six President Roosevelt look-alikes.[4]

But perhaps this version of the events is not completely accurate. In the spirit of complete fairness to President Roosevelt, let's look seriously for a moment at what he *said* he was doing. In his message to the Senate Committee on the Judiciary recommending his "practical assistance" plan for overworked Justices, he expressed great concern about working conditions, saying: "The judiciary has often found itself handicapped by insufficient personnel with which to meet a growing and more complex business. . . . The simple fact is that today a new need for legislative action arises because the personnel of the Federal Judiciary [are] insufficient to meet the business before them. A growing body of our citizens complain of the complexities, the delays, and the expense of litigation in the United States courts."[5] This problem was complicated by what the President claimed was a problem "of aged or infirm judges."[6]

Given the increased demands on the judiciary, President Roosevelt thought that the wisdom of his proposal would be manifest to all. "If an elder judge is not in fact incapacitated, only good can come from the presence of an additional judge in the crowded state of the dockets; if the capacity of an elder judge is in fact impaired, the appointment of an additional judge is indispensable."[7]

Were the Justices grateful for the President's concern for their understaffed condition, their overcrowded dockets, and the complexity of their modern cases? After all, Chief Justice Charles Evans Hughes had once said that "the importance in the Supreme Court of avoiding the risk of having judges who are unable properly to do their work and yet insist on remaining on the bench is too great to permit chances to be taken."[8] Of course, Hughes said this before he was appointed to the Court, and it's possible that he had an interest in seeing a few of those sitting Justices retire. On the other hand, Justice Louis Brandeis, who at age seventy-nine was the oldest of the Supreme Court Justices—and still one of its most brilliant—might have taken the President's suggestions about elder judges personally.

At first, the public had to be content with guesses about what the Justices were thinking; not a word came from the marble halls of the Court. The day the President announced his proposal, the Justices heard oral argument as usual. They made no statement to the press. In fact, Chief Justice Hughes went so far as to ask the young head of the Federal Bureau of Investigation, J. Edgar Hoover, to prevent a news organization from distributing a six-year-old film clip of him talking about the Court.

While the Justices were keeping their counsel to themselves, everyone else was putting their two cents in. The main forum for the debate was the Senate Judiciary Committee, where hearings on the Court bill were in progress. But the debate was by no means limited to senators. The pros and cons of hiring more Justices were vigorously debated in newspapers and on the radio. Letters poured into the offices of members of Congress—a total of ten million pieces of mail by the time the fight was over. The issue made some strange bedfellows: former President Hoover, who was vigorously campaigning against the plan, was joined by Burton Wheeler, a liberal senator who had helped defeat Hoover in the last election. Leading supporters included a former Supreme Court Justice, John Hessin Clarke, and two future Supreme Court Justices, Senators Hugo Black and Sherman Minton. But as the hearings on the bill before the Senate Judiciary Committee dragged on, the Justices remained silent.

We might never have known what the Justices thought about the plan if a woman hadn't driven across the Potomac into Virginia to play with a new baby. Mrs. Brandeis, wife of the Justice, made this trip to see Senator Wheeler's newborn grandchild—and to tell the senator that he was right about the Court bill. This tip sent Senator Wheeler on a quick trip to the Court to see if Justice Brandeis shared his wife's view. Not surprisingly, Justice Brandeis believed that wisdom was a concomitant of age, and that President Roosevelt's assertions to the contrary were quite misguided. "Will you testify at the hearings?" Senator Wheeler asked. Justice Brandeis would not. But he had a counteroffer: "You call up the Chief Justice and he'll give you a letter."[9]

Senator Wheeler was surprised—and had a few reservations about placing the call. After all, Senator Wheeler had given Chief Justice Hughes an exceptionally hard time at his confirmation hearings seven years earlier. But overcoming his embarrassment, Wheeler placed the call, and Chief Justice Hughes agreed to write the letter. One last problem: it was now Saturday afternoon, and Senator Wheeler was to be the first witness in opposition to the Court bill on Monday morning. Could Chief Justice Hughes write the letter in time?

Perhaps to disprove the President's claim that the Justices were too slow in getting their work done, Chief Justice Hughes had the letter done by Sunday afternoon. As Senator Wheeler came by his office to pick it up, Hughes said slowly and solemnly, "The baby is born."

And the baby was diapered and ready to go the next morning, as Senator Wheeler took the stand before the Senate Judiciary Committee. Senator Wheeler looked so smug that the chairman of the committee whispered to the senator sitting next to him, "I don't know what he's going to spring on us, but it'll blow us out of the water."

"Mr. Chairman and members of the Committee on the Judiciary," Senator Wheeler began, "it is with some reluctance that I appear here this morning." Senator Wheeler went on to explain how he had always supported the President and his programs and had frequently disagreed with the Supreme Court's decisions. And yet, he said, "I thought it was a reflection upon the Court when it was stated that the Court was behind in its work, and when it was very strongly intimated, if not stated in so many words, that such a condition resulted from the age of the Members of the Court." He explained that after doing some investigating, he "went to the only source in this country that could know exactly what the facts were and that better than anyone else." Then he sprang it: "I have here now a letter by the Chief Justice of the Supreme Court."[10]

Finally, the judicial silence was ending. As Senator Wheeler recalled, "You could have heard a comma drop in the Caucus Room as I read the letter aloud."

One by one, Chief Justice Hughes struck down the arguments proffered by the President and his supporters. First, the Supreme Court was fully abreast of its work. "When we rose on March 15 (for the present recess)," he wrote, "we had heard argument in cases in which certiorari had been granted only four weeks before—February 15."[11] Second, the Justices were hearing all cases that it was appropriate to hear—and not rejecting important claims to keep their dockets clean. Third, though the records and briefs submitted during the course of a term may be voluminous, questions on *certiorari* raise issues of law—and in most cases the records need not be examined.

Then Chief Justice Hughes came to his last argument—the clincher: "An increase in the number of Justices of the Supreme Court, apart from any question of policy, which I do not discuss, would not promote the efficiency of the Court. It is believed it would impair that efficiency so long as the Court acts as a unit. There would be more judges to hear, more judges to confer, more judges to discuss, more judges to be convinced and to decide. The present number of Justices is thought to be large enough so far as the prompt, adequate, and efficient conduct of the work of the Court is concerned."[12]

In a stunning display of counterintuitive logic, Chief Justice Hughes had found the best argument that proved the President wrong, conclusively demonstrating that adding Justices to the Court would *not* improve its efficiency. The President's reasoning made superficial sense: if the workload is too great, increase the number of hands on board. But Hughes's more subtle analysis displayed the fatal flaw in this theory. In the world of the Supreme Court, the amount of work is *inversely* related to the number of Justices involved. Though the Justices might be overworked now, adding more hands would make things even worse.

An amazing argument—and yet it carried the day. According to Senator Wheeler, "The letter had a sensational effect. The newsreels photographed it, newspaper reporters clamored for copies, and it was all I could do to keep it from being snatched from my hands when the session was recessed."[13] Later that day the Vice President gave the President a call. "We're licked," he said.[14]

The VP was right. The Senate Judiciary Committee reported the Court bill unfavorably, and despite vigorous debate on the floor of the Senate, the wind had been knocked out of the President's sails. As Senator Wheeler reported, "The Bill was [finally] consigned to its mercy death on a vote of 70–20."[15]

And so the Court survived one of the greatest crises of its history. More than sixty years later, little has changed. There are still nine Justices on the bench, and we are still overworked and still, by some lights at least, underappreciated. Indeed, our workload has increased dramatically. In his famous letter, Chief Justice Hughes was proud to note that, of the 1,090 cases on the docket in 1935, the Court had disposed of 990 during the term. But in the October 2000 term, for example, the current Court had almost 9,000 cases on the docket.

Congress has taken some steps to ameliorate this situation. One such change was the creation in 1982 of the Court of Appeals for the Federal Circuit, with its national jurisdiction over patent and customs appeals, appeals from the Merit Systems Protection Board, and claims against the government. Inasmuch as cases decided by the Court of Appeals for the Federal Circuit will not ordinarily present a conflict with another circuit's holdings, our Court has fewer occasions to grant *certiorari* simply to resolve a circuit conflict. Our acceptance of a case for plenary review from the CAFC is more likely to be based on a serious concern about the correctness of the appellate court's ruling, rather than merely a concern about conflicting circuit rulings. No doubt, this helps explain why a much higher percentage of the cases we *do* review from the CAFC result in reversals than would otherwise be the case.

Perhaps the most important change by Congress affecting our workload occurred when it made our mandatory appellate jurisdiction discretionary in 1988. This reform has allowed the Court more choice over which cases it will hear. More needs to be done, however, in the long run. But I don't want to complain too much. For clearly, under Chief Justice Hughes's reasoning, the only solution to the current problem would be to *lessen* the number of Justices on the Court. And I'm not sure I could approve of quite that much efficiency.

CHAPTER FIFTEEN

Thurgood Marshall: The Influence of a Raconteur

I WAS FRESH OUT OF STANFORD LAW SCHOOL, WORKING AS A civilian attorney in the Quartermaster Corps in West Germany while John served in the Judge Advocate General's Corps there, on the day in 1954 that Thurgood Marshall changed the nation. He had been chipping away at the building blocks of a separatist society long before 1954, of course, but it was through *Brown v. Board of Education*[1] that he compelled us, as a nation, to come to grips with some of the contradictions within ourselves.

Like most of my counterparts who grew up in the Southwest in the 1930s and 1940s, I had not been exposed personally to racial tensions before *Brown*. Arizona did not have a large African-American population then; and, unlike Southern states, it never adopted a de jure system of segregation. Although I had spent a year as an eighth-grader in a predominately Latino public school in New Mexico, I had no personal sense, as the plaintiff children of the Topeka (Kansas) School District did, of being a minority in a society that cared primarily for the majority.

But as I listened that day on the radio to Thurgood Marshall talking eloquently to the media about the social stigmas and lost opportunities suffered by African-American children in state-imposed segregated schools, my awareness of race-based disparities deepened. I did not, could not, know it then, but the man who would, as lawyer and jurist, captivate the nation would also, as colleague and friend, profoundly influence me.

Although all of us come to the Court with our own personal histories and experiences, Justice Marshall brought a special perspective. His was the eye of a lawyer who saw the deepest wounds in the social fabric and used law to help heal them. His was the ear of a counselor who understood the vulnerabilities of the accused and established safeguards for their protection. His was the mouth of a man who knew the anguish of the silenced and gave them a voice.

At oral arguments and conference meetings, in opinions and dissents, Justice Marshall imparted not only his legal acumen but also his life experiences, constantly pushing and prodding us to respond not only to the persuasiveness of legal argument but also to the power of moral truth.

Although I was continually inspired by his historic achievements, perhaps I was affected most personally by Justice Marshall as raconteur. It was rare during our conference deliberations that he would not share an anecdote, a joke, or a story. Yet, in my ten years on the bench with him, I cannot recall ever hearing the same "TM" story twice. In my early months as the junior Justice, I looked forward to these tales as welcome diversions from the heavy, often troublesome task of deciding the complex legal issues before us. But over time, as I heard more clearly what Justice Marshall was saying, I realized that behind most of the anecdotes was a relevant legal point.

I was particularly moved by a story that Justice Marshall told during the time the Court was considering a case in which an African-American defendant challenged his death sentence as racially biased. Something in the conversation caused his eyebrows to rise characteristically, and with a pregnant pause he said, "That reminds me of a story."

And so it began, this depiction of justice in operation. "You know," he said, "I had an innocent man once. He was accused of raping a white woman. The government told me if he would plead guilty, he'd only get life. I said I couldn't make that decision; I'd have to ask my client. So I told him that if he pleaded guilty, he wouldn't get the death sentence.

"He said, 'Plead guilty to what?'

Justice Thurgood Marshall (1967–1991) in his chambers, rooms 121–123, taken during the 1978–1979 term.

"I said, 'Plead guilty to rape.'

"He said, 'Raping that woman? You gotta be kidding. I won't do it.'

"That's when I knew I had an innocent man.

"When the judge sent the jurors out, he told them that they had three choices: not guilty, guilty, or guilty with mercy. 'You understand those are the three different possible choices,' he instructed. But after the jury left, the judge told the people in the courtroom that they were not to move before the bailiff took the defendant away.

"I said, 'What happened to "not guilty"?'

"The judge looked at me, and said, 'Are you kidding?' Just like that. And he was the *judge*."

As he neared the end of his tale, Justice Marshall leaned forward, pointed his finger at no one in particular, and said with his characteristic signal of finale, "E-e-e-nd of the story: The guy was found guilty and sentenced to death. But he never raped that woman." He paused, flicking his hand. "Oh, well," he added, "he was just a Negro."

With the aid of this low-key narrative, Justice Marshall made his own legal position quite clear: in his view, the death penalty was not only cruel and unusual punishment in violation of the Eighth Amendment, but it had never been, and could never be, administered fairly and free of racial bias. Although I disagreed with Justice Marshall about the constitutional validity of the death penalty, his story made clear what legal briefs often obscure: the impact of legal rules on human lives.

Through his story, Justice Marshall reminded us, once again, that the law is not an abstract concept removed from the society it serves, and that judges, as safeguarders of the Constitution, must constantly strive to narrow the gap between the ideal of equal justice and the reality of social inequality.

Justice Marshall's stories served for me another function. Beneath his wit and charm and rambunctiousness, he was an intensely private man. There were sides to him that no one but his family will ever know. But over the years, as he shared stories of Klan violence and jury bias, of co-opted judges and dishonest politicians, I gained an insight—a peephole really—into the character of a man who was at once eternally at peace and perpetually at war.

"S-a-a-a-n-d-r-a-a-a," he called out once, "did I ever tell you about the welcome I received in Mississippi?"

It was early evening in a small town in Mississippi in the early 1940s, and he was waiting to hop the next train to Shreveport. "I was starving," he told me, "so I decided to go over to this restaurant and see if one of the cooks would let me in the back to buy a sandwich. You know, that's how we did things then; the front door was so inconvenient!" Before he could go over, Justice Marshall recounted, "a man of your race holding a pistol sidled up. 'Boy,' he said, 'what are you doing around these parts?' I said, 'I'm waiting to catch the next train.' He said, 'Listen up, boy, because I'm only gonna tell you this once. The last train through here is at 4:00 P.M. and you better be on it cuz niggers ain't welcome in these parts after dark.'

"Guess what," Justice Marshall added, a twinkle creeping into his eye. "I was on that train."

What Justice Marshall did not say, what he had no need to say, was how physically threatening and personally humiliating the situation must have been. Left unspoken, too, was the anger and frustration any grown man must have felt at being called "boy" and run out of town.

It is not surprising, really, that these sentiments were relegated to the backdrop. Unlike many national figures, Justice Marshall was not interested in publicizing the risks he had taken or the sacrifices he had made. Instinctively, he downplayed his own role, as though it were natural to hide under train seats, or earn twenty-four hundred dollars a year as a lawyer, or write briefs on a manual typewriter balanced, in a moving car, between his knees. To Justice Marshall, these hardships warranted no comment. They were simply the natural extension of a lifetime credo of "doing the best you can with what you've got."

But to those of us who have traveled a different road, Justice Marshall's experiences are a source of amazement and inspiration, not only because of what they reveal about him but also because of what they instill in us, and ask of us.

I have not encountered prejudice on a sustained basis. But I have experienced gender discrimination enough—such as when law firms would hire me, a "lady lawyer," only as a legal secretary—to understand how one could seek to minimize interaction with those who are intolerant of difference. That Justice Marshall never hid from prejudice but thrust himself instead into its midst has been both an encouragement and a challenge to me.

I asked him once how he managed to avoid becoming despondent from the injustices he saw. Instead of responding directly, he told me about the time he and his mentor, Charles Hamilton Houston, the vice dean at Howard Law School, traveled to Loudoun County, Virginia, to help a man on trial for his life. The man, George Crawford, had been indicted by an all-white grand jury for allegedly murdering a white woman from a well-to-do Virginia family, as well as her white maid. Despite their defense challenge to the exclusion of African-Americans from the jury, Crawford was convicted of murder by an all-white jury and sentenced to life.

"You know something is wrong with the government's case," Justice Marshall told me, "when a Negro only gets life for murdering a white woman."

After the trial, Justice Marshall said, the media asked if Crawford planned an appeal based on the exclusion of African-Americans from the jury. "Crawford said, 'Mr. Houston, if I have another trial, and I got life this time, could they kill me the next time?' Charlie told him yes.

"So Crawford told Charlie, 'Tell them the defendant rests.'

"I still have mixed feelings about that case," Justice Marshall added. "I just don't believe that guy got a fair shake. But what are you going to do? There are only two choices in life: stop, and go on. You tell me, what would you pick?"

Even now, I still think about Justice Marshall's backhanded response, wondering how one can confront, as he did, the darkest recesses of human nature—bigotry, hatred, and selfishness—and emerge wholly intact. Although I probably will never completely understand, part of the answer, I think, lay in his capacity for narration itself. His stories reflected a truly expansive personality—the perspective of a man who immersed himself in human suffering and then translated that suffering in a way that others could bear and understand. The past that he related—doused in humor and sadness, tragedy and triumph—was but a mirror of himself: a man who saw the world exactly as it is, and pushed on to make it what it can become.

No one could help but be moved by Justice Thurgood Marshall's spirit. No one could avoid being touched by his soul.

As I continue on the bench, a few seats down from where he once sat, I think often of Justice Marshall. I remember the morning we first met, and the afternoon he left the bench. I remember the historic lawsuits he brought, and the thoughtful opinions and dissents he wrote. I recall his unwavering commitment to the poor, the accused, and the downtrodden, and his constant, impassioned repudiation of the death penalty.

More than that, though, I think of the raconteur himself. Occasionally, at conference meetings, I still catch myself looking expectantly for his raised brow and his twinkling eye, hoping to hear, just once more, another story that would, by and by, perhaps change the way I see the world.

CHAPTER SIXTEEN

Warren E. Burger

———

A CHIEF JUSTICE IS ALWAYS A SPECIAL FIGURE IN AMERICAN history. Indeed, only sixteen Justices have held that position since our Constitution was ratified. Warren E. Burger was the fifteenth Chief Justice, and his seventeen years in that capacity (1969–1986) were distinguished by his energy and his efforts to improve the judicial system throughout the United States. His life and his service as Chief Justice have left their imprint on many aspects of our legal system.

Warren Burger graduated magna cum laude in 1931 from St. Paul College of Law, the earliest forerunner of William Mitchell College of Law. He was the president of his law school fraternity, Phi Beta Gamma, which, with uncanny foresight, conferred upon him the title of "Chief Justice." He could not have attended a traditional day law school—he was a husband and father and found it necessary to hold a full-time job in the insurance industry to support his family. If it were not for the opportunity that St. Paul's offered him to attend classes at night, he could not have entered the legal profession.

Throughout his career, Warren Burger had a profound interest in raising the quality of the work of the judicial branch by improving the management of the courts. As Chief Justice, he worked to make the Supreme Court—and all courts—more responsive to the needs of those who use them, and his legacy was to the most fundamental aspect of the law: its inner workings, the machine itself. He understood that justice involves not only making good law but also administering it swiftly and efficiently. To Chief Justice Burger, this meant a judicial

Chief Justice Warren Burger and President Ronald Reagan in the Oval Office at the White House, September 17, 1981.

Chief Justice Warren Burger at a White House reception for Associate Justice designate Sandra Day O'Connor, September 24, 1981.

system in which the procedures by which justice is dispensed are as expedient as the system allows. It also meant a system in which the participants are professionally, as well as ethically, trained, and in which they have studied and mastered their craft.

Chief Justice William Rehnquist has called his predecessor the greatest judicial administrator of our time. Chief Justice Burger left his mark on every facet of our judicial system. He presided over the Court during a time when caseloads were increasing and the bar and the federal judiciary were growing rapidly. Yet the system within which they operated had remained unchanged, partly out of neglect, partly out of a reverence for tradition that sometimes hampers our progress.

As early as his confirmation hearings, the Chief Justice was reflecting on how he might deploy that office in the cause of improving the operation of our legal system. When a senator asked his views on the duties of the Chief Justice, he answered that he would, of course, be responsible for deciding cases. But he added: "The Chief Justice of the United States is assigned many other duties, administrative in nature. I would think he has a very large responsibility to try to see that the judicial system functions more efficiently. . . . I would expect to devote every energy and every moment of the rest of my life to that end should I be confirmed."[1]

The Chief Justice did indeed, as he sought, "ma[ke] our system work better." Where he saw potential for reform, he identified the precise need, offered specific proposals to address it, and produced concrete results. This task was not easy. In a system built on precedent and tradition, and in an area without an obvious constituency to attract the attention of legislators, change is hard-won. Chief Justice Burger wisely preferred that he risk some false starts rather than make no starts at all.

The Chief Justice recognized that the responsibilities of the bench had grown tremendously, and that judges were dedicating more and more precious time to administrative duties. Soon after assuming office, he gave his first speech to the American Bar Association. In those remarks, which led to the establishment of his *Annual Report on the*

State of the Judiciary, he pointed out the need for professional administrators who would provide "careful planning and definite systems and
organization" to ensure more efficient administration of justice, and
who would permit judges to concentrate on their essential task of judging.[2]

To achieve that goal, he urged the creation of an Institute for Court
Management. Today, the institute has trained hundreds of court administrators employed throughout the state and federal judicial systems. Chief Justice Burger also helped create the offices of circuit
executives and state court administrators, who have further alleviated
the administrative burdens of federal and state judges and improved
the efficiency of the courts.

In recognition of the fact that it was not only the execution of administrative tasks but also the efficiency of court procedures that
should be restructured, Chief Justice Burger became instrumental in
working to expand the jurisdiction of federal magistrates, who have
proven invaluable in the critical and time-consuming procedures of issuing warrants, conducting pretrial discovery, and providing information to those who use the courts. He also perceived that the practice of
assigning different aspects of the same case to different judges was an
uneconomical as well as a needlessly depersonalizing procedure. As a
result, he promoted the current, much improved method of consoli-
dating and assigning all aspects of a case to a particular judge.

Sensitive to the fact that the health of the entire legal system—both
state and federal—depends on a strong state judiciary, Chief Justice
Burger identified the need to strengthen state courts. He therefore proposed creating the National Center for State Courts, now in Williamsburg, Virginia, which makes available data and research relating to
matters of importance to the state judiciary.

And when Chief Justice Burger became concerned that Congress
was less responsive than it might be to the needs of the judicial branch,
he began a personal campaign of letters to and meetings with members of Congress, in order to communicate better the needs of the judiciary. In response, Congress authorized a substantial increase in new
district and appellate court judgeships. It also created the Commission

on Revision of the Federal Court Appellate System, which has studied, among other things, proposals to restructure the circuit courts.

Chief Justice Burger did not devote his efforts solely to judges and the courts. He also was an ardent proponent of heightened ethical and professional standards for the practicing bar. In a keynote address to the American Inns of Court, he voiced his view that members of the legal profession are "quasi-public servants" and "officers of the court" with a grave responsibility: "What [i]s imperatively needed [i]s more emphasis on professional ethics, on manners and deportment in the courtroom and in the practice; in short, the necessity for civility in what is inherently a contentious human enterprise."[3]

The Chief Justice demonstrated his own commitment to the legal profession by pressing for meticulous ethical training, so that lawyers, like doctors, would be equipped with the ability to identify symptoms that reflect serious underlying problems. And he advocated the certification of trial lawyers, based on the English model in which trial lawyers—barristers—are trained in advocacy. The American Inns of Court are themselves the product of the Chief Justice's idea for improving the skills of the working bar.

Warren Burger reminded us often that it is "the law school . . . where the ground-work must be laid." Legal education today is conspicuous for its breadth. We have seen the development of interdisciplinary offerings, which recognize the contributions that economics, psychology, literature, philosophy, and sociology can make to the law. But it is essential, in the face of these innovations, that law schools continue to insist on acquisition of the fundamental skills that every lawyer should master. Chief Justice Burger tenaciously adhered to the view that "laws are not ends in themselves but a means to an end—a tool."[4] Only advocates who know expertly how to use the tools of procedure, legal analysis, and advocacy will be equipped adequately to represent their clients and to help to shape and refine our legal principles.[5]

These positions hardly sound controversial today, for now we see the need for many of the reforms that Chief Justice Burger suggested. But at the time they were proposed, some of these ideas were greeted with skepticism, disagreement, even anger. The Chief Justice's efforts to employ administrative officers in courts were meant to ease the judiciary's workload, but many judges were loath to cede any part of their responsibilities to administrative staffs. And imagine the response from the bar when the Chief Justice observed that "people suffer because lawyers are licensed, with very few exceptions, without the slightest inquiry into their capacity to perform the intensely practical functions of an advocate."[6] Some legal academics were provoked by the Chief Justice's assertion that law schools should offer practical training to their students, and that lawyers, like carpenters and electricians, must learn their craft.

But as with most of the Chief Justice's campaigns for reform, his ideas, unpopular as they may have been initially, were necessary examinations of serious problems. They produced much needed improvements to our legal system. His efforts on behalf of more efficient courts have produced a corps of career administrators who have been invaluable in bringing organization and promptness to the way in which routine tasks are handled. The lack of courtroom training for lawyers has met with a much acclaimed remedy: as a result of the attention he called to the need for improving the quality of advocacy in our courts, the American Bar Association, the American College of Trial Lawyers, and the Association of Trial Lawyers of America jointly sponsored the creation of the National Institute for Trial Advocacy.

And it is in part as a result of Chief Justice Burger's urgings that clinical opportunities were widely introduced in law schools as an educational tool. It is just this sort of teaching that he was interested in implementing when he criticized modern legal education. "The shortcoming of today's law graduate," he said, "lies not in a deficient knowledge of law but that he has little, if any, training in dealing with facts or people—the stuff of which *cases* are really made."[7]

Of course, at the same time that he was spearheading reform both in the administration of courts and in the legal profession, Chief Justice Burger was fully engaged in leading the Supreme Court through a time of important development. During his years of active service, he wrote more than 250 opinions for the Court, many of which stand out as landmarks. In an area of special interest to me, the Chief's opinion in *Reed v. Reed* was the Court's first decision striking as unconstitutional under the equal protection clause a state law discriminating against women on the basis of gender.[8] *Reed* marked the Court's first solid departure from its consistent affirmation of governmental authority to classify by gender. To mention only a very few of his other opinions, his work on the Nixon-tapes case averted a constitutional crisis by compelling the President to release his tapes of conversations.[9] And his opinion for the Court in *INS v. Chadha* was a landmark case in the separation-of-powers context.[10]

What is perhaps not as well known is Warren Burger's deep love of history and of the Court. In 1974 the Chief Justice founded the Supreme Court Historical Society. He also created the position of curator of the Court and began a Supreme Court documentary-history project. He transformed the interior of the Court building into a vastly more attractive space that now includes displays of historical documents, portraits of the retired Justices, and busts of the retired Chief Justices. And among the many treasures in the Court secured by the Chief Justice, there is one in particular that we owe to him personally. In the Court's John Marshall Dining Room, where the Justices occasionally have lunch, there is a handsome bas-relief of Chief Justice Marshall. This was not commissioned by the Chief Justice, but sculpted by him.

Chief Justice Burger was a man of unusual talents and special qualities. He always had time to offer his colleagues a cup of tea and conversation. He loved to relax and reminisce with his law clerks. His former clerks recall Saturdays—regular working days—on which the Chief would prepare soup for them in a small kitchen off of his study. He would even insist on washing the dishes. He enjoyed a capacity for unstinting hard work and the vision to set long-term goals.

After his retirement as Chief Justice, Warren Burger continued forcefully and effectively to express his vision of an efficient legal system, staffed by capable lawyers and judges. He greatly enjoyed serving as chairman of the Bicentennial Commission to commemorate the two hundredth anniversary of the writing and ratification of our Constitution, the establishment of our three branches of government, and the adoption of the Bill of Rights. In so doing, he helped to reeducate us all about an event that he himself aptly described as "one of the greatest stories . . . in the history of human liberty."[11]

CHAPTER SEVENTEEN

Lewis F. Powell, Jr.

———

I WAS AT THE SUPREME COURT IN JANUARY 1972 TO WITNESS the investiture of Lewis Powell and William Rehnquist. I met the Powells at the reception following, but little did I dream then that I would know Lewis Powell as a colleague on the Supreme Court nine years later.

Lewis Powell was the ninety-ninth Justice to serve on the Supreme Court, and perhaps the most reluctant. It is reported that on the day he was sworn in, Nan Rehnquist asked Justice Powell's wife, Jo, if it wasn't the most exciting day of her life. Jo reportedly said, "No, it is the worst day of my life. I am about to cry." Lewis Powell had turned down an appointment to the Court in 1969 and was prepared to do so again in 1972. Luckily for the Court and the nation, he finally agreed to accept the nomination when President Nixon convinced him that it was his duty to his country to do so.

Justice Powell's family in America dated back to Thomas Powell, who came to the James River area of Virginia from England in 1635. The future Justice was born in Suffolk, Virginia, but lived most of his life in Richmond. He was an able student and a good athlete, playing basketball and baseball. He learned how to shoot and enjoyed hunting. He also learned as a youngster the demanding nature of life on a farm. His father bought a milk cow named Mollie. The younger Powell was directed to feed her, take care of her, and milk her. Anyone who has done that chore knows there is never a day off. Justice Powell said that one of his happiest days was some years later, when he went out to the barn and "found the damn cow dead."

Justice Lewis F. Powell, Jr., Associate Justice, 1972–1987.

Justice Powell attended college and law school at Washington and Lee University in Lexington, Virginia. He quickly demonstrated his leadership qualities, becoming president of his fraternity, managing editor of the student newspaper, and student body president. He graduated first in his class from law school, then did a postgraduate year at Harvard.

Upon completing his schooling, he returned to Richmond to practice law and after a couple of years joined the law firm of Hunton & Williams at the handsome salary of fifty dollars per month. Soon afterward he married Jo Rucker, a beautiful and talented graduate of Sweet Briar College. It was a marriage made in heaven, as they say, and one that remained joyous and loving for more than sixty years. Lewis and Jo had four wonderful children—Jody, Penny, Lewis III, and Molly—nine grandchildren, and one great-grandchild.

In 1941 the young lawyer volunteered to serve in the Army Air Force. He saw duty in North Africa, Sicily, and England. Eventually, he was assigned to military intelligence and served in the most sensitive and top-secret intelligence group, known as ULTRA. In the military service he made a very important contribution to the victory of the Allies, and it was a significant part of his life.

After World War II, Powell returned to Hunton & Williams, where he represented some important clients, including Colonial Williamsburg. Qualities of leadership emerged again at once—within his law firm, in the House of Delegates of the American Bar Association, and as chairman of the Richmond School Board. In that capacity he served during the years immediately following the Supreme Court's decision in *Brown v. Board of Education,* keeping the public schools open. Later, he became a member of the Virginia State Board of Education. He supported reform of the curriculum and strongly opposed those proposing massive resistance to the desegregation of the public schools. He became president of the Colonial Williamsburg Foundation and, in 1964, president of the American Bar Association.

Justice Powell served on the Supreme Court of the United States from January 1972 to June 1987. He wrote more than five hundred opinions, many very significant. It was a great privilege to serve on the

Court with him for six full years. No one did more than Lewis Powell to help me get settled as a new Justice. He found us a place to live. He allowed me to hire one of his two secretaries as my chamber's secretary. Most important, he was willing to talk about cases and the issues. His door was always open. I miss those visits and discussions still today.

Lewis was very hardworking and attended to every detail. He was concerned in every case about the equity at the bottom line—about reaching a fair and just result. He brought to his task a lifetime of experience as a lawyer and as a leader. He was enormously kind and thoughtful. But underneath that gentlemanly exterior was a firmness and resolve. When he decided on a course of action, he would hold his ground.

Lewis was an excellent dancer, and I had the privilege of dancing with him several times. He once asked me to speak at a meeting of the Richmond Bar Association. When he introduced me, he said: "Now, on my tombstone, it will say, 'Here lies the first Supreme Court Justice to dance with another Justice.'"

Lewis Powell followed the precept of another famous Southerner, General Robert E. Lee: "Do your duty in all things. You cannot do more. You should never do less."[1]

Another observer of Lewis Powell said, "For those who seek a perspective grounded in realism and leavened by decency, conscientious in detail and magnanimous in spirit, solicitous of personal dignity and protective of the public trust, there will never be a better Justice."[2]

I would add: For those who seek a model of human kindness, decency, exemplary behavior, and integrity, there will never be a better man.

PART FOUR

—

Women and the Law

As the first woman Justice on the Supreme Court, I've received innumerable requests from groups around the country asking me to comment on some aspect of the role of women in America, both today and in the past. It is a subject in which I have more than a passing interest.

In my life span, I have witnessed a sea change in public attitudes about women. When I went to law school in the middle of the last century, there was only a handful of women students in the major law schools around the country. Women's work was still thought to be largely at home or, for some, as schoolteachers or nurses. World War II dramatically opened up opportunities for women. My own career unfolded at this time, and I was a beneficiary of the changing attitudes about "women's work." This year, for the first time in the United States, there are more women in law schools than men.

The chapters in Part Four reflect some of the history of these remarkable strides.

CHAPTER EIGHTEEN

Women in Society:
The American Experience

———

*T*HE STRUGGLE OF AMERICAN WOMEN TO GAIN ADMISSION to the working world and to attain basic civil rights has been marked by laborious, often divergent efforts and punctuated by periods of rapid change. Although American women still have a way to go, in recent years doors firmly shut for centuries have swung open and permitted our entry. We scarcely blink today at the notion of a female astronaut, engineer, lawyer, surgeon, or legislator.

This recent access to the working world has presented women with an unprecedented array of new blessings and burdens. On the one hand, we have largely shed the stereotypes that once branded us, in the words of the Court on which I now sit, "unfit for many of the occupations of civil life."[1] On the other hand, we have struggled with the difficulties of balancing our role in the workplace with the biological realities of pregnancy and the practical requirements of raising families. American women still endeavor to find an appropriate balance between equality and recognition of gender distinctiveness. Nonetheless, the path we have taken to date can offer opportunity for our own further reflection as a nation—and insight to the outside observer. For although the experiences of every country have been and will be distinct, I believe that one can safely make generalizations about the experience of American women that may prove useful.

In order to explore the tremendous advances made by American women in this century, it is important to stake out the starting point.

Belva A. Lockwood, in *Frank Leslie's Illustrated Newspaper*, April 5, 1879, the
year she became the first woman admitted to the Supreme Court bar.
She ran for President of the United States in 1884 and 1888
on the Equal Rights Party ticket.

Here, as always, the past serves as prologue; the situation of women in the late eighteenth, nineteenth, and early twentieth centuries in the United States provides crucial context and demonstrates just how far we have traveled.

When the wife of future President John Adams implored her husband in 1776 to "remember the Ladies" in drafting our new nation's charter, her remarks fell on deaf ears. John Adams's curt dismissal of her plea prompted Abigail Adams to respond: "I cannot say that I think you very generous to the Ladies, for whilst you are proclaiming peace and good will to Men, Emancipating all Nations, you insist upon retaining an absolute power over Wives."[2]

The American Constitution, signed on September 17, 1787, was produced by fifty-five men. Although subject to the Constitution's terms, women were "unacknowledged in its text, uninvited in its formulation, [and] unsolicited for its ratification."[3] In permitting each state to determine the qualifications of voters for Congress, the Constitution implicitly endorsed laws in virtually every state that prohibited women from voting. To be sure, provisions of the Constitution were broadly framed and did not, in and of themselves, aggravate the plight of women. Nonetheless, it is fair to say that, in setting out the contours of American government in 1787, the Framers of the Constitution envisioned no role for American women.

Nor did the ratification of the Bill of Rights in 1791 have much effect on the legal status or rights of women. Although the Bill of Rights did not specifically deny equal rights to women, its Framers did not contemplate meaningful protection for them, either. The carefully drawn limits of the bill circumscribed only the federal government; the states were free to continue as before in fashioning the political and legal rights of their citizens. States drew their legislation primarily from the English common law. Only in the case of unmarried women were the laws in this country somewhat more generous than in England, and then only with respect to property ownership.

America inherited from England a tradition in which gender defined "the geography of social life."[4] As the great political observer Alexis de Tocqueville described matters in the 1830s, "the Americans have applied to the sexes the great principle of political economy which governs the manufactures of our age, by carefully dividing the duties of man from those of woman, in order that the great work of society may be the better carried on."[5] Men dominated the public arena of political and commercial activity; women, for their part, occupied the private realm of domestic and spiritual life.

The law respected such boundaries. The notion of two distinct spheres had firm roots in the belief—embraced by virtually every major theologian and philosopher of the time—that women were subordinate, probably less intelligent, and definitely weaker than men. By law, wives could not hold, purchase, control, bequeath, or convey property, retain their own wages, make contracts, or bring legal actions. In the words of the English poet Alfred, Lord Tennyson, a wife stood in legal relation to her spouse as something just "better than his dog, a little dearer than his horse."[6]

Within their limited realm, however, women held what can fairly be described as lofty status. The message from press and pulpit alike was that women, though intellectually inferior to men, were morally and spiritually superior. Much of their exclusion of women from public life in the nineteenth century was justified in the name of preserving the sanctity of this domestic sphere. Married women's domesticity became a source of patriotism, as the home was equated with a "nursery of citizenship."[7] The physical well-being of women—and, not coincidentally, the protection of women from the cruel and heartless world—became social preoccupations. Embracing their moral role, many nineteenth-century homemakers organized in maternal and charitable societies. Marriage and membership in the unskilled labor force remained mutually exclusive alternatives, and women generally did not challenge their plight.

The law reinforced a rigid distinction between genders, and did so most vehemently with respect to women's efforts to join the bar. In 1874 Belva Lockwood, who had managed to gain admission to the National Law School by appealing directly to President Ulysses S. Grant, was rejected by the United States Court of Claims with the simple announcement: "Mistress Lockwood, you are a woman."[8] The Virginia

Supreme Court reacted similarly, determining that Lockwood was not a "person" within the meaning of the state bar licensing statute.[9]

Myra Bradwell suffered a like fate. In rejecting her application to the state bar in 1869, the Illinois Supreme Court proclaimed that "God designed the sexes to occupy different spheres of action, and . . . it belong[s] to men to make, apply, and execute the laws."[10] The Supreme Court of the United States wholeheartedly agreed. Concurring in the Court's judgment, Justice Bradley wrote: "Man is, or should be, woman's protector and defender. The natural and proper timidity and delicacy which belongs to the female sex evidently unfits it for many of the occupations of civil life."[11]

The situation was similar for other professions. In many institutions, any excuse for excluding women would suffice. Princeton's graduate program, Yale Medical School, and the Brooklyn and Bronx bar associations all justified their ban on women by their alleged inability to afford separate rest rooms.[12]

The marital relationship during this period, at least as it was reflected in law, was characterized by male dominance. Upon marriage, women suffered what Blackstone termed "civil death," as their individual identities merged into their husbands' in the eyes of the law.[13] The married woman by herself often was legally classified with "lunatics, idiots, . . . and infants."[14]

Men were under a legal duty to support their wives, but the law rarely stepped in to enforce this obligation. A typical case is *Miller v. Miller*.[15] After failing to provide for his wife, Mr. Miller signed a written contract agreeing to give her an annual allowance. When he breached his contract, Mrs. Miller took him to court. The Iowa Supreme Court declined to enforce the agreement, asking itself: "What element could be introduced into a family that would tend more directly to breed discord than this contract?" Judges took a similar stance toward domestic violence.

Early English law had recognized the husband's right to discipline his spouse, provided that he "neither killed nor maimed her."[16] Most of the state courts of the United States adopted this or comparable legal principles. The Supreme Court of Mississippi approved the role of husband as disciplinarian in 1824, stating: "Let the husband be permitted to exercise the right of moderate chastisement, in cases of great emergency, and use salutary restraints in every case of misbehaviour, without being subject to vexatious prosecutions, resulting in the mutual discredit and shame of all parties concerned."[17]

Not until the late nineteenth century did some states begin to criminalize wife beating. Even then, although there were hundreds of societies for the protection of children and animals in Victorian America, only one—in 1886 in Chicago—specifically protected battered women.[18] In most cases women were left simply to forgive and try to forget.

This, then, was the situation of American women until all too recently: they could not vote; they were excluded from the working world, due in part to their supposed mental inferiority and in part to notions of their "moral" superiority, which required their protection and insulation from economic competition and political affairs; they generally lacked power to own or sell property; and their husbands— their lords and undisputed legal masters—were permitted to discipline them as they would children. Socially and legally, America reflected and reinforced a highly gender-stratified order.

Against this backdrop, it is clear that women in America have come very far indeed. Today women outnumber men as eligible voters in national elections. The need for effective laws preventing spousal abuse and domestic violence recently has come into sharp focus. In my own lifetime I have witnessed a revolution in the legal profession that has resulted in women composing nearly 30 percent of attorneys in this country, and over 50 percent of law school students.[19] This progress is truly amazing when you consider that, at my graduation near the top of my class at Stanford Law School in 1952, the only position I was offered at a national law firm was that of legal secretary. Yet, I have since served as a state senator, a state judge, and a United States Supreme Court Justice. It is astonishing to contemplate how much change has occurred so quickly.

Women's efforts to secure for themselves the right to vote by appealing to the newly drafted Thirteenth, Fourteenth, and Fifteenth

Amendments were unsuccessful. In the only Supreme Court case addressing the issue,[20] the Court resoundingly and unanimously rejected the notion that the spirit of equality in the Fourteenth Amendment somehow compelled the extension of the vote to women. After local authorities in Missouri refused her request to register to vote in the 1870s, Virginia Minor sued. Minor lost at every stage of the litigation. In rejecting her arguments, the Supreme Court ultimately concluded that the U.S. citizenship guaranteed in Section 1 of the Fourteenth Amendment did not inevitably include the right to vote, because although women were undeniably citizens, they had been "excluded from [voting] in nearly all the States by the express provision of their constitutions and laws."[21]

After the *Minor* decision was handed down, women activists concluded that the broad, egalitarian language of the first section of the Fourteenth Amendment held out only hollow promise. For change to come, it had to come from without, rather than within, the existing Constitution.

The turn-of-the-century Progressive reform movement, which developed in response to deplorable conditions in the newly industrialized American cities, provided a crucial social impetus to this change. As in the antislavery movements of the previous century, women constituted the bulk of membership in the numerous national organizations established to improve modern society for all classes of people. Progressive organizations lobbied several state legislatures to enact legislation setting maximum hours and minimum wages for male and female workers in various occupations.

These social welfare laws initially ran afoul of the Supreme Court's freedom-of-contract jurisprudence. The Court repeatedly struck down as unconstitutional legislation aimed at protecting bakers, miners, and the like on the grounds that laws limiting their hours interfered with their ability to work *more*. The Court perceived any interference, however altruistically motivated, as an unconstitutional incursion on the rights of workers and employers to fix their relationship contractually.

There is some irony in the fact that the tide of judicial hostility to protective legislation ultimately was reversed by appeals to paternalis-

tic stereotypes about women. As the argument ran, women were fragile, they could not be depended upon to represent their own interests
in the business world, and they needed legislative help. Freedom of
contract meant little where women were concerned, because they were
unable to fend for themselves in the workplace. The Supreme Court
observed in 1908 that "history discloses the fact that woman has always been dependent upon man. . . . In the struggle for subsistence
she is not an equal competitor with her brother."[22] Only after the Court
accepted women's special need for protection as a rationale for pierc-
ing the logic of freedom-of-contract jurisprudence did it gradually
begin to defer to protective legislation for the working classes generally. Such change, however, would not come for decades.

In the meantime, the new political sophistication of women working in the trenches for legal reform ultimately helped them to secure
the right to vote in the Nineteenth Amendment to the Constitution.
That amendment was an outgrowth of a remarkable alliance between
Progressives, who touted women's need for protection in the workplace, and pioneer feminists like Elizabeth Cady Stanton and Susan B.
Anthony, who sought full and equal citizenship for women. The 1920
passage and ratification of the Nineteenth Amendment, which required a two-thirds vote of both houses of Congress and ratification by
three quarters of state legislatures, remains the single greatest political
triumph of the women's movement in the United States.

As all too often happens after a great victory, however, the women's
movement fragmented upon winning the battle over the right to vote.
No longer blessed with a clear goal, the movement became sharply
split along two lines: descendants of the Progressives, who advocated
special protective legislation for women in recognition of gender distinctiveness, and descendants of Stanton and Anthony, who sought absolutely equal rights and equal treatment, neither more nor less. The
quest for the vote had been but a temporary goal unifying feminists of
widely divergent philosophies. Several of the organizations that had
led the fight for the vote turned against social welfare legislation, la-
beling its notions of women's special fragility sexist and demeaning.
As a result of this deep ideological divide, women did not tend to vote

in blocs. Thus, the period between World War I and World War II was a confusing time for women, who still lacked economic independence, political experience, and—with some notable exceptions—meaningful education, but who no longer enjoyed a consensus on how best to improve their situation.

After the tide of its freedom-of-contract jurisprudence receded in the 1930s, the Supreme Court entered a period in which it deferred to legislative judgments regarding the differences between the sexes. Despite the extension of the vote to women, many of these laws continued to enforce the exclusion of women from much of the working world. In 1948 four women challenged the constitutionality of a Michigan statute forbidding a woman being a bartender unless she was "the wife or daughter of the male owner" of the bar. The Supreme Court rejected the claim that the statute violated the equal protection clause, reasoning that "despite the vast changes in the social and legal position of women," the state could unquestionably forbid all women from working as bartenders.[23] As late as 1961 the Court reaffirmed Florida's practice of restricting jury service to men, unless women registered separately. Gwendolyn Hoyt, who was convicted by an all-male jury of murdering her husband, argued that she was entitled to a jury made up of men and women. In rejecting her contention, the Supreme Court reasoned that, "despite the enlightened emancipation of women from the restrictions and protections of bygone years, and their entry into many parts of community life formerly considered to be reserved to men, woman is still regarded as the center of home and family life."[24]

True victory for women at the workplace did not come until after Congress passed civil rights legislation in the early 1960s, and it arrived partly by accident. The Civil Rights Act of 1964, an outgrowth of the Kennedy and Johnson administrations' concerns about racial discrimination, was passed at a time when women's issues were not at the forefront of national attention. Indeed, the provision of the act barring gender-based discrimination by employers was not part of the original legislation. As the story goes, a congressman named Howard W. Smith introduced an amendment offering protection against sex discrimination in a last-minute effort to *defeat* the entire legislation, because he believed that none of his peers would vote for protection for women. When the act as amended passed both houses of Congress, Congressman Smith, whose overriding purpose had been to prevent the antidiscrimination laws from going into effect, became an unwitting hero of the women's movement.

The late 1960s and early 1970s saw great activity in the women's movement, when an increasing proportion of American women found traditional roles less fulfilling than the prevailing culture assumed. National surveys revealed that a scant 10 percent of American women wanted their daughters to lead lives like theirs.[25] Changes in longevity and access to birth control altered the pattern of women's lives. At the turn of the century, the average woman lived to be forty-eight and could contemplate living ten to fifteen years after her last child left home. By the 1960s, however, a typical mother had her last child at age twenty-seven and could anticipate spending about two thirds of her adult years without children under age eighteen.[26] Thirty-eight percent of all women were in the workforce.

As women increasingly looked beyond the home for fulfillment, the revitalized women's movement once again had a single issue that could unify people of disparate philosophies: passage of an amendment to the Constitution that would guarantee that American women would not face official discrimination on the basis of gender. With little debate, twenty-two states quickly ratified the Equal Rights Amendment, or ERA, by the end of 1972; eight others ratified in 1973, three in 1974, and one in 1975.

Just as the women's movement began stirring mainstream America and prompting calls for the ERA, however, the Supreme Court managed to find greater protection for women in the Fourteenth Amendment than decades of prior cases had presumed existed, thus diminishing the immediate sense of need for the ERA. Together with the radicalization of the women's movement in the 1970s, the Supreme Court's doctrinal turn contributed to the ultimate failure of the ERA in 1982.

The first case in which the Court struck down a state law that discriminated against women was *Reed v. Reed.*[27] *Reed* involved a challenge to an Idaho law giving men an automatic preference as administrators of estates. The case signaled a dramatic shift in the Court's approach to matters of gender. Rather than defer to any legislative judgment, the Court determined that the distinction drawn in the Idaho law was "the very kind of arbitrary legislative choice forbidden by the Equal Protection Clause of the Fourteenth Amendment."[28]

In subsequent cases, inspired in part by the pioneering litigation efforts of my colleague Justice Ruth Bader Ginsburg, the Supreme Court made emphatically clear that it would no longer accept without question the story that women are fundamentally different from men. In 1972, while striking down a federal statute making it easier for men to claim their wives as dependents than it was for women to claim their husbands as dependents, Justice Brennan wrote: "There can be no doubt that our Nation has had a long and unfortunate history of sex discrimination. Traditionally, such discrimination was rationalized by an attitude of 'romantic paternalism' which, in practical effect, put women, not on a pedestal, but in a cage."[29]

Two years later the Supreme Court struck down a Utah statute providing that noncustodial divorced parents were required to pay child support for girls only until they reached the age of eighteen, but for boys until they reached the age of twenty-one. The state justified this distinction by arguing that women matured faster, married earlier, and tended not to require continuing support through higher education. The Court took a hard look at these justifications and concluded: "A child, male or female, is still a child. No longer is the female destined solely for the home and the rearing of the family, and only the male for the marketplace and the world of ideas. . . . Women's activities and responsibilities are increasing and expanding. Coeducation is a fact, not a rarity. The presence of women in business, in the professions, in government and, indeed, in all walks of life where education is a desirable, if not always a necessary, antecedent is apparent and a proper subject of judicial notice."[30]

In 1976 the Supreme Court made its more searching standard of review for gender-based classifications explicit, ruling that such laws would be upheld only if they served important governmental objectives and were substantially related to the achievement of those objectives.[31] For the next decade the Court invalidated a broad range of statutes that discriminated on the basis of gender—for example, a federal statutory provision allowing widows, but not widowers, to collect survivor's benefits;[32] a state law permitting the sale of beer to women at age eighteen but to men not until age twenty-one;[33] a state law requiring men but not women to pay alimony after divorce;[34] a federal provision allowing benefits for families with dependent children only when the father was unemployed, but not when the mother was unemployed;[35] and a state statute granting only husbands the right to manage and dispose of jointly owned property without spousal consent.[36]

It is impossible to exaggerate the extent to which these cases changed the landscape of gender law. Until 1970 the Court generally assumed that state legislatures and Congress *did* have good reasons for writing sex-based distinctions into the law. After 1971 the Court refused altogether to entertain that presumption.

The volume of cases in the Supreme Court dealing with gender discrimination has declined somewhat since my appointment in 1981. In *United States v. Virginia*,[37] we struck down the Virginia Military Institute's male-only admission policy on equal protection grounds. But several of the cases brought before the Court have involved not constitutional challenges under the Fourteenth Amendment but rather interpretations of statutes such as the Civil Rights Act. In one case[38] we held that, under the Civil Rights Act, once a law firm makes partnership consideration a privilege of employment, the firm may not discriminate on the basis of sex in its selection of partners. We also have made strides in dealing with sexual harassment at the workplace. In 1986 the Court first held that sexual harassment is a form of sex discrimination that is actionable under the Civil Rights Act.[39] In 1993 we reaffirmed that standard and made clear that plaintiffs need not demonstrate psychological or physical injury in order to establish a hostile working-environment claim.

In all of its recent cases, the Court has looked askance at the loose-fitting generalizations, myths, and stereotypes that previously kept women at home. The Court has preferred a person-by-person assessment of job qualifications, rather than the overinclusive generalizations of the past.

The women's rights movement in America today is by no means a coherent or uniform endeavor. Perhaps because women have advanced so dramatically in the working world in recent decades, the sense of urgency that prevailed in the 1960s and 1970s has given way to fragmentation along traditional lines.

One area of disagreement focuses on women's roles as parents and professionals. As an empirical matter, women professionals still bear primary responsibility for children and housekeeping, spending roughly twice as much time on these cares as do their professional husbands. As a result, women encounter special difficulties managing both a household and a career.

Today American women are confronted by "the juggle." While many women are able to balance a profession and home admirably, it is nonetheless true that time spent at home is time that cannot be billed to clients or spent making contacts at social or professional organizations. Women still may come up against what has been called a "mommy track" or a "glass ceiling" in their chosen professions—a delayed or blocked ascent to partnership or management status due to family responsibilities. Women who do not wish to be left behind often face a difficult choice. Some forgo family life altogether in order to attain their career aspirations. Others decide that the demands of a career require delaying family responsibilities at the very time in their lives when bearing children is physically easiest. Personally, I chose to have and enjoy my family early on and to resume my career path somewhat later. But the ideal choice, to the extent that it exists, is certainly not self-evident, and American women are forced to make substantial trade-offs that American men largely bypass.

In recognizing and responding to this fundamental difference in the experiences of genders, modern courts and legislatures face some of their most difficult challenges. There is a fine, often perilous line between crafting responses to genuine differences and coddling and sustaining pernicious stereotypes. If society does not recognize the fact that only women can bear children, then "equal treatment" ends up being unequal. On the other hand, if society recognizes pregnancy as requiring special solicitude, or if society inevitably links the biological ability to bear children with the assumption of full child-rearing responsibilities, it is a slippery slope back to "protectionist" legislation and the predominant nineteenth-century worldview that barred women from the workplace altogether. At this, the beginning of the twenty-first century, these are the problems for U.S. women that loom largest.

Several insights can be drawn from our history. First and foremost, the experience of women in the United States demonstrates that dramatic change can occur only when members of a large group surmount their individual differences and unite in pursuit of a concrete goal. The two most significant accomplishments of the American women's movement—winning the vote and gaining mass entry to the working world—were the products of a rare consensus among adherents of widely divergent philosophies. In both cases, unity was born of tremendous adversity. In both cases, however, the period following the ultimate achievement of these goals was one of great fragmentation and disarray. Generally speaking, there is tremendous tension between valid recognition of differences between genders—as, for example, in the pregnancy context—and the harmful stereotyping to which women were subjected through much of our history. Women in the United States have long had various and sometimes conflicting approaches to reconciling this tension, and it has only been when they have cast such fundamental differences aside and forged common ground that they have achieved meaningful change.

Second, real change, when it comes, stems principally from attitudinal shifts in the population at large. Rare indeed is the legal victory—in court or legislature—that is not a careful by-product of an emerging social consensus. Courts, in particular, are mainly reactive institutions. Although the power of judicial review is said by some to be the "cornerstone" of our constitutional law, courts are rarely the first to ponder the constitutional questions that come before them. State and federal legislators and executives typically must decide, as a preliminary mat-ter, whether the laws they enact or the actions they undertake are con-stitutional. The judiciary has no role to play until someone with a personal stake in the matter challenges the government action or prac-tice in court. Thus, a court's agenda is critically shaped by the issues and concerns of individual litigants. To be sure, almost every political, economic, or social problem of great import ultimately wends its way into the Supreme Court's halls. However, it is important to realize that we almost never work on a blank slate; legal change is most frequently a delayed response to changes in the agenda of the people.

The third point is really another way of stating the second. It is un-settling, at times, to hear some modern feminists couch their reform agenda in terms of protection and recognition of their uniquely female perspectives. When gender distinctiveness becomes a mantra, I worry that, in our voyage from the eighteenth century to the present, we have not really traveled very far at all.

There still *are*, however, limited situations in which treating women and men identically may result in unequal treatment for women, and these situations require unremitting attention. Despite myriad ad-vances in modern reproductive technology, it remains the case that only women are biologically capable of bearing children. If pregnancy were a speedy, painless endeavor, this distinction might lack legal relevance. Because it is not, however, some accommodation on the part of the working world is necessary. Statutes that take this particular distinction into account, unlike statutes harping on women's frail dispositions, do not, in my view, perpetuate discrimination. Rather, they help to elimi-nate it. In recent years the Supreme Court has confirmed this intuition, upholding a California pregnancy disability-leave statute that effectively allowed women, as well as men, to have families without losing their jobs.[40] Unfortunately, there is still work to be done to level the playing field with respect to child care responsibilities and to ensure that men *and* women are able to avoid the cruel dilemma of choosing between home and the working world.

Society as a whole can benefit immeasurably from a climate in which all persons, regardless of gender, have the opportunity to earn respect, responsibility, advancement, and remuneration based on ability. Women are still engaged in a struggle against social attitudes that impose barriers to the achievement of this goal. In large part, success depends on changing minds at home, in the streets, and at the workplace, not just in legislatures and courts. Each and every one of us has a role to play in completing that task.

CHAPTER NINETEEN

The Women's Suffrage Movement
and Its Aftermath

*I*T IS DIFFICULT TO IMAGINE THAT NOT SO MANY YEARS AGO, and well within living memory a woman's right to vote was not protected by our Constitution. It is hard to remember that a right that women today have taken for granted all our lives is one that some of our grandmothers never enjoyed. The history of the suffrage movement is a colorful and entertaining one, and a tale from which we can draw many lessons.[1]

The impetus for much-needed organization in the women's movement came in the summer of 1840. At the World Anti-Slavery Convention in London, the United States was represented by a delegation that included a number of women. Trouble began even before the convention opened. Despite strong objection by some of the American leaders, and following a heated debate on the floor, it was ruled that only the male delegates should be seated. Among the women forced to sit passively in the galleries were Lucretia Mott, an ardent abolitionist and a founder of the first Female Anti-Slavery Society, and Elizabeth Cady Stanton, the young wife of an abolitionist leader. After the sessions, the two women talked of the irony of workers devoted to the antislavery cause being denied a voice in the convention simply because they were women. They recognized the need for concerted action.

Elizabeth Cady was the privileged daughter of a New York judge. She spent many hours as a small child crouched in the corner of her father's office listening to people plead for help with legal problems.

Cover of *Official Program: Woman Suffrage Procession*,
Washington, D.C., March 3, 1913.

And thereupon _Richard Crowley_ Esq., the Attorney of the United States for the said District, prayed the process of the said _District_ Court for the arrest of the said _Susan B. Anthony_ and it was granted ; and on the _27th_ day of _January_ in the year of our Lord one thousand eight hundred and seventy-_three_ of the _January_ term of _said Court_ at the _City_ of _Albany_ came the Marshal of the United States for the Northern District of New York, and brought into the said _District_ Court the body of the said _Susan B. Anthony_ upon the said process : and the said

Susan B. Anthony

being duly arraigned upon the said I-_dictment_ called upon to plead thereto, pleaded that she was _not_ guilty of the offenses charged therein, in manner and form as the same are therein set forth, and of this she put _herself_ upon the country, and said United States of America did the like. _at the May term of said District Court held at the City of Rochester on the 22nd day of May,_ And _thereupon_ the said _Richard Crowley_ the Attorney of the United States, for the Northern District of New York, moved that the said Indictment and the issue joined thereon be transmitted to the _Circuit_ Court of the United States for the said Northern District of New York for disposal therein, and the said motion was granted.

Wherefore let a jury be summoned, empanelled and sworn to try the said issue at the _June_ term of said Court in the year of our Lord one thousand eight hundred and seventy-_three_ at the _Village_ of _Canandaigua_ in the said District.

And now on the _17th & 18th_ days of _June_ of the term of _June_ one thousand eight hundred and seventy-_three_ aforesaid come as well the Attorney of the United States for the said District as the said _Susan B. Anthony_ and come also the jurors aforesaid ;

and the said jurors to speak the truth of the matters within contained being chosen, tried and sworn upon their oaths say, that the said _Susan B. Anthony_ is guilty of the offenses charged in the said Indictment in manner and form as the same are therein set forth. And _thereupon the 19th_ _day of June of said term_ the said _Susan B. Anthony_ being present in open Court, and having heard the said verdict is inquired of by the Court if she has anything to say why the judgment of the law should not be pronounced upon _her_ according to the said verdict : and no sufficient answer being given, His Honor the Judge of the said Court, in the presence of the said _Susan B. Anthony_ does here adjudge and sentence that the said _Susan B. Anthony_ for the said offenses of which she stands convicted as aforesaid _be imprisoned in the_ _and pay a fine of_ _one hundred dollars and the costs of_ _this prosecution_

Charles Mason
Clerk.

Transcript of the sentencing of Susan B. Anthony, 1873.

Some of those people were women who complained that their husbands and fathers had disposed of their property or spent their earnings on liquor or had the sole right to guardianship of their children in the event of a separation. Judge Cady was forced to explain, time and again, that they had no legal redress.

Young Elizabeth was forever marked by that lesson. Years later, she married Henry Stanton, an abolitionist leader, and moved to Seneca Falls, New York. Looking back in 1898, she wrote: "My experiences at the World Anti-Slavery Convention, all I had read of the legal status of women, and the oppression I saw everywhere, together swept across my soul, intensified now by many personal experiences. It seemed as if all the elements had conspired to impel me to some onward step. I could not see what to do or where to begin—my only thought was a public meeting for protest and discussion."[2] Within a few years after the London convention, however, during Lucretia Mott's visit to Seneca Falls, Stanton, Mott, and several other women gathered and decided to call their own convention. The following day an announcement appeared in the *Seneca County Courier* of a "woman's rights convention" to be held in July 1848.

Elizabeth Cady Stanton shouldered much of the responsibility for organizing and animating the convention. As she prepared for the upcoming meeting, she read to her husband the draft of a proposed resolution demanding that women be given the right to vote. Henry, the passionate abolitionist, warned her that, if she presented it to the convention, he would have nothing to do with it and would go so far as to leave town to avoid embarrassment. Suffice it to say that Henry left town. In fact, only Frederick Douglass, the black abolitionist leader, approved of Elizabeth's daring resolution and promised to support its introduction at the convention.

Despite the fact that only one issue of the Seneca Falls newspaper had carried the brief notice, some three hundred people journeyed to the convention from within a fifty-mile radius. But when the conventiongoers arrived at the little Wesleyan chapel where the meeting was to be held, they found the door locked. Not to be discouraged, the

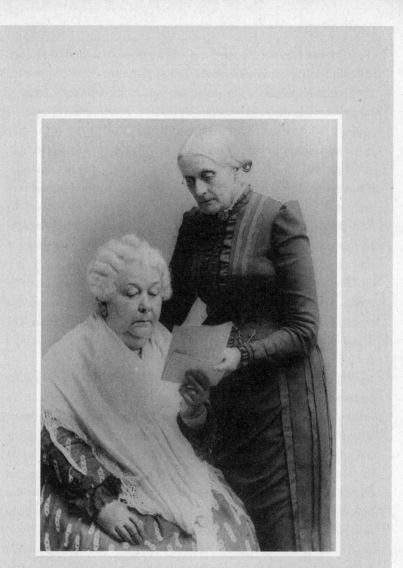

Elizabeth Cady Stanton (seated) and Susan B. Anthony (standing).

crowd boosted one of Elizabeth's nephews through a window to open the hall, and the convention proceeded as planned.

Eloquent speeches and rousing discussion filled the days. Some of the liveliest was inspired by Stanton's reading of Resolution nine of the convention's Declaration of Sentiments: "Resolved, that it is the duty of the women of this country to secure to themselves their sacred right to the elective franchise."[3] Resolution nine carried by a small margin; it was the only resolution *not* to pass unanimously. One of the conventiongoers, young Charlotte Woodward, was the only woman at the Seneca Falls convention who lived to cast a vote in a national election. In 1920, at the age of ninety, she reportedly declared, "I am going to the polls if they have to carry me."

The birth of the women's movement in the United States is commonly dated from the Seneca Falls convention. Additional women's rights conventions followed, and the movement picked up steam. The first National Women's Rights Convention was held in 1850, and a similar convention followed every year for ten years.

It gradually became clear, however, that women agreed on their dissatisfaction with the current state of affairs but had yet to develop an ideology or a set of goals to guide their cries for change. Few felt as strongly as Elizabeth Cady Stanton about the importance of securing the vote. For many, more pressing concerns included women's inability to control property and earnings, their limited opportunities for higher education and employment, and their lack of legal status. But how could women bring about a change in the laws without the right to vote?

The Civil War and the emancipation of former slaves brought the question of suffrage to the forefront. If newly freed blacks were to be guaranteed the same civil rights, including suffrage, as all other citizens, there was no reason that women, too, should not be swept up by the momentum and included in the resulting expansion of the right to vote.

The reformers were in for quite a shock, however. A draft of the Fourteenth Amendment introduced in Congress in 1866 would have incorporated *into* the Constitution, for the first time, a restriction explicitly based on gender. Although the first section of the amendment held out initial promise—in broad language, it appeared to endorse the notion of constitutional equality and full rights of citizenship—the second section dashed any hopes that the amendment would ensure gender equality. The draft declared that the right to vote should not be "denied to any portion of [a state's] *male* inhabitants."[4]

The reformers realized that if this proposal were adopted, yet another constitutional amendment would be required to give women the right to vote in federal elections. Elizabeth Cady Stanton recognized what a monumental task this would be; she believed that the women's suffrage movement would be set back a full century if the proposal were adopted. Even though it was not, she wasn't far wrong. Women did not get the vote for another sixty years.

Angered by the lack of progress, Stanton decided to take matters into her own hands. In 1866 she declared herself the first female candidate for Congress. No one challenged her right to run, but she received only 24 of the 22,026 votes cast.[5] Following in Stanton's footsteps, a young woman named Victoria Woodhull obtained permission in 1871 to present a petition to the U.S. House of Representatives' Judiciary Committee, arguing that the recent amendments had secured the vote for women as well as blacks. Under Section 1 of the Fourteenth Amendment, she claimed, women are "citizens" of the United States just as men, and thus are guaranteed the same rights and privileges of citizenship—including the right to vote. The committee, of course, rejected the petition, and the Supreme Court in turn rejected the argument in 1875. Under the Constitution, the Court ruled, women had no right to vote.[6]

Despite these setbacks, many women embraced Victoria Woodhull's claim that women were entitled immediately to exercise the right to vote. Susan B. Anthony resolved to dramatize the issue by voting in the presidential election of 1872. She did so and was joined by several other women, but their punishment was swift and sure. Within weeks, all were arrested. Anthony planned to rely on the Fourteenth Amendment for her defense, which she claimed had confirmed her right to cast a ballot. But at her trial the judge ruled that women were incompetent to testify in court, and Anthony was prohibited from speaking in her own defense. The judge concluded that her vote, cast by "a person of the female sex," was per se "against the peace of the United States of America and their dignity."[7] Because she had indeed voted, she was admittedly guilty and there remained no issue to be presented to the jury. The judge instructed the (male) jurors to enter a verdict of guilty.

In another respect, however, Susan Brownell Anthony was the clear victor; her treatment at the hands of the judicial system won for her the sympathy even of those who had been opposed to her original act. Letters of support and funds for her defense poured in. The following year one newspaper even called her "America's best-known woman."[8] As with many of contemporary society's widely recognized figures, one had only to speak or print the name Susan and it was evident to whom one referred.

At the same time, change was taking place on another front: in the states. The first major victory for women's suffrage occurred in the territory of Wyoming, where a bill to enfranchise women was signed into law in 1869. Contrary to predictions, the state elections that followed did not result in disaster and dissolution of the existing order. And an interesting development occurred: once women enrolled as voters, their names began to appear on the list of prospective jurors. Women's presence on Wyoming juries actually stirred up more excitement than their presence at the voting booths!

When Wyoming sought statehood in 1890, pressure was applied in Washington to repeal women's suffrage. And indeed, the bill to admit Wyoming to the Union met tremendous resistance in both houses of Congress. One senator from Texas even predicted that allowing women to vote would result in a disastrous reversal of traditional gender roles: women would "do military duty" and "work the roads," while men would be forced to "nurse the children" and "stay at home while the ladies go out and make stump speeches in canvasses."[9] Wyoming leaders replied that they would rather remain outside the Union than join without the women. The bill to admit

Wyoming passed by a vote of 29 to 18, and women enjoyed the right to vote in one state of the Union.

Following Wyoming's example, Utah in 1870 enacted a law granting women the right to vote. It was revoked in 1887, but women in Utah regained the right to vote when Utah was admitted to statehood in 1896 under a constitution that provided for women's suffrage. By that time, both Colorado and Idaho had joined the states that granted women the right to vote, and other Western states had granted limited suffrage rights on specific issues.

The suffragists then turned their attentions to the remaining territories—including Arizona and Oklahoma—but were not so successful. In Arizona, for example, as the territory prepared itself for statehood, the suffragists campaigned vigorously for a women's suffrage provision in the new state constitution. But once again, they met defeat; the fifty-two male delegates to the state constitutional convention rejected their pleas, at least in part for fear that President Taft would veto a statehood bill that provided for universal suffrage. Not to be discouraged, the Arizona suffragists turned to a newly established weapon of democracy: the voter initiative, by which voters themselves could place measures on the statewide ballot. One newspaper, the *Arizona Gazette*, had predicted that the effort to include universal suffrage in the proposed constitution would fail but that male voters would grant women the right to vote in a poststatehood election.

That is precisely how events unfolded. Arizona was admitted to the Union on February 14, 1912. In July 1912 petitions to place the women's suffrage issue on the ballot were filed.[10] In the November election Arizona voters approved the initiative granting universal suffrage by a margin of greater than 2 to 1. Just two years later, in 1914, Frances Willard Munds, who had been a vigorous lobbyist for a universal-suffrage bill before the Arizona territorial legislature, became the second woman in America to be elected to a state senate. And just six short years later, Arizona would be one of the thirty-six states to ratify the Nineteenth Amendment.

But the relatively enlightened views that permitted and even encouraged the enfranchisement of women in the Western states in the late 1800s were not universally shared. By 1900, concrete progress, measured by increases in the number of states granting women the right to vote, had slowed almost to a halt.

The necessary jolt came from England, where the women's suffrage movement was marked by militancy, sensationalism, and calls for direct action. One English suffragette went so far as to throw herself in front of the king's horse as it was winning the Derby, sacrificing her own life to garner attention for the suffrage movement.[11]

The American suffragists were quick to learn their lessons from the English. Under the leadership of Elizabeth Cady Stanton's daughter, Harriot Stanton Blatch, the movement resolved to draw in working women, who most stood to benefit from enfranchisement. From these alliances, the Women's Political Union was born. The union conducted open-air meetings, covered polls with propaganda, and held elaborate parades. On another front, the Woman Suffrage party, led by Carrie Chapman Catt, held suffrage bazaars and balls, sold suffrage calendars and buttons, and hung suffrage posters on every available surface. The pressure on nonsuffrage states quickly heated up. But opposition to suffrage heated up in tandem, and well-funded groups were dismayingly successful at killing suffrage motions or, if necessary, bribing or threatening state legislators to ensure defeat of the proposals. The time was coming once again to return the focus of the movement to a national pitch for a constitutional amendment.

Former President Grover Cleveland was eager to place (and keep) women on a pedestal. In his 1905 contribution to the *Ladies' Home Journal* opposing women's suffrage, he explained the truth as he saw it:

> Thoughtful and right-minded men base their homage and consideration for woman upon an instinctive consciousness that her unmasculine qualities, whether called weaknesses, frailties, or what we will, are the sources of her characteristic and especial strength within the area of her *legitimate* endeavor. They know that if she is not gifted with the power of clear and logical reasoning she has a faculty of intuition which

by a shorter route leads her to abstract moral truth; that if she deals mistakenly with practical problems it is because sympathy or sentiment clouds her perception of the relative value of the factors involved.[12]

By 1912, it had been sixteen years since either house of Congress had issued a report on the suffrage amendment. A small band of young, well-educated women descended on the capital city, determined to be heard. Eight states had granted full suffrage to women, and these voters became a formidable force, pressuring their delegates to support a national amendment. What followed in Washington were six years of lobbying, visits to President Wilson, picketing, parades, pilgrimages, and petitions.

When the suffragists discovered that President Wilson's 1916 address to Congress made no reference to suffrage, they decided to bring the issue to the forefront on their own. Five women procured seats in the front of the gallery. One of the women concealed a large yellow banner under her skirt, which she unrolled and dropped over the balcony at a predetermined moment. The banner demanded, MR. PRESIDENT, WHAT WILL YOU DO FOR WOMAN'S SUFFRAGE? President Wilson's speech faltered for only a moment, but the damage was done. By the time a page on the floor was able to jump up, catch one corner of the banner, and tear it down, the women were already busy handing out mimeographed reports on the episode to the press.

In the ensuing months suffragists were jailed repeatedly for picketing the White House. When the new Russian Republic extended the vote to women following the Bolshevik Revolution, suffragists taunted President Wilson with the lack of similar progress in the United States. Tensions mounted. To the surprise of the suffragists, some of the opposition they had once faced was absent. Liquor interests, long hostile to the suffragists, were busy fending off the likelihood of a national prohibition amendment and couldn't be bothered with the women's suffrage movement.

Progress, long overdue, came quickly. At its 1916 convention, the Republican party recommended the extension of suffrage to women but decided that this ought to be accomplished by the states. The Democratic party followed suit. In 1917 the House set a vote on the suffrage amendment. Meanwhile, the suffragists were busily lobbying behind the scenes in a well-organized effort to bring pressure to bear on the congressmen who would be participating in the decisive vote. By the end of 1917, six state legislatures had granted women the right to vote in presidential elections. States began sending resolutions to Congress calling for a federal amendment. Even New York, the most populous state in the Union, yielded to the demand for women's suffrage.

The vote on the amendment was set for January 10, 1918. As the day drew near, however, suffragists believed they were forty-five votes short of the two-thirds majority they needed. Their nerves were not eased by the fact that, on the day of the vote, several representatives who were believed to favor the federal amendment encountered a whole array of misfortunes, ranging from a train wreck to physical illnesses and injuries to the death of one representative's wife. On at least one occasion during the roll call, the opposition appeared to believe it had carried the day.

But when the dust settled, the suffragists at long last had cause to celebrate. The proposed amendment passed the House by the necessary two thirds, with just two votes to spare. That the vote was too close for comfort is highlighted by one hopelessly undecided representative's story. The representative told his brother that, if the child his wife was expecting turned out to be a girl, he would vote in favor of women's suffrage. Sure enough, his wife gave birth to a beautiful daughter—and the representative was recorded in favor of the amendment.

The suffragists faced their next hurdle with equal enthusiasm. Again, it appeared that they lacked ten votes to reach the necessary two thirds in the Senate. Many and various supporters of the amendment urged its passage: the Democratic and Republican National Committees, former President Theodore Roosevelt, members of the cabinet, and a number of states that had granted suffrage all pleaded for a vote in favor. Even President Wilson made a personal appeal to the Senate; this did not in the end tip the scales in favor of passage, however. The amendment fell one vote short in the Senate. The suffragists geared up for a renewed battle in the Sixty-ninth Congress.

In May 1919 the suffrage amendment once again passed in the House, this time by a vote of 304 to 90. A similar victory in the Senate was almost a foregone conclusion. Indeed, this time the amendment passed with two votes more than necessary. Seventy-one years after the Seneca Falls convention, the extension of the vote to women seemed, if not certain, at least probable. Only one hurdle remained: ratification in three fourths of the states.

By June 1920, thirty-five states had ratified the proposed amendment, and suffragists began to hunt about for a final state. Connecticut and Vermont seemed likely prospects, but the governors in both states were opposed to women's suffrage.

Thus it was that the suffragists turned to an unlikely setting for the last great battle of the suffrage movement: Tennessee. The governor of Tennessee, eager to be credited with passing the amendment, called an emergency session of the state legislature. Despite bribes, threats, and other machinations by opponents of suffrage, the measure passed the state senate.

Antisuffragists then turned their attention to the upcoming vote in the House. Once again they engaged in a great deal of maneuvering in hopes of ensuring a defeat. When the measure was brought to a vote in mid-August, however, they expected to prevail by only two votes. When one of their anticipated allies voted in favor, all attention turned to Harry Burn, a twenty-four-year-old representative of a rural district opposed to suffrage. Although his electors opposed the measure, Burn had only recently received a letter from his mother urging him in strong language to vote in favor of suffrage. Burn resolved that, if the measure required a single vote for passage, he would supply it. He did so, and the count in favor of suffrage stood at 49 to 47. The speaker of the House quickly changed his vote to yes, hoping to take advantage of a parliamentary maneuver allowing reconsideration of the issue. When opponents failed to muster enough votes to defeat ratification on reconsideration in the days that followed, the suffragists attempted to request reconsideration themselves, planning to vote it down immediately. When the House members assembled, however, they almost lacked a quorum: the antisuffragists had fled en masse across the Alabama border, hoping to prevent reconsideration. The suffragists pressed ahead without them, and the governor notified Washington of the vote.[13]

On August 26, 1920, Secretary of State Bainbridge Colby signed the Nineteenth Amendment into law.

That is the flavor, at least, of the seventy-year struggle for women's right to vote. But what was it all for? Suffragists were jailed, attacked, harassed, and divorced in their quest for their American dream of full citizenship and civil rights. So it behooves us to consider for a moment what we, in the ensuing years, have made of their ideals. Are we making good use of the vote? Have we reached full and equal citizenship in other respects? And in what ways are the suffragists' concerns still pertinent to our world today?

Like most revolutionary changes, suffrage took a while to sink into the popular consciousness. Women got the vote too late to have a significant impact on the 1920 elections. Indeed, several states refused to reopen their voter rolls to allow women to register in time. And in 1924 barely a third of eligible women voters turned out to vote in the national elections, leaving Calvin Coolidge the least supported President-elect of the twentieth century, with the votes of only 23.7 percent of the eligible population.[14]

Gradually, however, the women of America discovered their long-suppressed will to vote. By the time of the 1952 elections, my own generation of young women, who had had better access to higher education and work outside the home than our predecessors, and who had grown up with the vote, were at the polling booths. And in the presidential election that year the female majority showed itself as an independent and decisive electoral force. Not only did the female vote finally catch up with the male vote—at thirty million each, a 50 percent national turnout—but it also diverged from the male vote, giving the lie, for at least a substantial number of women, to the miserable prewar stereotype of women following their husbands or fathers, sheeplike, into the polling booth.

The period from 1920 to 1932 saw sixteen women elected to the House of Representatives, one to the Senate—and one, Florence Allen, to the Ohio Supreme Court, the first female state supreme court justice in American history. Judge Allen, who had been active in the suffrage movement twenty years earlier, also was the subject of a campaign led by Molly Dewson to have her nominated to the U.S. Supreme Court[15]—but that idea was apparently forty-odd years before its time.

There was still a long way to go when the United States entered World War II. A 1936 Gallup Poll found 80 percent of Americans— men *and* women—in agreement with the proposition that a wife should stay at home if her husband had a job.[16] Transforming voting rights into a broader equality was proving to be a slow, evolutionary process.

That process has continued, in fits and starts, to the present. According to a recent United Nations study, women remain 1.3 times as likely as men to be living in poverty in the United States—the worst ratio of eight developed countries studied.[17] It may take yet a few more generations before there is full gender equality in this country.

The distance we have yet to go should not, however, be allowed to overshadow the fact that we have come astoundingly far down the road since 1920. Let me give just a few examples of that progress, beginning with specific instances drawn from the states. In my home state of Arizona, Lorna Lockwood blazed the trail, first as legislator, then as our first female trial judge, and eventually as the first woman in the country to serve as Chief Justice of a state supreme court. Minnesota, in 1991, became the first state to have a majority of women on its supreme court.[18] And over the past few decades, the states have gradually consigned to the annals of history many of the old doctrines relating to marital property and family relations that kept women in positions of economic dependency and inferiority. At the same time, the states also have created a few new rights, such as pregnancy disability leave,[19] that have positively advanced the economic opportunities of women, and have taken a more active role in formerly neglected areas such as protecting victims of domestic violence.

Photograph of the Old Brick Capitol as the National Woman's Party,
c. 1921–1930, as viewed from its northwestern corner at First and A Streets, NE.
The name NATIONAL WOMAN'S PARTY can be seen on a plaque in the center.

But it is perhaps the overall statistics, federal and state, rather than individual cases and appointments here or there, that best reflect the extent of progress. Women today are not only well represented in law firms but are gradually attaining other positions of legal power, comprising 20 percent of judges, 25 percent of U.S. attorneys, 14 percent of state prosecutors, 23 percent of state legislators, 29 percent of state executives, 20 percent of mayors, 12 percent of U.S. congresspersons, and, of course, just over 22 percent of U.S. Supreme Court Justices.[20] Until the percentages come closer to 50 percent, we cannot say we have succeeded. Still, the progress has been astonishing.

Women on the international scene have shown spunk, wit, and determination as well. One of the last century's most inspiring books written about politics was Helen Suzman's *In No Uncertain Terms*. Suzman, for many years the lone voice against apartheid (and the lone woman) within the white South African parliament, offered the following quote from a fellow parliament member as an example of the prejudice she had to contend with: " 'The Hon. Member . . . must stop chattering. She is in the habit of chattering continually. If my wife chattered like that Hon. Member, I would know what to do with her. There is nothing that works on my nerves more than a woman who continually interrupts me. She is like water dripping on a tin roof.' "[21] That was in 1965, and the honorable member was "chattering" about the need to dismantle apartheid.

Sometimes the voices of democracy can do rather more than just grate on the nerves—as the maker of that statement, former South African President P. W. Botha, was later to learn. In due course, such voices prevail.

And that optimistic note is, perhaps, the key lesson of the suffrage movement, one that we must never forget.

CHAPTER TWENTY

Women in Judging

———

I AM OFTEN ASKED WHETHER IT MAKES A DIFFERENCE THAT WE have women judges, and whether the justice dispensed by women judges is somehow different from the justice we would expect from men. In answering such questions, I sometimes reflect on those early days in Phoenix, Arizona, when it mattered a great deal to me as a young woman lawyer that another Arizona woman was on my state's highest court, and that she showed an interest in the progress of other women in the legal profession.

Justice Lorna Lockwood was the daughter of a well-known Arizona lawyer. She ran for and was elected to the Arizona legislature. Later, she was elected as the first woman trial judge in the state. Like other women judges in the 1950s, she was assigned to juvenile court. Eventually, she ran for and was elected to the Arizona Supreme Court. She became the first woman in the United States to serve as chief justice of a state supreme court. She was always interested in the women lawyers in the state and would encourage them. She also visited the women prisoners at the Arizona State Penitentiary and started a self-help program there. By her work and deeds, Justice Lockwood set many a young woman, myself included, on the path toward recognition in the legal profession.

The path for women judges began in Pennsylvania. In 1870 a young woman named Carrie Burnham applied to the law department of the University of Pennsylvania. She was rejected. When she asked to purchase tickets to his lectures and to study law, the dean of the law department replied: "I do not know what the Board of Trustees will do, but as for me, if they admit a woman I will resign for I will neither lecture to [Negroes] nor women."[1] For the next decade, she and her new husband, Damon Kilgore, fought a long, hard battle in the legislature and in the courts in order to win an opportunity for women to study and to practice law. In 1881 she was finally able to purchase a ticket to attend lectures at the University of Pennsylvania, and on June 17, 1883, Carrie Burnham Kilgore became its first woman graduate. The Philadelphia Court of Common Pleas was not impressed, however, with Mrs. Kilgore's law degree, because the next year it denied her motion to be admitted to its bar. Finally, in 1885, Carrie Kilgore convinced the state legislature to change the laws governing bar admission, and in 1886 she was admitted to practice before the Pennsylvania Supreme Court.

That same year, she became the first woman to serve in a state judiciary, when she was appointed to be a master in chancery. Two years later her husband passed away, leaving his fifty-year-old widow with two young daughters. Some urged her to put the children in a home so that she could further her career. She replied: "Yes, they shall be put in a home, and I shall continue my profession; but it shall be a home of my making. They have lost their father; they shall not lose their mother while I live."[2]

It was with this characteristic fortitude and courage that Carrie Kilgore charted the way for us women lawyers and judges. It has sometimes been a tough and lonely road. A friend wrote in 1890 that Mrs. Kilgore "regrets that no other women are practicing or studying law in Philadelphia, and says she would like to have a lady student in her office, and would give such a one a good chance with her after her admission to the bar."[3]

Even today, more than a century later, I can still say that it matters a great deal to me to have a second woman on the Supreme Court. And it is especially fitting that she should be Justice Ginsburg, a woman who has advanced directly in so many ways the progress of women. It was a happy day indeed when she was confirmed to join our Court.

Of course, our country arguably functioned perfectly well for almost two hundred years without a woman on the United States

Carrie Burnham Kilgore was the first woman to gain admission to law school and to receive the LL.B. (1883). After graduating, she was admitted to the Orphans' Court of Philadelphia and to the state Supreme Court and all the lower courts. She was admitted to practice before the United States Supreme Court in 1890.

Burnita Shelton Matthews, first woman to serve as a Federal District Court Judge, active status, 1949–1968.

Supreme Court. That all-male Court decided many seminal civil rights cases, among them *Brown v. Board of Education*, and a plethora of decisions striking down laws that discriminate against women. Even today, women represent only some 20 percent of judges in this country, but most observers nonetheless conclude that we have one of the most functional and fair judicial systems in the world.

My intuition and my experience persuade me that having women on the bench, and in other positions of prominence, is extremely important. The self-perception of women is informed by such examples, and by the belief of women that they, too, can achieve professional success at the highest levels.

Most of the early women legal pioneers faced a profession and a society that espoused the view that women were by nature different from men. Women were perceived, as Carrie Kilgore learned, to be best fitted for motherhood and home life—compassionate, selfless, gentle, moral, and pure. Their minds were attuned to art and religion, not logic. Men, on the other hand, were fitted by nature for competition and intellectual discovery in the world—battle-hardened, shrewd, authoritative, and tough-minded. Women were thought to be ill qualified for adversarial litigation, because it required sharp logic and shrewd negotiation, as well as exposure to the unjust and the immoral.

Even Clarence Darrow, one of the most famous champions of unpopular causes, had this to say to a group of women lawyers: "You can't be shining lights at the bar because you are too kind. You can never be corporation lawyers because you are not cold-blooded. You have not a high grade of intellect. I doubt you can ever make a living."[4] Another male attorney of the period commented: "A woman can't keep a secret, and for that reason if no other, I doubt if anybody will ever consult a woman lawyer."[5]

Breaking free of these stereotypes required some good examples. Recent sociological literature strongly suggests that positive role models play a significant role in professional and other achievements. One study, which focused on the role models of women attorneys, shows that women lawyers whose mothers were themselves professionals use their mothers as role models with much greater frequency than is the case with mothers who did not work.[6]

The earliest women judges were forced by necessity to learn their craft by simple trial and error. In 1925 Texas had an all-woman supreme court, although only for a brief moment. What happened was that the male members of the court disqualified themselves from a case involving the Woodmen of the World because they all were members of the fraternal order. So the governor appointed three women to a special supreme court to hear the case. This contemporary news account of the event illustrates the problems that pioneers sometimes face in the wild: "The courtroom was filled with lawyers and women when the special judges took their seat upon the bench. . . . Chief Justice Cureton of the Supreme Court administered the oath to the women. . . . None of the women raised her right hand, as is customary among men taking an oath of office. They did not seem to be flurried by the experience."[7]

The experience of these early judges is truly remarkable in light of the tasks that they faced, often without much help. For example, when Judge Burnita Matthews was appointed to the District Court for the District of Columbia, becoming the first woman federal district-court judge, she faced a docket that combined the work of a federal court with all the local matters currently handled by the D.C. Superior Court. Despite this heavy workload and difficult docket, she earned a reputation for having fewer of her rulings reversed on appeal than any of her colleagues.[8] We women lawyers and judges alike have good cause to be thankful that these early judges learned and practiced their craft so well, because we are the direct beneficiaries of their experience and example.

I am often asked whether women judges speak with a different voice. This is a question that generates widely differing responses. Undaunted by the troubling history of their view, many writers have suggested that women practice law differently than men.

As judges, we all strive to be dispassionate and objective in analyzing issues, to be impartial and analytical, to be courageous and independent when we resolve a case in a manner sure to be unpopular generally. Women, like men, can and do have all these attributes. We can agree with Judge Learned Hand that "it is as craftsmen that we get our satisfaction and our pay. In the universe of truth, we live by the sword, we ask no quarter of absolutes, and we give none."[9] Likewise, Judge Hand was indisputably right when he said, "Somewhere there lurks a craving to impress some form upon the stuff about us . . . this formless thing, wayward, unaccountable, inconsequent, wanton. . . . [and] the itch to leave upon an indifferent universe . . . the print of [our] hands upon the clay."[10]

As we judges put our hands upon the clay, some say that differences emerge in the ways in which women and men resolve some issues. Scholars have undertaken studies of the methods and decision making of women judges in comparison with their male counterparts. To my surprise, one author has surmised that my opinions differ in a peculiarly feminine way from those of my colleagues.[11] She concluded that my opinions reveal that I have been less willing to permit violations of the right to full membership in the community, that I view the shaping of the values of the community through governmental processes as an important function of the community, and that I employ a contextual approach and tend to reject so-called bright-line rules. I would guess that my colleagues on the Court would be as surprised as I am by these conclusions.

More generally, women attorneys have been characterized as more likely to seek to mediate disputes than litigate them, more likely to focus on resolving a client's problem than on vindicating a position, and more likely to sacrifice career advancement for family obligations. It is said: "Women tend to strive to preserve relationships, to empathize with a potential adversary, to have an ethic of caring that influences decisions about justice of an outcome."[12] I would say that such traits are found not only in women judges. Rather, as Judge Gertrude Mainzer put it: "I'm happy that there are differences between men and women, but I think it is the kind of person you [are], [your] intellect, where you come from . . . that applies just as much to men as to women." There is simply no empirical evidence that gender differences lead to discernible differences in rendering judgments.

The so-called new feminism is interesting but troubling, precisely because it so nearly echoes the old Victorian myth of the "true woman"—the myth that worked so well to keep women out of the professions for so long. It is a little chilling to compare these suggestions with Clarence Darrow's assertion that women are too kind and warmhearted to be shining lights at the bar. Indeed, such rhetoric threatens to establish new categories of women's work, to which women are confined and from which men are excluded. It's worthwhile to recall that, when the Philadelphia Court of Common Pleas resisted the "unfeminine importunity" of Carrie Kilgore's desire to practice law, it stated: "While a woman may doubtless perform [the law's] duties, . . . we think she can only do so by a sacrifice of those qualities which it especially behooves us all to cherish and protect."[13] Do we want to return to the days when women judges were routinely placed on family or juvenile courts because they were more caring?

My colleague Justice Ginsburg had this to say on the subject while speaking to a group of California women lawyers:

> Theoretical discussions are ongoing today—particularly in academic circles—about differences in the voices women and men hear, or in their moral perceptions. When asked about such things I usually abstain. Generalizations about the way women or men are—my life's experience bears out—cannot guide me reliably in making decisions about particular individuals. At least in the law, I have found no natural superiority or deficiency in either sex. I was a law teacher until I became a judge. In class or in grading papers over seventeen years, and now in reading briefs and listening to arguments in court for fourteen years, I have detected no reliable indicator of distinctly male or surely female thinking—or even penmanship.[14]

Another remarkable woman, Judge Pat Wald of the Court of Appeals for the District of Columbia, said recently: "We may be almost at the gates of real equality—when we can judge and be judged by the same standards of skill, craft, humanity and compassion that should exemplify all judges."[15]

So the question remains: *Do* women judges decide cases differently by virtue of being women? I would echo the answer of another woman judge, Justice Jeanne Coyne, formerly of the Minnesota Supreme Court, who says that "a wise old man and a wise old woman reach the same conclusion."[16] Are women from Venus and men from Mars? Or, as Ellen Goodman says, aren't we all living here together on earth?[17]

This should be our aspiration: that, whatever our gender or background, we all may become wise—wise through our different struggles and different victories, wise through work and play, wise through profession and family.

CHAPTER TWENTY-ONE

Women in Power

———

IT IS SAID THAT ONLY ABOUT 5 PERCENT OF THE POPULATION has real leadership qualities, and that women have these qualities to the same degree that men do. That statistic is misleading. In fact, each one of us will be a leader at some time in our lives. Whether we lead a family, a group of friends, a larger group, or a major segment of society, each of us will act in ways to influence others.

It is the individual who can and does make a difference even in this increasingly populous, complex world of ours. The individual *can* make things happen. It is the individual who can bring a tear to my eye and then cause me to take pen in hand. It is the individual who has acted or tried to act who will not only force a decision but also have a hand in shaping it. Whether acting in the legal, governmental, or private realm, one concerned and dedicated person can meaningfully affect what some consider an uncaring world. So give freely of yourself always to your family, your friends, your community, and your country. The world will pay you back many times over.

What, then, are the attributes of leadership? How do we exercise it? How do we develop it?

Leadership is synonymous with power. By power, I mean the ability to bring things about or to prevent them from occurring—the possession of control, authority, or influence over others. Power is the ability to do. It is clear that women today are becoming increasingly powerful in this country. In Arizona, for example, the top four elected officers as of the year 2000 were all women. This is a stunning and dramatic example of women in leadership, women with power.

I have been called the most powerful woman in the United States. If that's true, then I am perhaps the person most qualified to talk about how women exercise power. Yet I often feel that I'm the person least qualified to talk about the subject. Because I am the one exercising the power, I cannot assess objectively whether I exercise power differently than do men, or if my being a woman has had a special impact on the Supreme Court or on the law.

Subjectively, I can tell you that I do not believe either is so. In the exercise of my power as a Justice of the Supreme Court, there are institutional constraints that strictly limit what I can do. Concerns for the integrity of the Court, the operation of the collective decision-making process, and, most important, the law itself—as embodied in the Constitution, congressional statutes, and the Court's prior case law—exert an influence on my actions far greater than any uniquely feminine perspective I might bring.

I might also add that I work with eight very strong-willed colleagues. I don't think any of us exerts much power over the others. I certainly haven't found any Justice more or less willing to be persuaded by me because I am a woman. My power on the Court depends on the strength of my arguments, not on my gender.

Now, it might be that the law is unusual in this respect. The law is, after all, a system of rules that, by their very nature, constrain action. It may be that women in other spheres of influence have far more opportunity to express gender differences. Even if this is true, I believe that, in any position of real power, there always will be institutional constraints that have an enormous influence on the decision maker's behavior. That is the nature of power, and of its accompanying responsibility. It would be hard to say, for example, that the politics of Indira Gandhi, Golda Meir, or Margaret Thatcher differed, because of their gender, from the politics of male political leaders in their respective countries.

None of this is to say that women do *not* differ from men in the way they exercise power, only that the differences are subtle. We all bring to the seats of power our individual experiences and values, and part of these depend on our gender. I can give you a few examples of how, at least in a small way, my being a *female* Supreme Court Justice has made a difference.

The federal courts largely have control over their own rules of procedure, that is, the rules that prescribe how lawsuits in the federal courts are to be brought and how they proceed. Before my appointment to the Supreme Court, these rules used the male pronoun when referring to the various actors in our judicial system. That is no longer true. As a result of my request and suggestions, the Federal Rules of Civil and Criminal Procedure are now phrased in gender-neutral terms. Similarly, the Supreme Court publishes summaries of cases to be argued in front of the Court, along with the names of the attorneys making the arguments. Until I requested a change, these lists showed the names of male attorneys without any preceding title or designation, but female lawyers were listed as "Miss" or "Mrs." Now the men are listed as "Mr." and the women as "Ms." And my arrival at the Court triggered a change in the bronze doorplates on each Justice's chambers. Gone is the MR. JUSTICE. Now we are all known as "Justice" So-and-So. None of these changes has affected the way in which any lawsuits have proceeded, yet I believe they send a small but important signal.

There is indeed evidence that the election or appointment of women to public office may produce certain policy changes. For example, there is some indication that women are more likely than men to be interested in crime, health, and welfare issues, as well as issues related to abortion, child care, and education. Men in public office appear to be more interested in issues of war, defense, and taxation. There is also some indication that women as a group tend to be somewhat more "liberal" than men on issues of capital punishment, gun control, school busing, abortion, and amnesty.[1]

On the other hand, at least one study found almost no difference in the *voting* behavior of male and female members of Congress.[2] My own experience in the Arizona legislature was somewhat different. When I first entered the legislature, Arizona had some laws on the books that were truly gender-biased. Arizona is a community-property state: all assets of the partners to a marriage belong to both partners equally. Nonetheless, until the early 1970s, Arizona law gave exclusive control of those assets to the husband. Arizona also had laws that set maximum working hours for women, while imposing no such limitation on men. As a legislator, I developed amendments to these laws and was successful in getting them enacted. I believe the demise of those laws was inevitable. I am certain, however, that my efforts hastened the process.

Consistent with my own perceptions is a 1981 study of gender differences in conviction and sentencing by state trial judges. The study found no systematic differences in conviction or sentencing between male and female judges when looking across all criminal defendants. This was not true when the researchers considered the gender of the defendant as well. Female judges were no more likely to *convict* female defendants than were male judges, but they were much more likely to send female convicts to jail.[3] I believe this was true when I was a trial judge, and I think I know why. Male judges are more likely to believe a sob story from a female defendant. Female judges know better.

If the differences between men and women in the way they exercise power are subtle, the differences in the acquisition of power are not. As a matter of *fact*, women have not acquired power in anywhere near the numbers men have. To take an example close to home: while women now make up almost 30 percent of the legal profession, they account for only 20 percent of federal judges and law-firm partners, 10 percent of law-school deans and corporate general counsel, and 5 percent of managing partners at large firms.[4]

Even though the number of women in powerful positions is increasing steadily, there can be no doubt that it has been a struggle. And why is that? In the past there was a widespread belief—declining today, but certainly still there—that women are unfit for power positions. The image of the aggressive leader does not lie easily with traditional notions of femininity.

When Elizabeth Holtzman ran for Brooklyn district attorney in 1981, her opponent ran a radio commercial featuring a woman who said: "Liz Holtzman, she's a nice girl; maybe I'd like to have her as a daughter but not as a D.A." She tells of how people would meet her on the street and say, "I voted for you for Congress, I voted for you for Senate, but D.A., that's not a job for a woman. How can you cope with the pressure? How can you stand up to criminals?"[5]

My own political experience was similar. When I first ran for the state legislature, the women's movement was as active as it had been at any time since the first suffragists. As a result, the people of Arizona were willing to accept a woman in at least some positions of power. Nonetheless, there were certain rules one had to obey. It was simply a matter of political reality that, in order to get elected, a woman had to appear and act "feminine." People gave up their traditional notions only grudgingly.

Nor were these attitudes limited to the general public. They were prevalent within the power centers themselves. As a legislator, I never joined my male colleagues for a beer in the local pub at the end of the day, or for dinner at a popular bistro near the capitol. I did not try to participate in the annual basketball game between the Senate and the House members, or the annual fishing trip to Arizona's north woods. While I think I served as an effective legislator, I was never "one of the boys." Somehow, I sensed that the acceptance of women as leaders carried with it some reservations about the *social* interaction between the male and female members. My approach as a legislator was to try to develop as much background knowledge and expertise as possible in the subject areas of the legislation, and to develop community contacts that would provide the necessary public support for my positions. I also made efforts to entertain at my home all my colleagues at least once each legislative session, to try to keep our inevitable disagreements "agreeable."

I have mentioned that only 15 percent of partners at major law firms are women. The paucity of female partners can be attributed in part to the fact that it takes time to make partner, and that women have only begun to enter the legal profession in large numbers in recent years. But the "glass ceiling" does exist. Women come into firms ostensibly on the same partnership track as their male counterparts, but when it comes time for promotions to partner status, they are in some cases systematically overlooked. This may be outright sex discrimination. In many cases, however, I think that partners believe they are making gender-neutral decisions. They simply do not realize that their image of a "partner" may work to exclude women.

In my own case, the ceiling was considerably lower. I graduated near the top of my class from one of the better law schools in the country. My male classmates had no trouble finding jobs. I interviewed with several law firms in California but received no job offers—other than the previously mentioned job as a legal secretary.

By the mid-sixties, the situation for women lawyers was not much better. I remember having a conversation with the senior partner of a large Denver law firm in 1966. He told me how hard they were working to attract and hire an African-American man as a lawyer. When I asked whether the firm had any women lawyers, he looked surprised. "Why, no," he said. "We don't expect to ever hire any women lawyers. Our clients just would not accept them."

In 1989 I had the pleasure of returning to the law firm that offered me a secretarial position on the occasion of its one hundredth birthday—and recounting that story to the assembled partners and guests. I also told them that, in 1981, one of their former partners, William French Smith, who was then attorney general of the United States, telephoned me in Arizona to ask whether I could go to Washington, D.C., to discuss a position there. Naturally, knowing of his long association with that law firm, I assumed it was a secretarial position. But was it secretary of commerce or secretary of labor?

It is important to note that being a woman is not necessarily a disadvantage. Both Senator Barbara Mikulski and Congresswoman Connie Morella believe that it has become a political advantage. "Women are perceived as being more community-minded and more honest," Senator Mikulski says. Consultant Barbara Franklin believes there is such a need for talent that she doesn't see how we are going to manage without a big influx of women.[6] I heartily agree. It is inevitable that women will expand their share of political power. We *will* have a female President.

But we're not quite there yet. One important factor is child rearing. The fact is that private and personal family concerns inhibit women from entering the fray more than they do men. Studies indicate, for example, that child-rearing considerations are a more important factor for women than for men in deciding to run or be considered for office. It was true for me and is still true for many women. For better or worse, the private sphere is more interconnected with the public sphere for women than it is for men.

I did not seek public office until my children were in school and at an age when they did not need a parent at home all day. It simply did not occur to my husband or to me that he should be concerned with the child care needs at home. We grew up in a different generation. But my eventual return to the job market necessitated that our three sons learn to be self-sufficient to a degree that would not have been true had I remained at home. They learned to cook and, when necessary, wash their clothes, and even to iron a shirt now and then. They have continued to use these skills in their adult years. Today's young people are clearly prepared to share the personal concerns of home and children on a more equal basis than were their parents.

Along with this change in the behavior of at least some men, the advent of more widely available child care and more flexible family-leave policies is, in many cases, making it less difficult for a woman to balance career and family—less difficult but still not easy. We still have a way to go before women will be on an equal footing with men in this regard.

There is another reason that women acquired power slowly, and it is closely related to the broad-based cultural explanation. A paucity of women in positions of power creates a vicious cycle. When women are grossly underrepresented in government and in the law and in the corporate boardroom, other women are less likely to believe that they belong in positions of power. For years our society's sexism fed on itself, and the powerlessness of women became a self-fulfilling prophecy. Because women were denied power for so long, it was hard to break the barriers.

But just as failure may lead to despair, power begets power. Those who are perceived by others as having power tend to be better liked, to engender greater cooperation, and to be more effective as leaders. And they tend to inspire others.

Earlier, I defined power as the ability to do. For both men and women, the first step in getting power is to become visible to others—and then to put on an impressive show. The acquisition of power requires that one aspire to power, that one believe power is possible. As women then achieve power and exercise it well, the barriers fall.

That's why I'm optimistic. As society sees what women can do, as *women* see what women can do, there will be even more women out there doing things—and we'll all be better off for it. Certainly today women should be optimistically encouraged to exercise their power and their leadership skills wherever it *might* take them.

Democratic institutions—our constitutions, governments, and laws—are principles to which the citizens owe allegiance. That allegiance has to be earned and developed over time and with many generations.

A commitment of a nation to basic concepts of democracy, of individual liberty, of fairness to all people—women as well as men—depends at bottom on custom, tradition, and the efforts of millions of ordinary citizens. No matter how grand the principles set forth in our constitutions and laws are, we as citizens must be committed to working together to achieve our goals and to make them work in practice.

As my colleague Justice Breyer has said: "Government . . . is no more than its individual citizens, showing their 'public face,' working together to solve the joint problems . . . share[d] as a community."[7]

Women must show *their* public face. We must help to work out our own community problems. We must insist on having equal voices and equal responsibilities. The treatment of women in a society is a critical measure of that civilization. I believe that society as a whole can benefit immeasurably from a climate in which all persons, regardless of gender, have the opportunity to earn respect, responsibility, advancement, and remuneration based on ability.

Women in the United States and elsewhere are still engaged in a struggle against social attitudes that impose barriers to the achievement of this goal. In large part, success depends on changing minds at home, in the streets, and at the workplace—not just in legislatures and the courts. Each and every one of us has an important role to play in completing that task.

—

PART FIVE

The Legal Profession
and the Courts

Earlier portions of this book have alluded to various aspects of the judicial system in the United States, both federal and state. In this part, I outline the basic organization and structure of that system and discuss some of the many challenges it faces.

All Americans can take pride in the fact that ours is basically as good a judicial system as can be found in today's world. Still, it has its problems. And so, besides describing how the system is constructed, I discuss here a few of the deficiencies in how it works: problems with our jury system, a lack of professionalism on the part of some lawyers, and a neglect of law beyond our borders.

These problems are by no means insuperable. But they must be vigorously addressed if we are to continue to improve the quality and delivery of justice.

CHAPTER TWENTY-TWO

Organization and Structure of
the American Judicial System

———

THE JUDICIARY IN THE UNITED STATES HAS TWO MAJOR components: the federal courts, including the Court on which I sit, and the courts of the various states. The structure of the two systems is remarkably similar and has been so for over two hundred years. At the base in each system are the state and federal trial courts, which are the courts of original jurisdiction. Although they are responsible for applying the law to the facts in each case, their distinctive function is to supervise the fact-finding process. Above the trial courts in the judicial hierarchy are the state and federal courts of appellate jurisdiction. Their main concern is to correct mistakes of law made by the courts beneath them; thus, generally, they have no fact-finding responsibilities. Frequently, there is a lower appellate court (most often called the court of appeals), and then a higher court (usually, but not always in the states, called the supreme court) with largely discretionary power to review the decisions made below. At the pinnacle of both systems is the Supreme Court of the United States. Almost exclusively a court of appellate jurisdiction, our Court considers cases from both the lower federal courts and the state courts.

This basic organization came into being with the passage of the Judiciary Act of 1789, which established a system of national courts to operate alongside the preexisting system of state courts. The act was an attempt to address the problem of effectively integrating local and national judicial authority in a geographically extensive territory. The problem had been a long-standing one in colonial America, and was particularly acute during the Articles of Confederation period that followed the Revolutionary War. Our Constitution, written in 1787, finally provided the necessary lawmaking authority for Congress to develop the integrated system we have today. Brief mention of some of these historical influences will help explain how our system came into being.

During the prerevolutionary period in America, the colonies developed their own judicial systems. Despite the enormous influence of the English common-law legal system, each colony had its local variations and customs to which strong attachments developed. This preference for local institutions and local law meant that authority in the American colonies was badly fragmented, which posed a problem for the colonies in their relations with one another and also in their relations with the Crown. There was a need for some overriding judicial authority to deal with legal issues arising in the colonies. Ever practical, the English revived an old institution—the Royal Privy Council—and sowed the seeds that resulted in the establishment of the judiciary as a separate and coequal branch of government under the Constitution of 1787.

The Privy Council originated in England during medieval times. It was the institution through which the Crown exercised judicial authority over possessions outside the realm. From 1660 to 1775, when the American Revolution broke out, the Privy Council exercised jurisdiction in ordinary appeals from the American colonies. One of its foremost powers in this regard was "disallowance": the authority to invalidate colonial legislation. Disallowance was one of the major forerunners of our fundamental concept of judicial review. Another important function of the Privy Council was the resolution of border disputes that often raged with great intensity between the colonies. These disputes seldom could be resolved except through the offices of a judicial body superior to the colonial courts, because those courts were both ill suited to the task and frequently disinclined to perform it impartially.

The beginning of the American Revolution in 1775 launched a new and uncertain era for the colonies. They began referring to themselves as "states" and conducting themselves much more as independent sovereignties than as constituent elements of a new nation. The judicial systems of the former colonies were as deeply afflicted by this lack of unity as any branch of government. Disliked and reviled though it may have been, the Privy Council undeniably had brought a measure of coherence to the workings of both the legislative and judicial processes in the colonies. Its absence meant that, quite literally, a vacuum existed, for the Continental Congress lacked the authority to fill the void.

The delegates to the Constitutional Convention of 1787 brought with them vast experience in government, as well as considerable knowledge of the law and the operation of the colonial judicial systems. Perhaps because of this, one matter seemed to inspire general agreement at the outset: almost all believed that there should be a single national court to exercise appellate jurisdiction. The drafters accepted the view that the court ought to possess independent constitutional status as a coequal branch of the national government. This outlook was to a large extent a product of thinking that evolved from Montesquieu's separation-of-powers doctrine. But it also reflected practical dissatisfaction with the ineffectiveness of the Continental Congress.

Ultimately, the Framers of the Constitution decided to vest judicial power "in one supreme Court, and in such inferior Courts as the Congress may from time to time ordain and establish."[1] The Constitution also specified the method for selection of federal judges, namely, nomination by the President and confirmation by the Senate. The independence of the judges was assured by granting them tenure for a term of "good Behaviour" and, very pragmatically, by ensuring that their salaries would not be cut by a disapproving legislature.

The concerns that led to the authorization of one Supreme Court and the power in Congress to establish inferior federal courts flowed naturally enough from the states' colonial history. But there was still the question, to which the history of the Privy Council furnished insufficiently exact precedent, of how to secure the enforcement of national authority once either the Supreme Court or an inferior federal court rendered a decree. For this purpose, the Framers included the supremacy clause, a provision that made the Constitution, laws, and treaties of the United States "the supreme Law of the Land."[2] By this mandate, the judges of the various states were bound directly to uphold the law of the United States even if that meant overriding state law. This clause forged a powerful link between the authority of the Supreme Court and the obligations of state judges. It was the hinge on which the maintenance of a uniform and supreme national law turned.

As we saw earlier, the first Congress of the United States passed the Judiciary Act of 1789, one of the most important statutes ever enacted. The organizational framework of the national judiciary established by this act remains largely intact today. The Judiciary Act fixed the composition of the Supreme Court, established a system of lower federal courts, and defined the jurisdiction of each of these courts in relation to each other and to the preexisting system of state courts.

Today the lower federal courts are organized into two tiers, designated as district courts and circuit courts of appeals. The district courts serve as general trial courts of limited jurisdiction. This means that the district courts can hear cases only if there is an express grant of jurisdiction by Congress. There are ninety-four United States district courts throughout the country, with from two to twenty-eight judges each. They mainly handle claims arising under federal law and suits between citizens of different states. Beneath the district judge in the hierarchy are bankruptcy judges and magistrates. The specialized matters they deal with are subject to review by district judges.

In several instances the jurisdiction of the district courts is concurrent with that of the state courts. This means that a plaintiff has the right to bring an action either in state court or in federal district court. The prime example of this type of concurrent, original jurisdiction is diversity of citizenship, that is, cases that involve litigation between citizens of different states.

In other instances, the federal district courts exercise original jurisdiction exclusive of the state courts. Federal-court jurisdiction often is made exclusive to signify that the national interests involved are so important that the state courts should not be permitted to adjudicate in the area. One example is judicial administration of federal intellectual-property law, that is, the patent and copyright laws.

There are now thirteen United States circuit courts of appeal, with 179 judicial positions. These courts provide appellate review of cases from the district courts and from certain federal administrative agencies. For all practical purposes in the federal judicial system, review of a case by the court of appeals will be final, because only a small percentage of such cases are reviewed by the Supreme Court.

In addition to the federal courts, the administrative agencies of the federal government provide another major set of adjudicative bodies. Federal agencies function in highly specialized areas such as tax, securities, labor, and international trade. These agencies have a system of adjudicative proceedings and internal appellate review that resembles the function and structure of the federal and state judicial systems. The major difference is that, once a litigant completes the review process within the agency, there generally is a right to judicial review of the claim.

The state court systems are created and established by state constitutional and statutory provisions. The systems differ from state to state. At the local level, the organization of state courts can be somewhat complex because of the variety of needs. Trial courts of general jurisdiction, frequently referred to as superior courts, typically have countywide jurisdiction over both criminal and civil cases. In addition to superior courts, most localities have specialized courts of lesser jurisdiction. They, too, handle civil and criminal matters. Their jurisdiction, however, either is limited by the amount in dispute or the seriousness of the offense charged or is specialized along subject-matter lines, such as probate, juvenile, or domestic-relations cases.

Above the local courts in each state are appellate courts. All states have a supreme court that is the court of last resort in the jurisdiction. Approximately half of the states have an intermediate court of appeals or a system of regional appeals courts. Frequently, this intermediate court of appeals is the court to which one can appeal as a matter of right. In such states, review before the supreme court of the state is largely, if not entirely, discretionary: the court hears only those cases that are important enough to justify its attention.

Except in criminal cases, the only recourse after taking a case to a state supreme court is to seek review by the Supreme Court of the United States—a privilege that is rarely granted. In criminal cases, however, a state defendant has the right to petition for a writ of habeas corpus in federal district court and, in effect, can obtain a second level of appellate review by the federal judiciary. As one might expect, federal habeas corpus jurisdiction has been one of the biggest sources of friction between the state and federal judicial systems.

The Judiciary Act of 1789 provided that the Supreme Court should consist of a Chief Justice and five Associate Justices. As discussed previously, the size of the Court varied from six to ten members until 1869, when Congress fixed its membership at nine, where it has remained ever since.

The Supreme Court has both original and appellate jurisdiction. Original jurisdiction is very limited, however, extending only to certain cases involving ambassadors and other foreign ministers and consuls, and to cases involving disputes between states. Over the past two hundred years, cases invoking the Court's original jurisdiction have not been numerically significant. The Supreme Court's appellate jurisdiction extends to cases from the federal courts of appeal as well as cases from the state court systems that involve issues of federal law. This latter aspect of the Court's jurisdiction is of great significance, because it is a primary means by which the authority of the national government is brought to bear against the states. The objective in such cases is to assure that state courts fulfill their obligation under the Constitution to recognize federal law as the supreme law of the land, even when it means displacing state law. This aspect of the Court's appellate function traces its lineage to the Royal Privy Council, which, as mentioned, had the power of disallowance over colonial legislation.

For the most part, the Supreme Court has discretion over the exercise of its jurisdiction. Parties generally must petition the Court and request that their cases be heard. The Justices themselves decide which of these petitions will be granted.

Over two centuries the primary structural characteristics of state and federal courts have been remarkably stable. To be sure, rapid population growth, economic and social change, and shifts in the balance between federal and state power, among other factors, have brought about changes in the organization and operation of the nation's judicial system. But on the whole these changes occurred within the organizational and jurisdictional framework set in place in 1789.

Today, as in 1789, the state courts handle the great bulk of the nation's cases—more than 27 million new filings annually. The major reason for this is that state courts are courts of general jurisdiction; while they come in many forms, they are open to hear virtually any type of case, whether it arises under state, federal, or international law. Moreover, state courts are more widespread geographically, operating in virtually every county in the United States.

The Supreme Court of the United States, too, functions today much as it has over the past two centuries, hearing cases from both the state and federal courts. Annually, it receives approximately seven thousand requests for review, of which only about one hundred are granted. In the remaining cases, the judgment below remains in effect.

The cases for which review is granted generally are selected by the Court for consideration based on the impact that an opinion will have on the development of the law in a particular area. Most cases are chosen for review because lower courts are in disagreement about the interpretation of a federal statute or a provision of the United States Constitution. Because one of the most important functions of the Supreme Court is to ensure uniformity in federal law, when such conflicts become too sharp the Court must step in to prevent unfairness to the public or an adverse impact on the administration of the law. In other situations, a case will be accepted for review simply because it presents an issue of such clear national significance that speedy resolution is vital to the functioning of state or national government.

The limited numbers of cases that are actually reviewed by the Supreme Court, and the nature of the reasons that such review is granted, make clear the Court's unique role. Unlike most lower appellate courts, state and federal, the Supreme Court's function is not to correct every error that is called to its attention. Thus, a determination not to grant review in a particular case in no way indicates our Court's approval of the lower court's decision. All it means is that the judgment below becomes final for purposes of that case. The Supreme Court's focus is, and must be, broader, for our primary purpose is to guide and shape the development of federal law generally, so as to enable lower courts to perform their responsibilities more effectively and fairly and to guarantee equal justice to all citizens.

CHAPTER TWENTY-THREE

Juries: Problems and Solutions

———

THE JURY SYSTEM IN THIS COUNTRY IS ONE OF THE MOST enduring aspects of our legal system as a whole. The only time most Americans—other than lawyers and litigants—see the inside of an actual courtroom is when they are called to serve as jurors. Juries have a proud history, both in this country and in England, where the jury as we know it developed. Today Great Britain, Australia, Canada, New Zealand, and the United States continue to use juries to hear evidence and determine the facts in many criminal cases, although only the United States and New Zealand continue to require use of juries in most civil cases. The Russian Federation is experimenting with the use of juries in serious criminal cases in several provinces, and plans to expand the use to all parts of the country.

Juries usually do their job very well and on occasion show extraordinary courage in the face of hostile or corrupt judges, delivering the verdict that justice demands, even if it is not the verdict the judge wants. As a trial judge I presided over many jury trials, both civil and criminal. In all but two or three cases I felt the jury reached an entirely appropriate verdict. And the jurors were almost always conscientious and sincere in trying to do a proper job.

But juries also have the ability to disappoint us. One of this country's great observers of human nature, Mark Twain, once complained that juries had become "the most ingenious and infallible agency for *defeating* justice that human wisdom could contrive."[1]

Our federal Constitution and all of its state counterparts guarantee the right to trial by jury.[2] And I believe deeply that the right to trial by

The Holdout (The Jury) by Norman Rockwell. Detail of *Saturday Evening Post* cover, February 14, 1959.

Trial by Jury by Thomas Hart Benton (1964).

jury is fundamental to our system of justice. I also think, however, that there are serious problems with the way juries operate in the United States today. These problems lead some to question whether we should do away with juries for certain categories of cases, or even altogether. In my opinion, the problems, though serious, are not insurmountable. Solving them will require serious effort and commitment on the part of lawyers, judges, legislators, and interested citizens. But it will be well worth the effort to preserve the institution of the jury.

To understand juries today, one has to understand a little bit about where they came from.[3] Prior to the thirteenth century, "trial by ordeal" was the norm in England, at least for serious crimes. This took a number of forms, none of which seem very appealing today. Perhaps the best known of these was tying up the accused and throwing her into water. If she floated, she was found guilty. If she sank, she was declared innocent. Talk about a no-win situation!

After about the year 1220, an accused person could opt for trial by jury rather than by ordeal. But trial by jury looked considerably different in 1220 than it does today. In those early days, a judge still decided the case. Jurors functioned more as witnesses than as finders of fact. They frequently were chosen precisely because they had personal knowledge of the case and the parties, and their primary role was to supply the judge with relevant information—about both the facts and the credibility of the parties and other witnesses—rather than to reach any conclusions.

The jury evolved considerably over the next several hundred years, losing its character as a supplier of facts, and taking on instead its now familiar role as finder of facts. One of the defining moments for the modern jury occurred in 1671. William Penn, the founder of Pennsylvania, was on trial in England for his preaching, which allegedly had caused an unlawful assembly and a breach of the peace. Of course, he was really on trial for being a religious nonconformist. The government put on evidence that Penn had been preaching to a group of Quaker worshippers on Gracechurch Street, and asked the jury to find him guilty as charged. The jury returned a verdict of "guilty of speaking in Gracechurch Street" but did not convict Penn of either unlawful assembly or breach of the peace. The judge told the jury that he would not dismiss them until they reached a "proper" verdict, and instructed them to reconsider. Again, they refused to convict, eventually declaring Penn not guilty.

The judge had to accept the jury's verdict, but he was so incensed that he fined the jurors forty marks each and ordered them sent to prison until they paid. One of the jurors, Edward Bushell, filed a writ of habeas corpus contesting his incarceration, and in a landmark decision Chief Justice Vaughan ruled that jurors could never be punished for their verdict.[4] Bushell's case has since stood for the principle that, however strongly a judge may disagree with a jury's verdict, the judge has no power to change the jury's mind.

By the eighteenth century, juries in England and in prerevolutionary America looked a good deal like they do today—except that only white men, and often only those who owned property, were eligible to serve as jurors. Support for jury trials in this country was enthusiastic and widespread. The Declaration of Independence listed deprivation of "the Benefits of Trial by Jury" as one of the intolerable outrages that King George had committed against the colonists. When it came time to draft the Constitution, the Federalists and Anti-Federalists, who could agree on little, agreed on the importance of preserving trial by jury.

Some of the enthusiasm probably stemmed from the famous trial of John Peter Zenger, a newspaper publisher who was tried in 1735 for libeling New York's royal governor. Zenger was jailed for eight months before his trial began, bail having been set by a progovernor judge at an outrageously high sum. When the trial finally began, the governor had Zenger's lawyer disbarred on a technicality, further infecting the trial with unfairness. But despite the governor's outrageous tactics, the jury, drawn from the local population, acquitted Zenger. That trial was remembered as a great example of a local jury's ability to resist a tyrannical government.

Juries continued for a long time to be composed entirely of white, property-owning, men. African-Americans first sat on an American jury in 1860, in Massachusetts.[5] Post–Civil War events led to some improvement: the Civil Rights Act of 1875 made it illegal for state or federal officials to discriminate on the basis of race in selecting jurors, but in practice many states flouted these requirements.

Sex discrimination has a similarly sorry history in jury eligibility. It was only after women secured the right to vote in 1920 that they achieved any serious hope of serving on juries at all. But discrimination persisted. A 1949 Massachusetts statute allowed trial judges to exclude women from any trial in which the judge thought that women would "likely . . . be embarrassed by hearing the testimony or by discussing [it] in the jury room."[6] As late as 1966, three states still had statutes excluding women from jury service. And even where women had the nominal right to serve on juries, the Supreme Court in 1961 unanimously upheld so-called affirmative registration plans, which required women to fill out a special application to be eligible for jury service, even though men were automatically eligible.[7] That case was overruled in 1975.[8] It is difficult to believe that the Supreme Court accepted the notion of equality of opportunity to serve on a jury a scant six years before I took my seat on the Court.

The world is a very different place now than it was in 1220, or in 1789, or fifty years ago. We therefore should not be surprised to learn that aspects of the jury system that worked well in those times work less well today and need some repairs. What *should* surprise us is that so little of the necessary repair work has been done.

There are three aspects of the jury system that need particular attention. First, *the conditions of jury service*. When citizens are called for jury service, they often view it as a burden rather than a privilege. And for good reason: when they arrive at the courthouse, they frequently are treated more like sheep than people, and the system can seem designed to disrupt their lives to the maximum possible degree. Second, *jury selection*. The process of selecting a jury out of the citizens called for jury service on a particular day has changed from a necessary safeguard against potentially biased jurors to a way for highly paid jury consultants to attempt to ensure a jury favorable to the side paying their fees. And third, *the conduct of the trial itself*. Too often jurors are allowed to do nothing but listen passively to the testimony, without any idea what the legal issues are in the case, and without being permitted to take notes or participate in any way, finally to be read a virtually incomprehensible set of instructions and sent into the jury room to reach a verdict in a case they may not understand much better than they did before the trial began.

To some extent, of course, the problem of jury confusion is unavoidable: some cases are just complicated, and the best-run trial in the world would still pose a serious risk of leaving the jury behind. Great Britain, Australia, and Canada have solved the problem by not submitting most civil cases to juries. In this country, I think the problem can be alleviated to a significant extent by making some fairly simple changes.

The problem of juries ill equipped to handle difficult cases stems in part from the second problem that I mentioned: jury selection. Jury selection proceeds on two levels: "peremptory" challenges, in which jurors are excused by the attorneys at their discretion and with no reason given, and "for cause" challenges, in which jurors are excused for potential bias. In my view, jury selection in this country has gone astray on both fronts, and both problems contribute to the bad impression some have of our jury system today.

First, the availability of peremptory challenges has given rise to "scientific" jury selection, which has led some to believe that a skilled jury consultant can virtually guarantee a verdict by stacking the jury with people who fit the ideal "demographic profile." Some say, accordingly: in England, where jury selection is limited, the trial begins when the jury is seated, while in America, the trial is already over.

Second, unlimited "for cause" challenges, coupled with the extensive publicity that accompanies some of our legal system's most important and high-profile cases, leads courts to search for the most ignorant, poorly informed citizens in the community to serve as jurors, because only those citizens are likely to have avoided forming any opinion about the case.

There is, of course, nothing particularly new about lawyers seeking to use peremptory challenges to stack the odds in their clients' favor. Clarence Darrow said many years ago that a defense lawyer should try to exclude, among others, the "almost sure to convict Scandinavian," but that persons of Irish descent were "always the best jurymen for the defense."[9]

What has changed is the lengths to which parties who can afford it will go to attempt to ensure a favorable jury. Jury consulting is estimated as a two-hundred-million-dollar-a-year industry,[10] and these consultants will do as much as the party can afford to assemble profiles of jurors thought most likely to be favorable or unfavorable to that party's case. In a recent highly publicized pretrial proceeding, for example, the lawyers compiled an eighty-page questionnaire containing nearly three hundred questions, ranging from the obvious to the somewhat obscure, such as: "Have you or anyone close to you undergone an amniocentesis?" After the several hundred prospective jurors filled out the questionnaire, the lawyers, the trial consultant, and the defendant used the resulting data to compile a complex jury chart listing each panelist's qualifications.[11]

Some scholars have questioned whether "scientific" jury selection really helps the party using it any more than does the old-fashioned lawyer's-instinct approach.[12] But whether it does or not, I believe its prevalence has contributed to the sense that jury trials may be unfair because parties with more money can tilt the odds overwhelmingly in their favor. Most citizens involved in litigation, whether as a criminal defendant accused of murder or as a civil plaintiff suing a large corporation, cannot possibly afford this kind of preparation. One cannot help but think that it *may* work, at least sometimes, and therefore that wealthy parties can give themselves an advantage, through the use of peremptory challenges, that is unavailable to the less well off.[13]

The other aspect of jury selection that I find troubling comes about as a result of the massive publicity that certain cases create. Over a hundred years ago, Mark Twain found it extraordinary that sensible, fair-minded people should be excluded from jury service simply because they had read news reports of a particular event. He complained that, "in our day of telegraphs and newspapers [the jury] plan compels us to swear in juries composed of fools and rascals, because the system rigidly excludes honest men and men of brains."[14]

Of course, news travels considerably faster today than in Mark Twain's day of telegraphs and newspapers. The result is that the media is saturated with information about any high-profile case, making it nearly impossible to find jurors who have not at least heard about it, and perhaps formed some initial opinions about the proper outcome. After all, when most people hear of interesting, newsworthy events, they tend to think about them and form views on them.

It is unfortunate that in high-profile cases in this country, which sometimes are high-profile precisely because they are very important, courts are forced to look high and low for jurors who never read newspapers, never watch or listen to the news, and never give much thought to issues of public importance. I'm not saying that those jurors are incapable of deciding cases properly. But I am saying that they probably are unrepresentative of their community, because they probably are, on average, considerably less-well-informed citizens than a random cross section would provide.

Finally, there is the problem of the treatment of the jurors themselves. There's a famous *New Yorker* cartoon where the jury foreman says to the judge: "We the jury find the defendant guilty, and we sentence him to jury duty."[15] I suspect that, when most people receive a jury summons, they do not think of it as representing an opportunity to "increase [their] natural intelligence" or to "exercise a powerful influence upon the national character," which is how Alexis de Tocqueville idealized jury service in America.[16] Instead, most see it as a hassle. It means getting time off from one's job or finding someone to look after one's responsibilities at home; going to the courthouse early in the morning, only to sit in an uncomfortable waiting room for most of the day; and perhaps having to repeat this ritual day after day until either being selected for a trial or being finally excused. It means loss of money, loss of time, and serious disruption of one's life. It is no wonder that jury service has lost some of its luster since Tocqueville wrote his famous work.

If we want juries to decide cases responsibly, and if we want people to look upon jury duty as an important aspect of being a citizen rather than as an enormous burden on their lives, we must treat jurors with the respect and consideration their crucial role in the legal system deserves.

These are some of the problems with the jury system in our country today. What can be done about them? The first level for reform is in the courtroom. Trial judges can accomplish a great deal on their own, just by using common sense. Trial judges can and should exert considerable influence over the selection of prospective jurors. In some jurisdictions, judges conduct all of the questioning of prospective jurors and, where written questionnaires are used, exercise control over the scope and nature of the questions.

For another thing, jurors should be given general instructions on the applicable law *before* the case begins. How are they to make sense of the evidence and the mass of information that the parties will put before them, unless they know in advance what they are looking for? Jurors are not mere receptacles in which information can be stored, to be retrieved intact when the jurors finally are told what to do with it. Jurors are people, and people organize information as they receive it, according to their existing frames of reference.[17] Unless they are given proper frames of reference at the *beginning* of a case, jurors are likely either to be overwhelmed by a mass of information they are incapable of organizing, or to devise their own frames of reference, which may well be inconsistent with those that the law requires.

And when jurors do get their detailed instructions at the end of the trial, we should not simply assume that they can remember, with perfect clarity, what is likely to be a fairly long discussion of unfamiliar principles. Rather, each juror should be given a written copy of the instructions to use during deliberations. That way, jurors who learn better by listening can rely on the judge's spoken instructions, while those who learn better by reading can rely on their written version. It should go without saying that instructions should be delivered in plain and simple English, rather than "legalese," as much as possible.

Jurors should be allowed, and encouraged, to take notes at trial. I frankly cannot understand the resistance to this practice. Some have complained that jurors' notes may be inaccurate, and that jurors will miss important testimony while they're trying to write something down. But again, common sense tells us otherwise. All of us have been through lecture classes in college or even high school, and I suspect that almost all of us took notes in those classes. I cannot imagine going through a class *without* taking notes. Taking notes is a way for a person to make sense of the information being received; to write down things that seem important, so that memory of them will not fade; and, perhaps most important for a juror, to take an active, rather than a passive, part in what is going on.

There are many more things a judge can do in the courtroom to make better use of juries, and trial judges around the country should experiment. Just because something has "always been done" a particular way does not mean that's the best way to do it. If common sense tells us to change something, we should change it.

It is incumbent upon those who oversee their jury systems to make sure that jury service, for whatever length of time, is bearable. A *New York Times* article has reported the typical conditions of jury service as follows: "For the princely sum of $15 a day, New York City jurors often spend hours waiting in crowded hallways, then are ushered into rooms with harsh lighting and bad ventilation and are offered seats on hard benches or chairs with the springs poking out."[18] This is no way to treat the individuals who make up what Tocqueville called "the most energetic means of making the people rule, [and] the most efficacious means of teaching it to rule well."[19] Fees must be adequate, accommodations must be adequate, and courthouse personnel must be adequately trained in anticipating and responding to the legitimate needs of the people comprising the jury pool.

If we want the citizens of this country to respect the jury system, and to see it as a valuable opportunity to participate in democratic governance, we must ensure that that participation is not overly burdensome and intolerably uncomfortable. Legislators and court administrators must take on the responsibility of informing themselves about the conditions of jury service and must be willing to spend the money to improve those conditions when necessary.

We should also start taking action concerning peremptory challenges. Lawyers in England—the country that gave birth to the jury as we know it here—have long been suspicious of the use of peremptory challenges in this country. One barrister has argued that "the jury system is, or in any event is intended to be, . . . a trial by your peers selected at random from all walks of life. And I think it's wrong that a person should try and engineer a better jury for himself, by exercising the right of challenges."[20]

In considering possible ways of addressing the problems that peremptory challenges can cause, we should not be blind to the fact that England did away with peremptory challenges completely in 1988.[21] As a result, jury selection in England, which was always less extensive than in this country, now usually is over in a matter of minutes.[22] Contrast that with the marathon jury-selection proceedings that have become all too common in this country, where the process can last for several months. Some commentators, as well the late Justice Thurgood Marshall, have argued that the benefits of peremptory challenges are not worth the costs and have recommended that we follow England's lead.[23] I am not prepared to abolish *all* peremptory challenges; the person whose life or property is at stake must have the assurance that the jurors selected can render a fair, impartial verdict. But thoughtful debate about this issue is overdue.

As to challenges for cause, one must wonder, in light of the problems that publicity can create in selecting a jury, whether it is absolutely necessary to find jurors who know nothing about a case that, as Mark Twain said, "the very cattle in the corrals . . . and the stones in the streets were cognizant of."[24] This is exactly the situation in some of the higher-profile cases in this country, where publicity can be so widespread that hundreds of potential jurors must be called to seat twelve jurors and some alternates. When an apparently reasonable juror tells the court that, despite some awareness of events relevant to the trial, he or she can decide the case fairly and on the basis of the evidence presented at trial, why should the court not believe it?

When courts assume that any person with more than the most passing familiarity with well-known events is inherently biased, they are likely both to exclude jurors who could decide the case fairly and well, and to guarantee an ill-informed, and probably unrepresentative, jury. Courts should at least begin to question the propriety of linking knowledge with bias. Bias is, of course, a good reason to excuse a juror for cause. But merely having read or seen some report of a case is not.

Another important question, and one that has spurred considerable controversy, is whether jury verdicts should always be unanimous. The Supreme Court of the United States has held that the Constitution is satisfied when a twelve-member jury agrees by a vote of 9 to 3 in criminal cases, although six-member juries must be unanimous.[25] Many states authorize nonunanimous verdicts for civil trials, although as far as I am aware only Louisiana and Oregon authorize nonunanimous verdicts for felony criminal trials.[26] Great Britain has adopted a variant of the nonunanimous verdict in criminal trials, providing that unanimous verdicts are preferred but that 10-to-2 verdicts may stand, as long as the jury has deliberated for what the judge deems a reasonable time.[27]

Some commentators have expressed vehement opposition to any experimentation with nonunanimous verdicts, arguing that the peculiar genius of the jury is to require that a group of diverse individuals *all* agree that the facts of a case point to a particular outcome, and that any lessening of the unanimity requirement will tend to reduce deliberation and devalue the jury's dissenting voices.[28] After all, they argue, if ten jurors agree, who cares what the two dissenters think? On the other hand, under the English system at least, the jury does have some incentive to achieve unanimous agreement, if only to conclude deliberations sooner. And allowing nonunanimous verdicts would reduce the risk of wasting large amounts of time and money on complex trials resulting in hung juries.

These and other changes should be considered on their merits, and decisions should be made in each state about how the institution of the jury can best be preserved and improved.

Juries are a great institution, with a proud history. But we need to make sure we do not remain so wedded to practices hailing from the twentieth century, or the eighteenth, or the thirteenth, that we make it difficult for juries to do their job well. We need to take this issue seriously, to think hard about ways in which juries can be made to work better, and not to fear change simply because it is different.

CHAPTER TWENTY-FOUR

Professionalism

———

*I*T IS HARDLY A SECRET THAT MANY LAWYERS TODAY ARE DIS-satisfied with their professional lives. The pressures associated with the increasing commercialization of law practice have made lawyers, as a group, a profoundly unhappy lot. As one *New York Times* article concluded: "Job dissatisfaction among lawyers is widespread, profound and growing worse."[1]

An examination of the research on lawyers' overall well-being is deeply troubling. Attorneys are more than three times as likely as non-lawyers to suffer from depression, and they are significantly more apt to develop a drug dependency, to get divorced, or to contemplate suicide. Lawyers suffer from stress-related diseases, such as ulcers, coronary artery disease, and hypertension, at rates well above average. Unsurprisingly, a recent RAND Institute study of lawyers in California found that they were "profoundly pessimistic about the state of the legal profession and its future" and that only half would choose to become lawyers if they had it to do over.[2]

This dissatisfaction with the present state of the legal profession is not limited to those within the legal community. Lawyers increasingly have been the subject of public derision. A lawyer in Texas recently filed a lawsuit claiming that he had been the victim of housing discrimination. Apparently, after several unpleasant experiences, the property company had adopted a policy of never selling new homes to attorneys. In economics, lawyers are typically described as creating "deadweight loss," not an altogether flattering term. And a recent study characterized the portrayal of lawyers in popular films today as that of "bad people and bad professionals. . . . Many . . . are unethical, disloyal or incompetent."[3] Few Americans can even recall that our society once sincerely trusted and respected its lawyers.

I believe that a decline in professionalism is partly responsible for this state of affairs. Dean Roscoe Pound said that a profession is "a group . . . pursuing a learned art as a common calling in the spirit of public service—no less a public service because it may incidentally be a means of livelihood."[4] On graduation from law school, aspiring attorneys do not simply gain the means to a comfortable livelihood. They also assume the obligations of professionalism: obligations to their clients, obligations in their dealings with other attorneys, obligations toward legal institutions, and obligations to the public. Personal relationships lie at the heart of lawyers' work. Despite our vast technological advances, the human dimension remains constant, and these professional responsibilities will endure.

Lawyers must do more than know the law and the art of practicing it. A great lawyer is always mindful of the moral and social aspects of the attorney's power and position as an officer of the court. That point was reaffirmed by a case that our Court decided a few years ago. The narrow question presented was whether a criminal defendant has a right to present, through his lawyer, a story that the lawyer knows to be false. The Court unanimously held that there was no such right.[5] The Constitution requires lawyers to represent their clients zealously, the Court said; but nothing in the Constitution justifies advocacy so zealous that it exceeds the bounds of the law.

It has been said that a nation's laws are an expression of its people's highest ideals.[6] Regrettably, the conduct of lawyers in the United States has sometimes been an expression of the lowest. Increasingly, lawyers complain of a growing incivility in the profession, and of a professional environment in which hostility, selfishness, and a win-at-all-costs mentality are prevalent. One lawyer who recently stopped practicing explained his decision to leave the profession in these bleak terms: "I was tired of the deceit. I was tired of the chicanery. But most of all, I was tired of the misery my job caused other people. Many attorneys believe that 'zealously representing their clients' means pushing all rules of ethics and decency to the limit."[7]

This complaint is not unique. In a *National Law Journal* study, over 50 percent of the attorneys surveyed used the word *obnoxious* to describe their colleagues.[8] Indeed, sometimes attorney conduct is not simply rude but downright scandalous. Two lawyers from prominent New York firms recently turned a deposition into an actual brawl.[9] And attorneys have been spotted exchanging invectives and even engaging in shoving matches in front of a court clerk's office[10]—a scene more reminiscent of combatants in a stadium than of professionals trained in the art of reason.

When lawyers themselves generate conflict, rather than addressing the dispute between the parties they represent, it undermines our adversarial system and erodes the public's confidence that justice is being served. Greater civility can only enhance the effectiveness of our justice system, improve the public's perception of lawyers, and increase lawyers' professional satisfaction. I fear that we have lost sight of a fundamental attribute of our profession, one that Shakespeare described in *The Taming of the Shrew.* Adversaries in law, he wrote, "strive mightily, but eat and drink as friends."[11]

In contemporary practice, however, we speak of our dealings with other lawyers as war—and too often we act accordingly. Consider the language that lawyers use to describe their everyday experiences:

"I *attacked* every weak point in their argument."

"Her criticisms were *right on target*."

"I *demolished* his position."

"If we use that strategy, she'll *wipe us out*."

"I *shot down* each of their contentions."

But one need *not* envision litigation as war, argument as battle, or trial as siege. Argument, for example, can be conceived of as discourse. When I ask a question during oral argument in the Court, it is meant not as an attack but as an invitation for counsel to address an area of particular concern. The most effective advocates respond accordingly, answering honestly and directly. Indeed, a good approach to oral advocacy is to pretend that each judge or Justice would like to vote in your favor—and will—but *only if* you can set the judge's concerns to rest by directly answering the question the judge finds troubling.

Trial, similarly, can be seen as an investigation in which the jury must choose among competing versions of the facts. Ranting and raving probably do little to convince. A more persuasive technique is to present yourself as a reasonable person who wants to see justice done; it just so happens that justice will be done by finding for *your* client, not opposing counsel's. All too often, attorneys forget that the whisper can be more dramatic (and compelling) than the scream.

Justice Holmes believed that "a lawyer [can] try [a] case like a gentleman"—or gentlewoman, I would add—"without giving up any portion of his [or her] energy and force."[12] Civility, however, is not a virtue that many of today's lawyers choose to advertise, as underscored by one lawyer's characterization of his "marketing strategy." Clients, he explained, are "not looking for a guy who coaches Little League. They don't want a wimp. They want a lawyer who means business, an animal who's going to get the job done, whatever it takes."[13] Such statements illustrate the brutality of some in the legal profession today. "Getting the job done" should go hand in hand with courtesy. A lawyer can "mean business" without remaking himself as an "animal."

The common objection to civility is that acting courteously will somehow diminish zealous advocacy for the client. Once, in fact, after I made some public remarks about the importance of civility, I received a letter taking me to task: "I want a [lawyer]," the correspondent wrote, "who could be capable of hating my opponents. I want a person [who] is willing and eager to stomp my opponents into the dirt. There should be absolutely *no* friendliness shown to the opposition."

I see it differently. In my view, incivility disserves the client because it wastes time and energy—time that is billed at hundreds of dollars an hour, and energy that is better spent working on the client's case than working over the opponent. It is hardly the case that the least contentious lawyer always loses. It is enough for the ideas and positions of the parties to clash. It is wasteful and self-defeating for the lawyers to do so as well.[14]

There is another aspect of professionalism that goes more to the heart of what it means to be a lawyer. Lawyers are dissatisfied with their careers not simply because of the long hours and hard work or even the decline in civility. Rather, many lawyers question whether, at the end of the day, they have contributed anything worthwhile to society.

Indeed, there is an old joke to that effect. It involves two men on a balloon expedition who became hopelessly lost in a storm. When the storm cleared, they found themselves floating above a one-lane road, with nothing in sight but wheat fields. There was no one, absolutely no one, around. Finally, they spotted a woman walking down the road.

"Hey!" they called down. "Wheeere aaare weee?"

To which the woman responded: "You're up in a balloon, about twenty-five feet off the ground."

"She's a lawyer," one man commented to the other.

"How do you know?" his companion asked.

"Well," he responded, "her answer was clear, precise, perfectly accurate—and totally useless."

I think we can all agree that perfect accuracy in the interest of utter futility is not the highest calling of the profession. Nor is it, in my opinion, the answer to why lawyers do what they do.

Rather, my answer is the same as the one I gave from the bench more than a decade ago:

> One distinguishing feature of any profession, unlike other occupations that may be equally respectable, is that membership in a profession entails an ethical obligation to temper one's selfish pursuit of economic success [even though that obligation cannot] be enforced either by legal fiat or through the discipline of the market. . . . Both the special privileges incident to membership in the profession and the advantage those privileges give in the necessary task of earning a living are means to a goal that transcends the accumulation of wealth. *That goal is public service.*[15]

Lawyers possess the key to justice under a Rule of Law—the key that opens the courtroom door. That key is not held for lawyers' own private purposes. It is held in trust for those who would seek justice, rich and poor alike. We can take pride in the legal community's present efforts to fulfill that trust. The bar is currently involved in greater amounts and more diverse types of pro bono work than ever before, and law schools are providing opportunities for their students to represent and advise those who, but for the students, would have no access to legal advice or legal remedies.

Nonetheless, a great and crying need for legal services for the poor remains. One recent estimate suggests that the legal needs of 80 percent of indigent Americans go unmet.[16] Perhaps more troubling, many Americans believe that the legal system is fundamentally unfair. The inscription above the entrance to the Supreme Court reads: EQUAL JUSTICE UNDER LAW. But a substantial number of our citizens believe that this lofty ideal rings hollow—that justice is reserved for the powerful, the educated, the elite. If that perception is to be changed, and the reasons for its existence eliminated, the legal community must dedicate even more of its time and resources to public service.

Certainly, life as a lawyer is a bit more complex today than it was a century ago. The ever-increasing pressures of the legal marketplace— the need to bill hours, to market to clients, and to attend to the bottom line—have made fulfilling the responsibilities of community service quite difficult. But public service marks the difference between a business and a profession. While a business can afford to focus solely on profits, a profession cannot. It must devote itself first to the community it is responsible to serve.

I can imagine no greater duty than fulfilling this obligation. And I can imagine no greater pleasure. "Happiness," Justice Holmes said, "cannot be won simply by being counsel for great corporations and having an income of fifty thousand dollars. An intellect great enough to win the prize needs other food besides success."[17] Ensuring that there is, indeed, "equal justice under law"—not just for the wealthy but also for the poor, the disadvantaged, and the disenfranchised—is the sustenance that brings meaning and joy to a lawyer's professional life.

CHAPTER TWENTY-FIVE

Broadening Our Horizons

———

W E LIVE IN A WORLD THAT IS CONSTANTLY SHRINKING. Cellular phones, fax machines, beepers, e-mail—all of these new forms of communications have made it much easier for us to talk to one another, no matter where we are. We need, however, more than technology to communicate with people from other nations. We need language skills. We need deeper understanding of foreign cultures. We need to know how to survive in an increasingly multinational environment.

Many of our schools recognize this need, and many parents are taking great interest in language training. High schools now offer more than French and Spanish. They are adding Japanese and Russian as well. American businesses have been in the forefront of this move toward what newspapers constantly herald as the "globalization" of trade. There are McDonald's restaurants in Moscow, Kentucky Fried Chicken franchises in Beijing.

American judges and lawyers, however, sometimes seem a bit more insular. We tend to forget that there are other legal systems in the world, many of which are just as developed as our own. This short-sightedness begins early in lawyers' careers. We learn in law school to look first at the decisions of our own state courts. If we appear in federal court, unless the Supreme Court has spoken to an issue, we look to the law of our local circuit and, perhaps, district. To a certain extent, that is perfectly appropriate because, in the common-law tradition, the only precedents that are truly *binding* in a given jurisdiction are decisions of our own courts.

Justice Sandra Day O'Connor (standing) and Justice Stephen Breyer (seated at O'Connor's right, with glasses) host a meeting with the Supreme Court of India at the Supreme Court building as part of the 2002 India–United States Judicial Exchange on October 15, 2002.

Justice Sandra Day O'Connor with Chief Justice of India B. N. Kirpal (center), with members and guests of the Supreme Court of India, during the India–United States Judicial Exchange at the Supreme Court building on October 15, 2002.

Justice Sandra Day O'Connor with
Chinese President Jiang Zemin, September 2002.

Nevertheless, I think that American judges and lawyers can benefit from broadening our horizons. I know from my experience at the Supreme Court that we often have much to learn from other jurisdictions. For example, even after *Erie v. Tompkins*[1] and the demise of general federal common law in 1938, the federal courts remain charged with the task of developing pockets of common law in discrete areas, like admiralty and maritime jurisdiction.

There also is ample precedent for looking beyond American borders in our search for persuasive legal reasoning. In this country's early years, it was commonplace for American courts to follow developments in English courts. Even today, first-year students of contract law cut their teeth on English cases like *Hadley v. Baxendale*.[2] Nineteenth-century cases, however, have become historical curiosities. At some point in our history, American judges and lawyers stopped looking abroad for persuasive authority. We have become more inward-focused. Other legal systems continue to innovate, to experiment, and to find new solutions to the new legal problems that arise each day; they offer much from which we can learn and benefit.

As the American model of judicial review of legislation spreads further around the globe, I think that we Supreme Court Justices will find ourselves looking more frequently to the decisions of other constitutional courts, especially other common-law courts that have struggled with the same basic constitutional questions that we have: equal protection, due process, the Rule of Law in constitutional democracies. Some, like the South African court, are relative newcomers on the scene but already have entrenched themselves as guarantors of civil rights. All of these courts have something to teach us about the civilizing function of constitutional law.

The first reason for U.S. lawyers and judges to pay attention to foreign law is that, more and more, foreign law is being applied in American courtrooms. Most commonly, foreign law matters in choice-of-law disputes. As international transactions increase, so do international disputes. Increasingly, courts have to choose not merely between the laws of two American states but between the laws of two or more countries.

A second reason for American judges and lawyers to study foreign legal systems is that we can discover ways of improving our own systems. Laws are organic, and they benefit from cross-pollination. We should keep our eyes open for innovations in foreign jurisdictions that, with some grafting and pruning, might be transplanted to our own legal system.

I have had the wonderful opportunity to participate in several legal exchanges—with judges and lawyers in Great Britain, France, India, Canada, and Australia, for example. We have compared approaches to criminal law, to administrative law, to court management, and to constitutional law. There are many interesting examples of borrowing foreign legal ideas one from another.

It is also important to mention how studying the law of other countries can reduce the costs of transnational litigation. Lawsuits do not always confine themselves to a single courtroom. Just as cases bounce from state to federal court in the domestic setting, parties may seek judicial remedies in the fora of several nations. By coordinating the rules that govern cross-border judicial proceedings, we can cut down on the time and expense of multinational litigation. Judges and lawyers do *not* have to leave this work to the State Department or to our foreign ministers.

There are, of course, many reasons why judges and lawyers should pay attention to foreign legal systems, starting with the three that I have just highlighted: to know how to apply foreign law in domestic courts, to borrow new ideas for our own legal institutions, and to enhance cross-border cooperation. Judges must be versed in other legal systems to do justice between the parties before them. Practicing lawyers must broaden their knowledge of foreign law simply to serve their clients better.

But the long-term considerations, I think, are the most important. The vibrancy of our common-law legal culture has stemmed, in large part, from its dynamism, from its ability to adapt over time. Our flexibility—our ability to borrow ideas from other legal systems—is what will enable us to remain progressive, with systems that can cope with a rapidly shrinking world.

PART SIX

The Rule of Law in the
Twenty-first Century

At the dawn of the twenty-first century there was profound optimism in our country. Many believed that the deep-rooted causes of global conflicts were being addressed effectively, that our technological supremacy would produce an entire world community of people sharing knowledge over the World Wide Web, and that economic prosperity was here to stay.

The events of September 11, 2001, and thereafter shattered our peace but not our faith in our institutions. We remain persuaded of the benefits of helping to shape a world in which democratic principles predominate in national governance, and in which the Rule of Law offers the best approach to secure freedom and equality for all people.

Fundamental to the Rule of Law in the United States is the role of an independent judiciary in enforcing the individual rights and liberties guaranteed by our Constitution. In Part Six I describe the role of the Constitution and the U.S. court system in our past—and envision it in our future.

CHAPTER TWENTY-SIX

Shield of Freedom:
The American Constitution
and Its Court

———

THE UNITED STATES HAS ONLY TWO NEXT-DOOR NEIGHBORS:
Canada and Mexico. I have lived most of my life much closer to
the Mexico side of our borders, for I was born in El Paso, Texas, and
grew up on a ranch in Arizona and New Mexico. That experience gave
me a great appreciation not only for the border but also for the history
and challenges that the United States and our neighbor to the south
share.

In the 1860s both Mexico and the United States were mired in
deadly conflict. Mexico faced a threat from without—in the form of the
French Intervention. The United States faced a threat from within—a
civil war—as the division over where, and then whether, to allow slavery pitted the North and South against each other.

From the fires of these two struggles emerged two men of tem-
pered steel. In the United States Abraham Lincoln fought to preserve
the young republic that he governed, managing to persevere in the face
of bitter strife and generals of indifferent quality in his own armies.
In Mexico, Benito Juárez fought to preserve the young republic that
he had governed after Napoleon III—the namesake of a famous
general—deposed the government and installed his own minion.

President Abraham Lincoln and President Benito Juárez each
share a place in the pantheon of their nations' heroes. They also shared

a vision for their respective countries: a vision of an independent federal union with individual opportunity for all, free of slavery and foreign invaders. Both Lincoln and Juárez were trained in the law and were strong advocates of individual liberty as guaranteed by a written constitution. As President Lincoln said, the Constitution "must be maintained, for it is the only safeguard of our liberties."[1]

In my first dwelling in Washington, D.C., on Virginia Avenue, my window provided a view of the magnificent statue of President Benito Juárez there. It is inscribed with Juárez's words: RESPECT FOR THE RIGHTS OF OTHERS IS PEACE. Each day I drove past that statue on my way to the Supreme Court, and it served to remind me of two of the many things, beyond a common border, that our two nations share: a common history of a struggle to gain independence and freedom from foreign rule; and a republican form of government backed by a written constitution reflecting the high value that we place on individual rights and on opportunities and responsibilities.

In the United States our regard and respect for the individual is manifested most particularly in the first ten amendments to our Constitution, which we call the Bill of Rights. Mexico's constitution also guarantees various individual rights, many of which are similar to those protected in the U.S. Bill of Rights. For example, both nations provide for freedom of speech and of the press, the right of peaceable assembly, freedom of religion, and the privilege against self-incrimination.

The primary difference in the treatment of these guarantees of individual liberty is in the nature and extent of their judicial enforcement. In the United States both the state and federal courts can review governmental action that is alleged to infringe on individual rights. A single decision of those courts can not only provide relief to the individual whose rights are infringed but also can determine the outcome of future actions in similar circumstances by virtue of the precedent that is established. Our courts can review legislation passed by Congress or the states to determine whether that legislation is itself constitutional. In Mexico, by contrast, the weight of precedent of a single court decision seems to be less. Courts in Mexico, as I understand it, also lack a general power to invalidate laws or official acts of government—although, through the writ of *amparo*, they can act in individual cases to enforce the constitutional rights of the particular applicant.

These differences in the power of judicial review lead to what is surely the most remarkable distinction between the judiciary in the United States and its counterparts in Mexico and in most other countries: judges in the United States are routinely called upon to address issues that would, in Mexico and elsewhere, be decided by the legislature or the executive branch. The range of issues that the Supreme Court of the United States faces each term is broad. Many of our cases arise from claims of specific individuals that their constitutional rights have been infringed. In each of these cases, the Court must look to the Bill of Rights, and to the Court's own precedents, in setting rules that will guide not only the parties involved but all state legislators, public schools, local and federal police, and state and federal courts and prosecutors.

Whether one agrees or disagrees with the rules the Court establishes, one must acknowledge that, in most other countries, it would be Parliament or Congress, rather than the High Court, that would take the lead in this sort of rule making.

It is tempting to ascribe the heightened involvement of judges in the United States in questions of individual rights entirely to the fact that a written charter of rights is appended to our Constitution. We would be mistaken, however, to believe that the American Supreme Court's immersion in individual rights flows entirely from the language of the Bill of Rights. Many nations have enacted far more detailed guarantees of individual rights without simultaneously producing judicial involvement of the degree current in the United States.

Mexico, for example, has a variety of guarantees of individual rights in its constitution yet does not allow judicial invalidation of its legislative acts. Canada has adopted a Charter of Rights and Freedoms that borrows some of the provisions of the U.S. Bill of Rights, but the use of similar language in our two charters does not necessarily imply that Canadian judges assume the roles of their United States cousins.

"Apt words have power," as the English poet John Milton said,[2] but even a poet—or a lawyer—recognizes that the power of words is shaped by those who use them, and by history.

The United States, like Mexico, cherishes its democracy and lauds the majoritarian "will of the people." But it also accepts—indeed, enshrines—the right of its unelected Supreme Court to use the Bill of Rights to declare illegal the actions of the democratically elected legislature or executive. Our nation, like Mexico, espouses the principle of federalism. We generally accept that the individual states are powerful sovereigns, virtually equal to the federal government. But the same United States that cherishes federalism has accepted the decisions of the Supreme Court that the Bill of Rights applies to the states despite the Constitution's ambiguity on the point. And finally, the Court has been able to use the Bill of Rights to push the country strongly in the direction of a racially integrated society, although many in the United States were reluctant to initiate those changes themselves.

The United States is a common-law country, not a civil-law country, and so in the United States a single case can be of great importance. Probably no case is more important than *Marbury v. Madison,* the case with which every law school in the country begins its course in constitutional law. In *Marbury,* decided in 1803, the Supreme Court declared that it had the authority to declare an act of Congress void if, in the opinion of the Justices, the act violated the Constitution.[3] That principle has survived to this day.

Marbury itself was *not* a case involving the Bill of Rights, but its holding is crucial to the Court's subsequent power in the field of individual rights. The power of the independent courts to declare unconstitutional the acts of another branch of government—the power of judicial review—as set forth in *Marbury* is the foundation of the courts' role in protecting individual rights. Without *Marbury,* the rulings of our Supreme Court on questions of discrimination, church-state relations, and freedom of speech or of the press would be less important and less enduring. Congress, when distressed by a ruling interpreting individual rights, could pass statutes contravening the spirit or letter of the decision, and the courts would be powerless to react.

But because *Marbury* established the courts, and especially the Supreme Court, as the final arbiters of the constitutionality of all acts of government, it is possible for an aggrieved individual to win a victory in the Supreme Court that neither Congress nor the executive branch can take away. As Chief Justice Marshall sweepingly asserted: "It is, emphatically, the province of the judicial department, to say what the law is."[4]

Marbury v. Madison, it should be noted, is in some ways a very anti-majoritarian decision. Alexis de Tocqueville praised judicial review as "one of the most powerful barriers that have ever been devised against the tyranny of political assemblies."[5] But Tocqueville also entitled the book in which he wrote those words *Democracy in America,* because he felt that democratic elections were a distinguishing feature of our nation's fledgling government. Yet the "political assemblies" whose decisions may be overturned as unconstitutional are democratically elected. The executive branch, whose actions also may be overturned by the Supreme Court, is headed by a President elected by the people of all fifty states. The Court that overrules other branches, in contrast, is undemocratically chosen and unrepresentative.

Indeed, it is an understatement to say that the Supreme Court is not democratically elected. The Justices of the Supreme Court are not elected *at all* (although some state court judges in this country are so chosen). Rather, the Justices are appointed by the President. And they serve not just for two years, as do the members of the House of Representatives, or for four years, as does the President, or for six years, as do the members of the Senate. Supreme Court Justices serve for life, or more accurately, as the Constitution provides, "during good Behaviour."[6]

The Supreme Court declares actions of the elected branches to be unconstitutional without itself being any more representative of the people as a whole than the elected branches. All of the current Justices are more than fifty years of age, whereas only 30 percent of persons in the United States who are of voting age have lived five decades.[7] All of the current Justices—indeed, all of the 108 Justices who have ever sat on the Court—are lawyers. But in the general population, as of 1999, only 1 in 283 was a lawyer.[8] And women in the United States constitute over half of the population and nearly half of the new lawyers,[9] while, in contrast, women on the Supreme Court are only 22 percent of that much smaller census.

Given the unrepresentativeness and the lack of political accountability of the Supreme Court, and given the power granted the Court by the doctrine of judicial review, it is probably unsurprising that the Court sometimes finds itself the center of public controversy. When the Court in the 1930s struck down as unconstitutional much of the New Deal legislation that President Franklin Roosevelt offered as a way to deal with a severely depressed economy, it met with a storm of criticism that subsided only upon the death of some of its most conservative members. When the Court in the 1950s struck down as unconstitutional the segregated school system of the Southern states, it was necessary to call out the National Guard to enforce some of the Court's edicts. When in the 1970s the Court struck down as unconstitutional limitations by states on abortions in the first three months of pregnancy, a new body of protesters took to the streets in opposition. And in 2000 the Court again set off widespread criticism when it held unconstitutional Florida's presidential election-recount procedures, and thereby determined the outcome of the election.[10]

But the Court, and its power of judicial review, survived all of this, and seem quite likely to survive current and future controversies as well. I think that the intertwined institutions of the Court and judicial review have proved so durable largely because the Court so often invokes the antimajoritarian doctrine of judicial review on behalf of the most antimajoritarian provisions of the Constitution: the Bill of Rights, approved in 1791. The members of the First Congress drafted the broad principles of that bill to assure individuals that a majority in the national government created by the Constitution four years earlier, however politically powerful that majority might be, could not take away certain liberties. The doctrine of judicial review has placed much of the interpretation and enforcement of those liberties in the hands of the Supreme Court, in part precisely because the Court is not part of the executive or legislative branch.

The impact of the Bill of Rights, as defended by the courts through the power of judicial review, does not stop there, however. Individual liberties are so important that the Bill of Rights has prevailed even in the face of another, sometimes competing principle nearly as dear to the American people. That principle—federalism—holds that the states are powerful sovereigns nearly equal to the national government. Federalism gives a great measure of independence to our fifty states. That is why the Bill of Rights originally was directed only at infringements of individual rights by the national government. But the Fourteenth Amendment, proposed and ratified in the wake of the Civil War, significantly extended constitutional limitations on state governments. The Court has ruled that among those constitutional limitations on state governments are the majority of the provisions of the Bill of Rights.

The Fourteenth Amendment, adopted in 1868, requires the fifty states to accord all citizens "due process" and "equal protection" under the law. Early in the twentieth century the Court began to suggest that the Fourteenth Amendment's promise of due process of law might implicitly incorporate certain of the individual rights contained in the Bill of Rights. In the 1930s and the decades that followed, the Court repeatedly enforced provisions of many of the amendments in the Bill of Rights against the states.

The Bill of Rights, then, triumphs on many occasions over two principles held in almost, but not quite, the same regard: the democratic rule of the majority, and federalism. In addition, there is a third factor—the specter of racism—that has played a large role in the history of the Bill of Rights, the Court, and the nation. The path has sometimes been tortuous, but almost everyone would agree that the United States has made significant strides in the past half century toward an integrated society, and that the Supreme Court has played a positive role in reducing discrimination against African-Americans, Hispanics, and other minorities.

In doing so, not surprisingly, the Supreme Court (and the lower federal courts charged with enforcing its decisions) relied heavily on the power of judicial review—and in the process did some damage to traditional notions of federalism and majoritarianism. The first step down the road was taken in 1954 in *Brown v. Board of Education*. In that case, individual students and their parents asserted their rights to a free and nonsegregated public-school education. The Court held that a state's maintenance of separate public schools for black and white elementary and secondary students denied the black students the equal protection of state law assured by the Fourteenth Amendment.[11] *Brown* called for an end to a system of segregation and discrimination that had become a way of life in a large part of the United States. That decision, and those that followed from it, caused the Court, under the banner of equal protection and due process, to take a leading role in the issue of race relations in the United States.

Moreover, as the issue of school desegregation in all its complexity came before the Court, individuals in increasing numbers began to seek redress through the legal system for other perceived social injustices. The battleground spilled over from the schools into the workplace, the voting booth, and the jury box. More often than not, individuals seeking to right injustices in such areas have invoked the Bill of Rights and the due process provisions of the Fourteenth Amendment. They have been aided in doing so by Congress, by a growing number of civil rights organizations that seek to influence policy through litigation, and by rules of procedure in the United States such as that permitting class-action lawsuits, by which a small group of plaintiff "representatives" can pursue a judicial remedy on behalf of a large number of absent persons who have the same rights at stake in the outcome of the suit.[12]

Congress contributed to the groundswell of individual-rights litigation by passing legislation supplementing various constitutional rights delineated in Supreme Court opinions. The most prominent example is the 1964 Civil Rights Act. That act provided a framework— for precluding discrimination on the basis of race, color, or national origin—that has been expanded by Congress repeatedly. Each of the new statutes has included provisions for enforcement in the courts, and each has been followed by substantial civil litigation on the part of aggrieved individuals. This in turn has led the lower courts, and ultimately the Supreme Court, to address further individual-rights issues not only in the common-law tradition but also in a fashion close to that of courts in a civil-law system: interpreting the statutes and resolving statutory ambiguities. In that respect, then, the involvement of the Court in social issues under the Bill of Rights is not entirely self-generated.

Today the judiciary in the United States addresses an extraordinarily wide range of issues involving pressing social concern. I suppose that our judges have become somewhat more comfortable addressing issues in suits arising under the Bill of Rights—not just those involving racism—in part because of their experiences in enforcing the civil rights legislation. When judges interpreting a statute routinely have to decide, for example, what steps a state hospital must take to assure that its services are equally accessible to the handicapped or an employer must take to see that jobs are distributed without racial discrimination, they begin to develop confidence in their expertise and ability to fashion remedies for violations of related constitutional provisions assuring freedom of religion or equal protection of the law.

That said, "humility is the most difficult virtue," as T. S. Eliot once noted[13]—and the breadth of cases now heard by judges in the United States has reminded us that humility is a virtue still worth pursuing. Faced with a staggering variety and complexity of problems, the Justices of the Supreme Court have in recent years learned—some would say relearned—that there are limits on our judicial authority, expertise, and ability to resolve social issues couched in terms of individual rights. By and large, we are not trained economists, educators, social workers, or criminologists. Our efforts to describe broad legal principles assured by the Constitution have sometimes run aground when the Court attempted to translate those principles into detailed, workable rules that achieve the constitutional goal. The authority of courts to enforce the Bill of Rights can be stretched too thin. One sure way to husband that authority is to invoke it only where necessary.

Thus, the Court sometimes avoids resolving constitutional questions, even with individual rights clearly at stake, when it determines that the question is simply best left to a controlled conflict between the elected branches of government. This "political question" doctrine was used by the Court, for example, to avoid ruling upon the constitutionality of the Vietnam War. It has also been employed to refrain from deciding various issues of basic sovereignty, such as the validity or territory of a foreign government, or the reach of the Constitution's guarantee that each state will have a republican form of government.

Mexico has its own counterpart to the doctrines of nonreviewability of certain questions and in general excludes from judicial review a broader range of issues than the United States. There is less judicial review of issues concerning the free exercise of religion, or of claims of election malfeasance or unwarranted dismissal of government employees, or of decisions of most decentralized administrative agencies—claims that would be reviewable in the United States.

Mexico's current President, Vicente Fox, has said recently that one of his principal goals is to improve his nation's justice system.[14] That goal, like our own efforts in the United States, requires unceasing efforts to select judges of the highest quality and to pay them adequately. It also requires us to try constantly to improve our methods of judicial administration, for justice delayed is justice denied.

The importance of the judicial branch to citizens in every country, and the crucial need for an independent judiciary free from political or private pressure, was eloquently expressed by Chief Justice John Marshall long ago: "The Judicial Department comes home in its effects to every man's fireside: It passes on his property, his reputation, his life, his all. Is it not, to the last degree important, that [the judge] should be rendered perfectly and completely independent, with nothing to influence or control him but God and his conscience?"[15]

I am sure that we do not always succeed in striking precisely the right balance between law and freedom. But we must never stop trying. Both north and south of our common border, we believe in law. At the same time, we believe in freedom. Each of these things, if unchecked, can destroy the other. It is, in the last analysis, the judicial branch that must preserve both law and freedom, keep each operating effectively for the common good, and assure justice.

CHAPTER TWENTY-SEVEN

The Life of the Law:
Principles of Logic and Experience
from the United States

———

THESE ARE TIMES OF TREMENDOUS CHANGE IN GOVERN-ments around the world. Since the mid-1980s, a remarkable number of countries in Latin America, Africa, and the Soviet bloc have turned from dictatorship to elected civilian government. I have been impressed by the strides these countries have taken toward their goals of liberty and democracy. But if they are to retain and build on their recent gains, the new governments must put into place a framework that can ensure the survival of basic freedoms. Of course, such a framework must be adapted to the political and cultural history of each country. Already, we see the post-Communist countries begin to differ significantly in their political, constitutional, and social development. Despite the important differences among nations and forms of government, however, some basic principles must be enforced if a government is to ensure the liberty of its citizens.

Since emerging from the grip of the Soviet Union, the developing nations of Central and Eastern Europe have looked to Western ideas about economic structure, the relationship among branches of government, and the relationship of the individual to the community for guidance in designing their own institutions and processes. The logic that guided our founders to establish certain safeguards within our system, and the experience we have had in the last two centuries, provide examples from which other nations can learn.

What from our own legal tradition and constitutional order must we recommend? The starting point, of course, is the notion that there must be free and fair elections of legislators and executive leaders. This is the basis on which a people can govern themselves.

But as countries in the former Soviet bloc and elsewhere labor to build the institutions that will ensure the development of free and stable democracies, there are three additional principles I believe they must put into place. First, they must create an independent judiciary that is separate from the influence or control of other branches of government. Second, there must be protection of the freedom of the press, so that the citizenry has access to the information necessary for debate and intelligent self-governance. Third, these emerging systems must provide an effective mechanism for enforcing basic individual rights, even against the will of the majority of citizens. Every country will place its own distinct stamp on the system it creates, but these principles transcend national differences.

On the surface, the model of government followed by most nations in Eastern Europe and the former Soviet Union differs quite substantially from the American political-legal system. Those countries generally have used the constitutions of Western Europe, rather than of the United States, as their starting point. The Anglo-American common-law tradition of lawmaking is alien to them. Their chief influences have been instead the federal German Constitution and the comprehensive codes of law in the Roman and Napoleonic civil-law tradition.

Yet despite these structural differences, American tradition and history have something to teach the Framers of new democracies. In designing our system in the late eighteenth century, the founders drew upon the experience and philosophy of Greece, Rome, France, and, of course, Britain. The principles that our founders formulated are now well enough accepted to provide a useful guide. These principles were, from the outset, rational and well-considered responses to the likely dangers posed by government. And, more than two hundred years after they were put into place, they have withstood the test of time and the various strains to which our own history has put them.

The first critical safeguard in the American system is the *independence of the judiciary*. The founders of our nation recognized that it is essential to the legitimacy of the judiciary—and to the legitimacy of the government itself—that the judiciary be a force free from potential domination by other parts of government. They had learned, from Montesquieu, that "there is no liberty, if the judiciary power be not separated from the legislative and executive."[1]

The model of government in the United States is based upon a separation of powers, which permits, and indeed requires, each branch of government to act as a check against possible overreaching by another branch. Thus, our judiciary is vested with the authority and independence to judge not only individuals but the legality of legislative and executive action as well. It is essential that the members of the watchdog branch be evenhanded, consistent, and incorruptible.

Even countries that do not employ the American separation-of-powers model, however, must take steps to safeguard the independence of the judiciary. Judges are entrusted with ultimate decisions over the life, freedoms, rights, duties, and property of citizens. These judges will never have the respect and trust of the citizens if they are believed to be acting as the enforcement arm of an oppressive government, or to be subject to corrupt influences.

The Communist legal system did not foster autonomous judicial action. Instead, judges were low-level operatives of party policy. The practice of "telephone" justice was common: a government official telephoned a judge to request a particular outcome in a case. Judges who refused to comply with such directives faced loss of their jobs, salary, housing, and the like. Whatever the ultimate structure given to the judicial branch, an emerging democracy would be wise to incorporate several measures taken by the United States to ensure the independence of its judiciary.

The first, and perhaps foremost, method of ensuring judicial independence is to place judges' salaries and positions beyond the reach of outside forces. Judges cannot perform their function with the necessary disregard for the government's preferred outcomes if the government has the ability to punish them. The reason that judges in the United States, unlike many countries, need not fear the displeasure of the government is that they are guaranteed their offices during good behavior and receive compensation that cannot be diminished while they are in office. Other branches of government cannot intimidate or threaten the judiciary, whose members are removable only through the drastic measure of impeachment. In the very rare instances when a federal judge is removed from office by impeachment for high crimes and misdemeanors, the entire process plays out in the full view of the public and, in this way, underscores the system's integrity.

Even the President, our most powerful government official, cannot control the actions of a federal judge. Because the President is responsible for the nomination of judges to the bench, he exercises great influence on the composition and general direction of the federal courts. But this influence is brief. Because judges' salaries and jobs are protected, a judge, once safely installed in office, is beyond the reach of executive displeasure or discipline. And even the President's nomination power is constrained by the requirement that the Senate give its advice and consent, and by the long tradition of senatorial courtesy. So the executive's power over the judiciary is both constrained and short-lived— a circumstance that Presidents often bemoan. In fact, President Eisenhower supposedly once remarked, in answer to a question about mistakes he had made during his presidency, that his two biggest mistakes were both sitting on the Supreme Court.[2]

Security in position and pay ensures that judges will not be afraid to enforce the law as they see it. Judges in some other countries, working without these safeguards, have found themselves removed from office or stripped of compensation or benefits to which they were previously entitled. For instance, it is reported that in 1991 a judge in a Balkan nation incurred the displeasure of government officials when he freed a former military official from investigatory detention for lack of sufficient evidence. The evening that his order went into effect, the judge was served with a draft notice to report immediately for combat duty.[3] In the same year, in the former Soviet Union, a judge was pressured—by telephone death threats, and visits from the police and a city council member responsible for the election of judges—to rule in favor of the police in a certain case. After ruling against the officers, the judge was notified that the new apartment she was to inhabit due to her election as a judge was no longer available.[4] Recently, in another Eastern European country, I was told that a judge lost his official car and his security when he ruled against the position taken by the government.

Safeguards for *both* position and compensation are essential, because unless both are protected, the safeguard is empty. The failure to guarantee judicial salaries undercuts the security of the permanent tenure even if it is ensured by the Constitution. In a number of newly formed democratic countries, the Ministry of Justice controls the financial and administrative functioning of the judiciary. Power over the purse strings, tenure, and working conditions of judges can too easily be converted into influence over the content of court decisions.

But it is not enough to guarantee the position and compensation of judges against the power of the political branches of government. Even though *our* political system in the United States is based on the belief that elected representatives are the rightful source of political authority, federal judges are not held accountable to the popular vote. Once appointed by the President and approved by the Senate, they are insulated from the pressure of politics—and, unlike other government officials, cannot be removed or stopped by the force of popular displeasure.

The experience in our country has borne out the wisdom of permitting judges to work without fear of recall. Judges have shown courage in enforcing the law, as they saw it, in the face of enormous public opposition. For example, in the late 1950s and 1960s, several judges of the Court of Appeals for the Fifth Circuit undertook to implement the Supreme Court's landmark school-desegregation decision, *Brown v. Board of Education.*[5] These judges worked against tremendous resistance in applying the equal protection clause to discriminatory practices in education, voting, jury selection, and employment. Their actions exposed them to abuse, ostracism, and even violence by those in the community who opposed their actions. They would never have been able to carry out their sworn duties if they had had to win a popular vote in order to retain their positions.

Many Central and Eastern European countries, like the Czech Republic and Bulgaria, have taken important steps to ensure the independence and legitimacy of their judiciaries. At first this may be discouraging work. For many years the judiciary functioned as merely an instrument of the government and the Communist party and provided no check to the power exercised by the party, the prosecutors, and the police. The citizens considered judges to be servants of the state, without authority to challenge the government's positions, and the stature of the judiciary fell accordingly. The honor and trust of the people, once lost, are hard to recover. But it can be done.

Our country's experience reflects a similar struggle to establish the legitimacy of our judicial branch. In our early days the founders had difficulty in justifying the position of the judiciary to the American public as a check against an overreach of legislative or executive power. Colonial judges, appointed by the English king, were remembered as instruments of tyrannical authority. Trust came slowly. Similarly, the people of Eastern Europe must learn to have confidence in a judiciary historically associated with an oppressive regime. But if the safeguards essential to protecting position and compensation are put in place, it is more likely that the citizens will learn to look to the judiciary as a bulwark of liberty.

An independent judiciary is necessary, but certainly not sufficient, to the maintenance of a free society. The second principle I want to emphasize is the *importance of a free press*. A judiciary that stands apart from the other branches of government is able to perform its function without fear of sanction. Likewise, a responsible press free from government control is able to perform its function of comment and criticism. Only an independent and vigorous and responsible press permits democratic institutions to correct themselves through the powerful forces of informed debate and public opinion.

The emphasis that our founders placed upon the freedom of the press is demonstrated by its enumeration in the very first provision of our Bill of Rights. That terse directive has been interpreted to place stringent limitations on the government's ability to regulate the activity of the press. We remain committed to the principle enunciated by Thomas Jefferson: "Truth is great and will prevail if left to herself; that she is the proper and sufficient antagonist to error, and has nothing to fear from the conflict unless by human interposition disarmed of her natural weapons, free argument and debate; errors ceasing to be dangerous when it is permitted freely to contradict them."[6]

Many of the emerging democracies in Europe and the former Soviet Union face daunting problems that make control and manipulation of the press very tempting for government. The problems of nationalism, the conflicts among different ethnic and cultural communities, and the rise of crime, unemployment, inflation, and various other social and economic challenges make open criticism of the government seem dangerous and destabilizing. These governments well know the power that the press and free information can wield, because one of the important reasons for communism's recent collapse was the influence of alternative examples presented by television, radio, and print.

Our founders, too, recognized the risk they took in protecting the freedom of the press because, as their own experience showed, speech is the tool of change and revolution. But if a country is to adapt itself to new times and new ideas, it must permit the unconstrained exchange of opinions. The leaders of newly forming democracies may fear criticism and wish to stifle the press. But only where the press is free to criticize—and the people are free to challenge—the government can freedom thrive, and the government be responsive to its citizens. A free press is a means by which government officials are held accountable for their actions. In my view, a responsible free press should be seen as a spur to more honest and more responsive performance. A healthy media reflects the views and the needs of the citizenry in a way that occasional elections or polls never can.

The proper functioning of a free press can take place only where the government and a privately owned media are separate. Where the government controls most information sources, little is left to free speech. The countries of Eastern Europe must take the necessary steps to remove the press from under the shadow of state ownership or domination, where it has suffered so long. The print press has made encouraging steps toward unfettered and active reporting. Television and radio, however, remain more significantly in the control of government. Only a few independent television or radio stations exist in Eastern Europe and the former Soviet Union, and each year heads of networks resign or are removed because of conflict with the government. The public's access to information cannot be sufficiently fostered if broad-based media outlets remain restricted by government oversight.

One happy development in recent times has been that the forces of technology have sped the progress of a free press by making it more and more difficult for a small group to control effectively the means of communication. Innovations like satellite broadcasting, global computer networks, faxes, and even photocopying machines make the flow of information easier and faster, and harder to restrain, than ever before. Recently this trend was illustrated most dramatically when Chinese reformers were able to use the Internet to get new information and support for their struggle.

Unfortunately, Eastern Europe has seen a spate of laws that punish criticism of government officials and the publication of state secrets. While the government typically justifies such laws as a way to protect the people and the government itself from possible irresponsibility by the press, the vagueness of the laws permits them to be used against any critic of the government. For example, it was reported that in Albania, in 1994, when the editor of an opposition newspaper was acquitted of charges of publishing official secrets, the judge who presided was arrested soon afterward. An appeals court then sentenced the newspaper editor to five months in prison.[7] Likewise, it was reported that a Romanian journalist who wrote satirical magazine articles was arrested and charged with "casting slurs upon the honor" of the President. The journalist was detained and then, ultimately, ordered to pay the maximum fine allowed by law for his authorship of "expressions which defame, insult and libel the constitutional institution of the Presidency of Romania."[8]

It is undeniable that freedom of the press brings with it some distasteful excesses. The press may pander to the market for works of thoughtless criticism, violence, pornography, and sensationalism. Our country, too, still struggles to balance the need for free speech with the need for some regulation. A recent issue under debate has been the tension between, on the one hand, the right of the press to report, the television networks to cover, and the public to learn factual information alleged against a criminal defendant, and, on the other hand, the right of the defendant to enjoy a fair trial with an unbiased jury. As we have seen only recently, permitting television in the courtroom can result in sensationalistic reporting of crimes and trials that may hamper the administration of a fair trial. Even in the United States we are far from settling the question of the appropriate division between privacy and access to information.

Protecting the freedom of the press is a dynamic area of the law. Shifting trends and the developing technology used by the press require reexamination of the underlying principle and its application in new contexts. This constant evolution requires effort and study and creates controversy. But I am optimistic about the capacity of newly formed democracies to discover, as we have, that although it may at times be difficult to strike the right balance, the preservation of freedom of speech justifies the effort.

The third, and last, crucial element necessary to the creation of free and stable democracies around the globe is not as easily summed up in a few words as "an independent judiciary" and "a free press." It is the principle that *certain fundamental rights, to which every citizen is entitled, must be placed outside the reach of political exigency.*

That is the purpose of our Bill of Rights. It has permitted us to place the most essential individual liberties beyond the reach of the majority and to guard the individual against the excesses of collective government. Although our Bill of Rights is only a few pages long and has been in force for more than two hundred years, great debates continue to rage over the proper meaning and implementation of its few words. But while we continue to dispute the exact contours of the rights it guarantees, we agree that our law protects certain, basic rights from any governmental intrusion.

As James Madison, who framed its ultimate shape, told Congress, the Bill of Rights was directed "sometimes against the abuse of the Executive power, sometimes against the Legislative, and in some cases against the community itself; or, in other words, against the majority in favor of the minority."[9]

This assertion points out a tension within the concept of democracy. Americans are committed to democracy—a form of government based upon the will of the people that is, by definition, majoritarian, in which the legislative and the executive are chosen by the people in free elections. Nevertheless, we have placed within our democratic system a mechanism to protect a range of civil and human rights, and to ensure that the will of the majority does not run roughshod over the rights of the minority. A government that seeks to protect the liberty of its citizens must remove some matters from the impulses of the political majority. Otherwise, all citizens must live in fear that they will one day find themselves in the minority, prey to the fears and passions of the political majority. It is the restraints placed on the majority by the Bill of Rights that make us free.

Such majoritarian pressures can be overwhelming—particularly in times of difficult social and economic change, such as those currently faced by some of the nations in the former Soviet bloc. Countries experiencing tension among national or other groups, particularly, must provide a staunch defense of individual rights that protect all people, regardless of race, nationality, or religion. Many Eastern European and Balkan countries have seen ethnic and national tensions lead to the eruption of a nationalism that endangers civil rights. For example, in the aftermath of revolution, free elections, and economic changes, some of the newly formed nationalist parties blame their country's problems on its minorities, with tragic results.

Governments must create a haven where citizens enjoy their constitutional and civil liberties in defiance of all the powers that the state or the masses can bring to bear. And these rights must be *enforceable*. For example, many of the emerging nations of Central and Eastern Europe are eager to provide their citizens with a wide range of civil and political rights. But if these countries do not provide the institutions and processes necessary for effective enforcement of these rights, their constitutions will represent nothing more than collections of grandiose statements that afford no real protection. This disjunction existed under former regimes, where constitutions were used to declare aspirations, rather than to delineate enforceable rights. The socialist constitutions glowed with promises. But because they provided no means of vindication in the courts or elsewhere, these guarantees meant little.

In our system—and our experience has proved its efficacy—it is the citizens themselves, through the courts, who enforce their rights. Enforcement is entrusted not to other government branches, agencies, or commissions that lack a personal stake in the aggrieved party's freedom but to the people. They take their claims to the courts, and the courts decide whether the actions of the executive or legislative branch have encroached upon some protected rights. The courts then have the power to halt the official conduct that violates those rights, and to order relief for past injury. Ready access to independent courts allows any citizen to press his or her claim. Even in the remote appellate part of the judicial system in which I work, any person, regardless of status or affiliation, may file a petition—handwritten, if the petitioner lacks the resources for a more formal filing—and that petition will receive careful and thorough consideration.

Some might ask how the United States puts so much emphasis on the will of the people in our democratic system and yet permits unelected, unaccountable judges to countermand the will of the representative executive and legislative branches. The debate over the countermajoritarian courts and judicial activism is familiar to us. But just as our system recognizes that the will of the people is the best law, it also acknowledges that there can be no liberty where the majority is free to tyrannize the minority. We, as a people, decided to withdraw certain rights from the consideration of the legislature in order to protect them from the vagaries of politics.

Citizens turn to judges, who are empowered to invalidate the laws that encroach on protected rights. The courts at times may act in ways contrary to the will of the majority, but in so doing they further the principles of our system by ensuring that all groups, including outsiders and minorities, enjoy certain baseline protections. Of course, the fact that the judiciary is the source of the protection for the most essential rights only intensifies the need for that judiciary to be independent. Where judges have the authority to strike down the action of the other branches, the way in which the judges are chosen and the conditions under which they perform their function are of the utmost importance.

And so, in the end, these bedrock principles—*an independent judiciary, a free press,* and *a mechanism that guarantees basic rights to all*—work together. An interlocking framework of principles must be in place if a nation is to ensure the liberty of its citizens. Unless judges are free to enforce the law without fear of reprisal, the other principles and goals of a free society can easily become empty promises. For instance, it makes little sense to expect elected officials to police unwarranted inhibitions on a free press, because government officials are often the source of these inhibitions. Where, however, the courts are free of political pressure, they can be entrusted to protect the freedom of the press.[10]

For their part, courts are unrepresentative and undemocratic. The very independence that protects them also insulates them from public control or ouster. A free press subjects them to the harsh glare of public scrutiny. There is no easy mechanism for the people or the government directly to sanction judges—but these judges know that their work will be observed and evaluated. The same is true for all public officials. As Judge J. Skelly Wright of the Court of Appeals for the District of Columbia reportedly once said, "Public officials, including judges, prosecutors, and the police, function best in a goldfish bowl."[11]

Especially in countries that are recovering from years under tyrannical regimes, a free press will help to restore faith in the institutions of government. Where the people believe that corruption, improper influence, and incompetence can be exposed, they can more readily trust public institutions.

A remarkable feature shared by the three principles I have discussed is how few words it takes to enunciate them, and how many years it takes to understand and implement them. Once the people agree on the precepts by which they will live, they must face the challenge of putting these precepts into practice. As the American experience illustrates, generation after generation will dispute their proper meanings. Such debate is an appropriate activity for a free society. The newly forming democracies around the world must learn to tolerate open criticism and disagreement about the proper relationship between the government and the people. They must fight against the habits from their past, from the time when the state suppressed frank appraisal of government.

It is regrettable but true that the recent histories of some of these countries will increase the difficulty with which they put their ambitious goals into practice. The United States was fortunate in its starting point. In fact, the American Revolution astonished many observers, because it was believed that the British system was more sound, and secured greater liberty, than any other system of governance in the world. We broke away from one of the freest societies ever created—but in embarking on our own grand experiment we were steeped in that tradition.

The countries of Central and Eastern Europe, in contrast, are emerging from intolerant and oppressive regimes. The history that these countries must surmount will certainly make their transition to a free and open government more difficult, if all the more glorious. No revolution, no matter how successful, erases memories of the past, former assumptions, and bad habits. The pervasive influence of the Communist order will continue to be felt for many years. Many official members of the new regimes played a role in the previous governments. Due to a recent history of oppression, these nations suffer from the absence of a culture that demands a strong and sometimes countermajoritarian judiciary and a free, often critical press. They are accustomed to constitutions that promise much but deliver few real freedoms. These countries must strive to change not only their institutions and processes but also their citizens' expectations of government.

While our constitutional and common-law traditions perhaps have a less direct influence on the countries of Central and Eastern Europe than do the Continental Western European traditions, these countries can draw upon our experience as a working model that put theory into practice. Fortunately, no country must formulate its political and legal systems from scratch. History has much to teach. And the assistance of the United States extends far beyond providing a role model for democracy. Both public and private groups are heavily involved in helping to smooth the transition to democratic self-government and a market economy. Our citizens' eagerness to see these countries achieve their goals has led to an outpouring of advice and support.

Both by its direct assistance and by its example, the United States demonstrates the liberty that a nation can achieve. One of our most respected jurists, Oliver Wendell Holmes, once observed, "The life of the law has not been logic: it has been experience."[12] At the time of its founding, the United States struggled to set out the logic of a system that could ensure liberty—and our experience in the last two hundred years has shown that it can be done.

We watch, expectantly, hopefully, as new countries from the former Soviet bloc, in Africa, and elsewhere throughout the world labor to construct their own free and stable democracies.

CHAPTER TWENTY-EIGHT

Through the Looking Glass
and into the Crystal Ball

---

*I*T IS A NATURAL IMPULSE, AS WE ENTER BOTH A NEW CENTURY
and a new millennium, to reflect on the most important developments in our society that came about in the past century, and to inquire about the changes that we should expect in the century to come.

One hundred years constitutes a good portion of the life span of our relatively young nation, and many of the freedoms and legal protections that we now take for granted were as yet unheard-of at the turn of the last century. America's worst years were those of the Civil War. In the decades that followed, our society was deeply—and officially—segregated by race. Women had not attained the right to vote. The courts had not recognized the intrinsic importance of free expression, a free press, or religious freedom. The Bill of Rights did not apply to the states in their treatment of criminal suspects and defendants.

All of that has changed, largely because of the decisions on individual rights issued by the Supreme Court of the United States in the latter half of the twentieth century. Those rulings, and the nation's response to them, are the defining moments of the legal system in the century behind us.

Most Americans, if they think of the Supreme Court at all, think of it in its late-twentieth-century role as the defender—and oftentimes creator—of individual rights. It is curious, however, that the Court did not assume that role until more than 150 years after the adoption of the Bill of Rights and more than 75 years after Congress enacted the Civil

West façade of the Supreme Court building, April 15, 1993.

Justice O'Connor and
her granddaughter
Courtney, 1995.

War amendments—the Thirteenth, Fourteenth, and Fifteenth Amendments to our Constitution.

The Framers of our Constitution were well schooled in the dangers of official oppression, and the Bill of Rights summarizes the personal and public liberties that they thought should lie beyond the government's reach. The first eight amendments to the Constitution provide for freedom of thought and belief; security from unreasonable searches of the home or person; protection against self-incrimination and the right to a speedy and public trial by one's peers; fair legal procedures before the deprivation of life, liberty, or property; and freedom from excessive fines or cruel and unusual punishments.

The Civil War amendments, adopted between 1865 and 1870, further defined our constitutional freedoms by abolishing slavery, by guaranteeing the right to vote regardless of race, and, in the Fourteenth Amendment, by providing that "no State shall make or enforce any law which shall abridge the privileges or immunities of citizens of the United States; nor shall any State deprive any person of life, liberty, or property, without due process of law; nor deny to any person within its jurisdiction the equal protection of the laws."

James Madison, who introduced the Bill of Rights, imagined an active role for the courts in implementing its guarantees. "Independent tribunals of justice," he wrote, "will consider themselves in a peculiar manner the guardians of those rights; [the courts] will be an impenetrable bulwark against every assumption of power. . . . They will naturally be led to resist every encroachment upon rights expressly stipulated for in the Constitution."[1] And in the words of Senator Jacob Howard, one of its key advocates, the Fourteenth Amendment was intended to grant "the humblest, the poorest, and the most despised of the race, the same rights and the same protection before the law as it gives to the most powerful, the most wealthy, or the most haughty."[2]

For much of its history, however, the Supreme Court had little to say about the Constitution's guarantees of individual freedoms.[3] At the turn of the past century, the Court's docket was dominated by property issues.[4] The constitutional questions that the Court did decide concerned the division of authority between the states and the federal government and the allocation of power among the branches of the central government.[5] These fundamental questions about our federalist system, and about the separation and balance of powers, are still very much a part of our docket. But as the twentieth century progressed, evolving notions of individual liberty, and efforts to balance that liberty with governmental power and the commands of citizenship, became the heart of judicial decision making.

Why did the Supreme Court assume this unaccustomed role? How were this nation's historical promises of equality suddenly brought to fruition? In the early 1900s, while the wounds from the Civil War were still healing, waves of immigration rapidly expanded both the size and the diversity of our nation's population. By the middle of the twentieth century, when individual liberties came to the forefront of the national consciousness, our country had also endured two world wars. Service in the military merged different ethnic and racial groups and prompted them to imagine the ways in which they might live and work together in peacetime as well. And women—who did not gain the right to vote until the passage of the Nineteenth Amendment in 1920—also had been integrated into the workplace during the wars. The changing face of the population, the forever altered role of women, and the hopes and expectations of a new generation of racial and ethnic minorities prompted the civil rights movement at midcentury. Much of that movement centered on litigation before the Supreme Court. The result was a range of rulings that had a profound impact on our society.

In the past fifty years the Supreme Court's decisions on individual rights have recognized for the first time many of the freedoms that most Americans today assume as our birthright. Among them are the right to speak freely and advocate for change, the right to worship as we please, and the privilege of political participation. For example, not until the 1960s did the Court acknowledge the constitutional right of the media to criticize public officials,[6] or hold that federal courts should consider constitutional challenges to the malapportionment of state legislative districts.[7] The latter decision led to the Court's announcement that the Fourteenth Amendment's guarantee of equal protection meant "one person, one vote" and required each vote cast in an electoral district to be of equal weight with every other.[8]

These were profoundly important changes. For instance, when I was first a resident of Maricopa County, Arizona, it had only two senators in the state legislature, despite the fact that one half of the state's population resided in that county. Legislative control of the state lay instead in the rural counties, which collectively had only a small percentage of the state's population. This situation was replicated throughout the United States for both congressional and state legislative districts. The Court's "one person, one vote" holding shifted the balance of power to urban America.

Many of the rights that form part of our popular culture about the police and the courts—and, consequently, our expectations about how the state will treat criminal defendants—resulted from the Court's criminal-procedure rulings of the 1960s. It was in that era that the Court first required the exclusion of illegally obtained evidence from state trials,[9] guaranteed all persons charged with serious crimes the assistance of an attorney,[10] applied the protection against self-incrimination to state-court defendants,[11] recognized the right to confront and cross-examine witnesses in state trials,[12] obliged the states to provide a speedy trial to criminal defendants[13] and a jury trial to those charged with serious crimes,[14] and extended the ban on double jeopardy to state criminal proceedings.[15]

In the 1960s and 1970s the Court also struggled with issues of personal privacy and procreative freedom, addressing in *Roe v. Wade*[16] a question that has deeply divided the American public: the breadth of constitutional protection for abortion rights. And under the equal protection clause, the Court began to strike down laws and regulations that discriminated on the basis of gender, as well as interpreting federal statutes to prohibit employment discrimination against women and to provide protection from sexual harassment in the workplace.[17]

The centerpiece of all of the Court's decisions on individual rights is *Brown v. Board of Education*,[18] mandating the desegregation of public schools. Just over a half century before, in *Plessy v. Ferguson*,[19] the Court had held that Louisiana's requirement of "separate but equal" accommodations for black and white passengers on railway trains was consistent with the Constitution. But in 1944 the Court announced that it would give closer scrutiny to laws that treated one race differently from another.[20] Shortly thereafter, the Court declared unconstitutional the exclusion of blacks from state primary elections, prohibited job discrimination against black railroad workers, and struck down a restrictive covenant that prevented blacks from choosing certain neighborhoods in which to live.

These decisions led up to the unanimous ruling in *Brown* in 1954 that state segregation of public schools was unconstitutional. By that ruling, the Court once and for all abandoned the idea that separate accommodations could be equal ones. *Brown* became the basis for subsequent decisions striking down forms of segregation throughout the South—in parks and beaches, traffic courts and theaters, railroad cars and bus terminals. And with the passage of the Civil Rights Act of 1964—prompted in large part by the social upheaval that followed the *Brown* decision—the Court and Congress finally acknowledged the need to give meaning to the Framers' promises of equality, although in a richly diverse nation that the authors of the Bill of Rights could never have envisioned.

Once judicial review became the tool for implementing reform, the Court's acknowledgment of a particular legal right often would lead other litigants to put forward their claims to new and different rights. The imperative to accord equal treatment, without regard to race or gender, has led to second-generation problems in defining the proper remedies for past discrimination. Recently, there have been challenges to affirmative action in the workplace and in the schools. Housing demographics have led to partial de facto resegregation of some schools. Some have begun to challenge the appropriateness of legislative and court-ordered remedies that favor minorities, and thus depart from the color-blind aspirations for our society that first found expression in the *Brown* decision.[21]

Certainly, much work lies ahead to erase the severe damage and distress caused by racial discrimination, and many questions remain unanswered about the ultimate sweep of the individual-rights decisions. But I believe that the hallmark of social change in the last century was the Supreme Court's increasing protection of the individual and its efforts to extend the benefits of American citizenship to every segment of society. So, too, in this new century, we will continue to ensure that individuals participate as equals in this country.

But we must also work to create a larger, more cohesive community out of our sprawling, ethnically diverse population. From a nation of fewer than 4 million people in 1791, America had grown to a nation of over 250 million by the bicentennial celebration of our Bill of Rights in 1991. Most of our citizens now live in urban, not rural, areas. Given our present-day proximity to one another, we must appreciate not only our differences but also our common needs and goals that draw us into an ever-tighter web of interdependence.[22]

In my view, the world will change even more dramatically by the end of the twenty-first century. Having protected, indeed exalted, the rights of the individual, we will be challenged by a world that is increasingly interdependent and that demands that we take part in a global community. There is much talk these days about the twenty-first-century economy, and about advances in technology and transportation that will bring the world closer together.

I believe that, just as in the past century the barriers that prevented women and minorities from fully participating in American society were removed, the next hundred years will alter many of the formal and informal barriers that divide the nations of the world from one another.

When the Bill of Rights came into being, as Thomas Jefferson said, this nation was "kindly separated" from much of the world "by nature and a wide ocean."[23] Those barriers have been breached. The earth seems to grow smaller as our national economies are increasingly linked together, and as more and more people can communicate instantaneously at the stroke of a computer key. Globalization, many of our leaders and scholars have commented, "is an inescapable truth of our time."[24]

We are rapidly forming new institutions that will enable close working relationships among nations. Trade agreements and treaties (such as the General Agreement on Tariffs and Trade, or GATT, and its recent offspring, the World Trade Organization, or WTO), economic partnerships (including the European Union and MERCOSUR), expanded forms of our traditional strategic alliances (such as NATO), and international organizations (like the United Nations and the World Bank) all will contribute.

When GATT was first drafted in 1947, there were approximately 23 signatories. Now there are nearly 150 members of what has become the WTO. It is a critical development in world history to have so many of these nations agree on such things as binding rules regulating trade, standards for the protection of intellectual property, and provisions for the resolution of international disputes.[25] To take a similar but smaller example: in our own hemisphere, the United States is a party to the North American Free Trade Agreement, or NAFTA, which removed the tariff barriers that formerly separated the combined trading population of 365 million people in this country, Canada, and Mexico. My home state of Arizona, situated as it is next to Mexico, clearly has felt the effects of that agreement. The interaction that NAFTA has produced between the people of Arizona and the people of neighboring Mexican states, like the interaction that GATT is producing among the nations of the world, is now a fact of life.

In recent years, the law has raced to catch up with the reconception of international markets and alliances, as standing international courts and alternative dispute-resolution bodies have multiplied. Each of the treaties and new international bodies incorporates a panel or tribunal to resolve the disputes that inevitably will arise among the signatory nations and their citizens. Differences might be resolved in the International Court of Justice, the European Court of Human Rights, the Inter-American Court of Human Rights, the Court of Justice of the Andean Communities, the Tribunal of the Law of the Sea, the International Labor Organization, the dispute panel systems of the WTO or NAFTA, the Administrative Tribunals of the United Nations, or more specialized bodies like the Iran–United States claims tribunal and the international criminal tribunals for Rwanda and the former Yugoslavia.[26]

We have not yet fully developed legal regimes appropriate to recent advances in technology, telecommunications, and transportation, and we are still formulating the necessary rules and procedures to maintain financial stability, enforce international contractual obligations, set industrial and product standards, and protect the environment. It will also take time for us to resolve how flexible borders will affect the domestic legal problems that the Supreme Court confronts, including questions of jurisdiction, immigration restrictions, antitrust and copyright violations, and the applicability of criminal laws to Internet transactions.

As an example, a citizen of Paraguay who had been sentenced to death by the Commonwealth of Virginia recently filed with the Supreme Court a claim that his conviction and sentence should be overturned on the basis of alleged violations of the 1963 Vienna Convention on consular relations. The petitioner, Angel Breard, alleged that the arresting authorities had failed to inform him that he had a right to contact the Paraguayan consulate. In addition, the republic of Paraguay itself instituted proceedings against the United States in the International Court of Justice, seeking adjudication of the Vienna Convention issue. Our Court ultimately concluded that Virginia's procedural rules governed the implementation of the treaty within that state, and we did not intervene to stay the execution.[27] We struggled to balance domestic state laws with this country's obligations under an international treaty, and to respect the jurisdiction of the International Court of Justice while still ensuring that our own precedents were followed. That effort exemplifies the challenges that we will face as international agreements proliferate and grow more and more relevant to the legal issues that have traditionally come before the Supreme Court.

To live together in a world with porous borders is the enormous challenge that we face in the future. It must be met with international legal systems that accommodate both our need to maintain internal authority and the obvious "gains from closer union"[28] that flow from participation in the global community.

Traditionally, the genius of the common law in the United States has been its capacity to evolve over time—case by case and issue by issue—as the courts apply basic legal principles developed over the past to resolve the challenges posed by new situations. This characteristic method of American courts has contributed enormously to the growth of law, freedom, and justice for all Americans.

In the last century the nation's legal institutions struggled—and, to a large degree, succeeded—in balancing individual rights against governmental power and established social norms. The courts played a central role in the racial integration of our society, in the recognition of gender equality, and in the protection of fundamental rights to freedom of expression and association, political participation, and due process of law.

In the new century, dramatic changes in the geographic and economic borders that have separated the United States from the rest of the world will alter our society even more fundamentally. How can the experiences of our past be brought to bear in constructing dispute-resolution mechanisms that will serve in resolving the global challenges of our future?

These are questions worth asking. The answers we provide will be a significant measure of our success in the new century. There is reason to hope the results will draw us closer together as a national community—and that we will play a leading role in finding better means of resolving issues and common concerns with the other nations of the world.

Epilogue

LIKE MOST CHILDREN HER AGE, MY GRANDDAUGHTER COURT-
ney is convinced that the world belongs to her alone. Approach-
ing life as only a child can, she is full of wonder and zest and utter disbelief in the word *no*. From time to time, as we sat together when she
was very young—I watching the evening news, she playing with her
building blocks—I wondered what the world looked like through her
eyes.

Initially, her vision was quite narrow. Unaware of the global events
unfolding on the television screen, she had concern only for her toys,
her food, her sleep, and the adults on whom she had come to depend.
But soon her perspective broadened. She began to form friendships,
and political and spiritual beliefs, and concern for the broader community that joins all of us around the globe. As I anticipate her development from child to adolescent to young adult, I think often of the
world I would like her to inherit.

I am optimistic about the world our children will discover. At a
time of heightened interest in a new global order, various countries
around the world have made enormous strides in the effort to build a
fair and equitable social order that affords all children and adults political freedom, economic opportunity, and meaningful legal protection.
A majority of all nations now has democratically elected leaders. The
United States has, I suppose, traveled longer on this journey, but other
countries are forging steadily ahead. Young and old, rich and poor, educated and illiterate, Eastern and Western, we share a common trait: a

hunger for liberty, a thirst for equality, a desire for sanctity from the encroaching reaches of the state.

As I read news accounts of the passage of new constitutions in various newly formed countries around the world, I gain insight into what the Framers of the United States Constitution must have experienced when they met more than two hundred years ago to write what has become the keystone of our democratic system. I feel the excitement. I sense the anticipation. I see the exhilaration. The peoples of many newly formed nations, like the founders of the American system, have recognized and committed themselves to what is fundamental: freedom of speech and expression; freedom of worship and association; freedom from arbitrary arrest and detention; freedom from government discrimination; and the right to participate in the political process, no matter what one's background, economic status, or views.

As I contemplate these global changes, I am reminded again of Courtney—or perhaps, more accurately, of the building blocks with which she used to play. I think of these blocks because, in my view, a country's ability to attain meaningful and lasting democratic reform depends largely on the blocks—the pillars—on which its new order is built. Rest a political system on an unstable foundation, and it will crumble under pressure and fall away like sand. But build that system on solid stones, and it will hold up and withstand the tests of time.

One of the strongest pillars of democracy is, I believe, the development of an educated citizenry. Establishing the right to vote is essential, but as we have discovered in the United States, citizens may not participate in the political process unless they understand it and believe they have a stake in the community. Nor can we be sure that the poor, the uneducated, the unskilled will respect or abide by the Rule of Law if they remain powerless and shut out. Although decent public education and job-creation programs strain government resources and taxpayers' wallets, their absence may engender even greater burdens: crime, homelessness, drugs, violence, alienation, despair. We cannot allow our children to languish. They are our legacies and our future. Democracy cannot flourish without them.

Democratic reform also requires a strong judicial system in which wrongdoers, no matter how influential, are punished, and victims, no matter how powerless, gain relief. Only with an independent judiciary can there be any assurance that justice will be served. Judges must be invested not only with the *authority* to decide cases. They must also be given the *ability* to apply the law as best they can, unencumbered by the vagaries of the political process and the threat of removal from public office.

In difficult cases, in unpopular cases, in cases that may draw criticism from the executive branch of government, the legislature, the media, or the general populace, it is essential that judges be insulated from public pressure. However much we believe in the strength and integrity of the human spirit, we cannot expect judges to do justice without establishing an institutional framework that guarantees them that their next decision, however loathsome or unpopular, will not be their last.

Attaining a good legal system is not easy. Corruption, racial and ethnic prejudice, disparity in legal representation, administrative delay, and process failure hinder even the noblest efforts to achieve reform. In the United States, where commitment to a fair and equitable legal system is deeply entrenched, justice still at times appears elusive. Equal justice under law still remains for some an unfulfilled promise, not a reality. And disturbing, saddening events still occur.

As John and I sat watching the Rodney King police-brutality case unfold on television in 1992[1] and the destruction of the World Trade Center on September 11, 2001, we wondered what effect these tragedies might have on the world in which our children and grandchildren will live. For most Americans, these incidents were a symbol of failure, a painful reminder of what we have yet to achieve. Yet they were also occasions for healing. In the aftermath of the violence that erupted in Los Angeles in the wake of the King verdict and in New York City after September 11, people immediately banded together to rebuild destroyed areas. The problems in our inner cities returned to the forefront of public discussion. In Los Angeles, black and white, indigenous and immigrant, began productive dialogues on where our democratic system had gone astray, and the reforms we yet require. In New York and across the world, productive discussions on how to prevent terrorism took center stage.

Out of such conflicts come redemption; from such setbacks emerge progress. America continues to grow in justice, I believe, because the tools for reform already are in place. It is precisely because our system embraces free speech that we sometimes witness such expressions of rage. It is precisely because we believe deeply in the Rule of Law that we are repelled by its malfunction. Racism and violence are never excusable. Nor can democracy tolerate terrorism, abuse, and injustice.

A nation's success or failure in achieving democracy is judged in part by how well it responds to those at the bottom and the margins of the social order. Those of us in positions of influence and power can never be complacent and comfortable with the status quo. However sturdy our foundation, however strong our legal and political institutions, we must acknowledge that our societies are not perfect.

Freedom and equality are not achieved overnight. Democracy takes work and time and constant effort. Liberty requires us to place ourselves in another's shoes, to see that things may not be as fair or as equitable as they appear from our own vantage points. Justice compels us to understand the rage, to feel the pain, to respond to the cries. Although it is easy to become impatient and disheartened by process failure and social discord, we must all take the long view of democratic change. The very problems that democratic change brings—social tension, heightened expectations, political unrest—are also strengths. Discord is a sign that progress is afoot; unease is an indication that a society has let go of what it knows and is working out something better and new.

When my granddaughter is a little older, I will tell her of my trips around the world. I will tell her of the determination and courage I have observed. I will tell her that the children she sees across the globe are the beneficiaries of hard work, vision, and sacrifice. I will tell her how lucky she is to inherit a world in which all children, no matter what color, national origin, or economic background, taste freedom and enjoy equality. I will tell her how fortunate she is to come of age in an era when countries in Europe, Africa, and Asia, as well as America, are more democratic and just than when I was born.

And she will, I imagine, look at me, her eyes older, wiser, and perhaps a bit jaded, and make a face and yawn as if it were always so.

Acknowledgments

My years at the Supreme Court have afforded me the motive, means, and opportunity to learn much that I had not known before about constitutional history, the history of our Court, the contributions of various Justices, and the progress of women in the country.

Along the way, my law clerks have joined me in that adventure, provided a treasure trove of materials for my study, and helped me immeasurably in ways that these pages only begin to reflect. I want to acknowledge particularly Jennifer Mason and Carolyn Frantz, who read the manuscript and offered many helpful suggestions. Crystal Nix, too, provided valuable insights. Kindly Linda Neary put all the text on computer disks. Franz Jantzen located photographs to enhance the material.

Finally, Kate Medina of Random House furnished useful recommendations and helpful support.

For all of this generous and capable assistance, I am profoundly grateful.

Notes

PREFACE

1. Wallace Stegner, *Where the Bluebird Sings to the Lemonade Springs* (New York: Random House, 1992), pp. 9–10.
2. *World Almanac and Book of Facts* (New York: Press Publishing Co., 2001), p. 486; Lyn Ragsdale, *Vital Statistics on the Presidency: Washington to Clinton,* rev. ed. (Washington, D.C.: Congressional Quarterly, 1998), pp. 422–429.
3. See "Court Not 'Seething,' Powell Says," *Richmond Times-Dispatch,* July 17, 1972, p. B1.
4. See Oscar Wilde, *The Picture of Dorian Gray* (London: Oxford University Press, 1999), p. 2.

CHAPTER 1 *What's It Like?*

1. E. B. White, "On Federal World Government and Other Matters" (July 3, 1944), in *The Wild Flag: Editorials from* The New Yorker (Boston: Houghton Mifflin, 1946), p. 31.

CHAPTER 2 *The Court's Agenda*

1. American Bar Association, *Perceptions of the U.S. Justice System* (Washington, D.C., 1999), p. 23.
2. Ibid.
3. See Lee Epstein et al., *The Supreme Court Compendium,* 2d ed. (Washington, D.C.: Congressional Quarterly, 1996), pp. 88–93, table 2-9.
4. Ibid.
5. Ibid.
6. Ibid.

7. See Richard J. Lazarus, "Restoring What's Environmental About Environmental Law in the Supreme Court," *UCLA Law Review* 47 (2000), pp. 703, 787–811, app. C.

8. 408 U.S. 238 (1972).

9. 349 U.S. 294 (1955).

10. Epstein, *Compendium*, pp. 88–93, n. 3.

11. *Florida Dept. of State v. Treasure Salvors, Inc.*, 458 U.S. 670 (1982).

12. Epstein, *Compendium*, pp. 88–93, n. 3.

13. Arthur D. Hellman, "The Supreme Court, the National Law, and the Selection of Cases for the Plenary Docket," *University of Pittsburgh Law Review* 44 (1983), pp. 521, 598.

14. See *Pennsylvania Bureau of Correction v. United States Marshals Service*, 474 U.S. 34 (1985).

15. See *Thomas v. Arn*, 474 U.S. 140 (1985).

16. U.S. Constitution, art. 3, sec. 2, cl. 2.

17. Wiley Rutledge, *A Declaration of Legal Faith* (Lawrence: University of Kansas Press, 1947), p. 6.

CHAPTER 3 *Judicial Appointment and Tenure: A History*

1. Charles Warren, *The Supreme Court in United States History* 178 (Boston: Little, Brown, 1923), p. 1.

2. "Justice Black's Speech," *New York Times*, Oct. 2, 1937, p. 1A.

3. U.S. Constitution, art. 1, sec. 2, cl. 2.

4. Henry J. Abraham, *The Judicial Process: An Introductory Analysis of the Courts of the United States, England and France*, 7th ed. (New York: Oxford University Press, 1998), p. 74.

5. See Joan Biskupic and Elder Witt, *Guide to the U.S. Supreme Court* (Washington, D.C.: Congressional Quarterly, 1997), pp. 846–847, 849; Lee Epstein et al., *The Supreme Court Compendium*, 2d ed. (Washington, D.C.: Congressional Quarterly, 1996), pp. 284–303, tables 4-8 and 4-9.

6. *Encyclopedia of the U.S. Supreme Court*, vol. 2, eds. Thomas T. Lewis and Richard L. Wilson (Pasadena, Calif.: Salem Press, 2001), p. 674.

7. Amy Goldstein, "Bush Curtails ABA Role in Selecting U.S. Judges," *Washington Post*, March 23, 2001, p. A1.

8. Henry J. Abraham, *Justices and Presidents: A Political History of Appointments to the Supreme Court*, 3d ed. (New York: Oxford University Press, 1992), p. 70.

9. Ibid.

10. J. Myron Jacobstein and Roy M. Mersky, *The Rejected: Sketches of the 26 Men Nominated for the Supreme Court but Not Confirmed by the Senate* (Milpitas, Calif.: Toucan Valley Publications, 1993), pp. 174–175.

11. Ibid.

12. *The Federalist 76*, ed. Clinton Rossiter (1961), p. 457.

13. U.S. Senate Committee on the Judiciary, *On the Nomination of Louis D. Brandeis to Be an Associate Justice of the United States: Hearing Before the Committee on the Judiciary*, 64th Cong., 1st sess., 1916; see U.S. Senate Committee on the Judiciary, *On the Nomination of Abe Fortas, of Tennessee, to Be Chief Justice of the United States: Hearing Before the Committee on the Judiciary*, 90th Cong., 2d sess., 1968.

14. John P. Frank, "Judicial Appointments: Controversy and Accomplishment," in *Supreme Court Historical Society*, 1977 Yearbook, p. 85.

CHAPTER 4 *The Supreme Court Reports*

1. William H. Rehnquist, *Grand Inquests: The Historic Impeachments of Justice Samuel Chase and President Andrew Johnson* (New York: William Morrow, 1992), p. 104.

2. Id. at p. 113.

3. Id. at pp. 114, 119–120.

4. Craig Joyce, "The Rise of the Supreme Court Reporter: An Institutional Perspective on Marshall Court Ascendancy," *Michigan Law Review* 83 (1985), pp. 1291, 1295.

5. Id. at p. 1301.

6. Id. at p. 1303.

7. Id. at p. 1303.

8. Id. at pp. 1304–1305.

9. Id. at p. 1307.

10. Id. at pp. 1309–1310.

11. Id. at pp. 1312–1313, and n. 120.

12. Id. at p. 1314.

13. Id. at pp. 1320–1321.

14. Id. at p. 1313.

15. Id. at p. 1322.

16. Id. at p. 1320.

17. Id. at p. 1334.

18. Id. at pp. 1343–1347.

19. Id. at p. 1338.

20. Id. at p. 1340.

21. Id. at pp. 1348, 1350.

22. Id. at pp. 1350, 1352, n. 375.

23. Id. at p. 1359.

24. Id. at p. 1361.

25. Id. at p. 1354.

26. U.S. Constitution, art. 1, sec. 8, cl. 8.

27. *Wheaton v. Peters,* 8 Pet. 591, 668 (1834).

28. Id. at pp. 668, 698.

29. Id. at p. 1385.

CHAPTER 5 *Magna Carta and the Rule of Law*

1. Winston S. Churchill, *The Birth of Britain* (New York: Dodd, Mead, 1956), p. 257.

2. "A Confirmation of the Great Charter, and the Charter of the Forest, Statutes Made at London the Tenth Day of October, Anno 25 Edw. I. and Anno Dom. 1297," in *The Statutes at Large from Magna Charta to the End of the Eleventh Parliament of Great Britain, Anno. 1761* (London: Printed for Mark Basket, and by the assigns of Robert Basket, and Henry Woodfall and William Strahan, 1762), p. 274 (all spellings have been Americanized).

3. John Winthrop, *The History of New England from 1630 to 1649,* vol. 1 (Boston: Phelps and Farnham, 1825), p. 160.

4. John Adams, "A Defence of the Constitutions of Government of the United States of America Against the Attack of M. Turgot, in His Letter to Dr. Price, Dated the Twenty-second Day of March, 1778," in *The Works of John Adams* (Boston: Little, Brown, 1851), p. 404.

5. U.S. Constitution, art. 1, sec. 7.

6. U.S. Constitution, amend. 14.

7. U.S. Constitution, amend. 14.

8. U.S. Constitution, amend. 14.

9. J. C. Holt, *Magna Carta,* 2d ed. (Cambridge, New York: Cambridge University Press, 1992), p. 461 (as translated from the original Latin text).

10. U.S. Constitution, amend. 5.

11. *Solem v. Helm,* 463 U.S. 277, 284–285 (1983).

12. *Duncan v. Louisiana,* 391 U.S. 145, 151 (1968).

13. *Smith v. Bennett,* 365 U.S. 708, 712 (1961).

14. Holt, *Magna Carta,* p. 461.

CHAPTER 6 *The Constitution*

1. National Constitution Center, "NCC News and Events: National Poll" (1999), available at http://www.constitutioncenter.org/sections/news/8b4. asp.

2. Ibid.

3. Ibid.

4. Alexander Hamilton, *The Federalist 1*, ed. Clinton Rossiter (1961), p. 33.

5. "Fundamental Orders of Connecticut—1638–39," in *The Federal and State Constitutions*, ed. Francis Newton Thorpe (Washington, D.C.: Government Printing Office, 1909), p. 519.

6. U.S. Constitution, preamble.

7. See, e.g., Harold H. Burton, "The Cornerstone of Constitutional Law: The Extraordinary Case of Marbury v. Madison," *American Bar Association Journal* 36 (Oct. 1950), p. 36.

8. U.S. Constitution, art. 6, cl. 3.

9. U.S. Constitution, amend. 1.

10. U.S. Constitution, amend. 14, sec. 1.

11. George Washington, "First Inaugural Address" (1789), in *The Inaugural Addresses of the Presidents*, ed. Renzo D. Bowers (St. Louis: Thomas Law Book Co., 1929), p. 24.

12. *Marbury v. Madison*, 1 Cranch 137, 177 (1803).

13. 347 U.S. 483 (1954).

14. *Gideon v. Wainwright*, 372 U.S. 335 (1963).

15. Leonard Baker, *John Marshall: A Life in Law* (New York: Macmillan, 1974), p. 745.

16. Chester J. Pach, Jr., and Elmo Richardson, *The Presidency of Dwight D. Eisenhower* (Lawrence: University Press of Kansas, 1991), p. 153.

17. Anthony Lewis, *Gideon's Trumpet* (New York: Random House, 1964), p. 202.

18. *Dred Scott v. Sandford*, 19 How. 393 (1857).

19. See *Chisholm v. Georgia*, 2 Dall. 419 (1793).

20. See, e.g., *A. L. A. Schechter Poultry Corp. v. United States*, 295 U.S. 495 (1935) (striking down the National Industrial Recovery Act of 1933).

21. *Roe v. Wade*, 410 U.S. 113 (1973).

22. *New York Times Co. v. Sullivan*, 376 U.S. 254, 276 (1964).

23. President Eisenhower, for instance, had to employ the National Guard to implement *Brown v. Board of Education*, 347 U.S. 483 (1954). See Walter F. Murphy et al., *American Constitutional Interpretation* (Mineola, N.Y.: Foundation Press, 1986), p. 776.

24. Franklin D. Roosevelt, "Address on Constitution Day" (1937), in *The Public Papers and Addresses of Franklin D. Roosevelt* (New York: Random House, 1941), p. 359.

25. James Madison, "House of Representatives Debates—June 8, 1789," in Bernard Schwartz II, *The Bill of Rights: A Documentary History* (New York: Chelsea House Publishers, 1971), pp. 1031–1032.

26. Learned Hand, *The Spirit of Liberty* (New York: Knopf, 1960), p. 190.

CHAPTER 7 *The Ratification*

1. See generally Gordon S. Wood, "Interests and Disinterestedness in the Making of the Constitution," in *Beyond Confederation: Origins of the Constitution and American National Identity*, eds. Richard Beeman, Steven Botein, and Edward C. Carter II (Chapel Hill: University of North Carolina Press, 1987), p. 69.

2. Jackson Turner Main, *The Anti-Federalists: Critics of the Constitution, 1781–1788* (Chapel Hill: University of North Carolina Press, 1961), p. 286.

3. See Herbert J. Storing, *The Complete Anti-Federalist*, vol. 1 (Chicago: University of Chicago Press, 1981), pp. 3–6.

4. Id. at p. 54.

5. John Fiske, *The Critical Period of American History, 1783–1789*, 4th ed. (Boston: Houghton Mifflin, 1889), p. 339.

6. See Max Farrand, ed., *The Records of the Federal Convention of 1787*, vol. 2 (New Haven, Conn.: Yale University Press, 1990), pp. 563–564, 631–634.

7. Ibid., pp. 369–370.

8. Ibid.

9. See Fiske, *Critical Period*, p. 307, n. 5.

10. See id. at pp. 306–310.

11. See id. at pp. 314–315.

12. See Richard D. Brown, "Shays' Rebellion and the Ratification of the Constitution in Massachusetts," in Beeman, Botein, and Carter, *Beyond Confederation*, pp. 113, 123.

13. J. Elliot, *The Debates in the Several State Conventions on the Adoption of the Federal Constitution*, vol. 2 (Philadelphia: J. B. Lippincott & Co., 1876), p. 8.

14. Id. at p. 134 (emphasis added).

15. Id. at p. 102.

16. Edward Dumbauld, *The Bill of Rights and What It Means Today* (Westport, Conn.: Greenwood Press, 1957), p. 3.

17. Elliot, *Debates*, vol. 2, p. 177.

18. Id. at pp. 177, 181.

19. Storing, *Complete Anti-Federalist*, p. 15.

20. Alexander Hamilton, *The Federalist 84*, ed. Clinton Rossiter (1961), pp. 513–514.

21. See J. Elliot, *The Debates in the Several State Conventions on the Adoption of the Federal Constitution*, vol. 3, pp. 441–442 (comments of George Mason during the Virginia debates, June 14, 1788).

22. Elliot, *Debates*, vol. 2, p. 552.

23. Elliot, *Debates*, vol. 3, p. 22.

24. Id. at p. 171.
25. Id. at p. 659.
26. Id. at p. 259.
27. Id. at p. 659.
28. Dumbauld, *Bill of Rights*, pp. 173–205.
29. See generally Lawrence M. Friedman, *A History of American Law*, 2d ed. (New York: Simon & Schuster, 1985), pp. 557–563.
30. *United States v. Darby*, 312 U.S. 100, 124 (1941); see also *United States v. California*, 297 U.S. 175 (1936).
31. *National League of Cities v. Usery*, 426 U.S. 833, 843 (1976), quoting *Fry v. United States*, 421 U.S. 542, 547 n. 7 (1975).
32. *Garcia v. San Antonio Metro Transit Authority*, 469 U.S. 528 (1985).
33. *New York v. United States*, 505 U.S. 144, 188 (1992) (quoting James Madison, *The Federalist 39;* emphasis added).
34. *Printz v. United States*, 521 U.S. 898, 935 (1997).
35. *Truax v. Corrigan*, 257 U.S. 312, 344 (1921) (Holmes, J.).

CHAPTER 8 *The Evolution of the Bill of Rights*

1. Philip B. Kurland and Ralph Lerner, eds., *The Founders' Constitution*, vol. 1 (Chicago: University of Chicago Press, 1987), p. 470.
2. See, e.g., *Stromberg v. California*, 283 U.S. 359 (1931).
3. See *Benton v. Maryland*, 395 U.S. 784 (1969).
4. See *National Socialist Party of America v. Skokie*, 432 U.S. 43 (1977).
5. See *Hazelwood School District v. Kuhlmeier*, 484 U.S. 260 (1988).
6. See *Virginia Bd. of Pharmacy v. Virginia Citizens Consumer Council, Inc.*, 425 U.S. 748 (1976).
7. See *Wooley v. Maynard*, 430 U.S. 705 (1977).
8. See, e.g., *Miller v. California*, 413 U.S. 15 (1973).
9. See *Tinker v. Des Moines Independent Community School Dist.*, 393 U.S. 503 (1969).
10. See *Texas v. Johnson*, 491 U.S. 397 (1989).
11. See, e.g., *Barnes v. Glen Theatre, Inc.*, 501 U.S. 560 (1991).
12. See, e.g., *Katz v. United States*, 389 U.S. 347 (1967).
13. See *Kyllo v. United States*, 533 U.S. 27 (2001).
14. 381 U.S. 479 (1965).

CHAPTER 9 *The Judiciary Act of 1789 and the American Judicial Tradition*

* An earlier version of this was published as Sandra Day O'Connor, "The Judiciary Act of 1789 and the American Judicial Tradition," *University of Cincinnati Law Review* 59 (1990), p. 1.

1. Felix Frankfurter and James M. Landis, *The Business of the Supreme Court: A Study in the Federal Judicial System* (New York: Macmillan, 1927), p. 4.

2. Charles Warren, *The Supreme Court in United States History*, rev. ed. (New York: Macmillan, 1937), p. 17, quoting "Address Before the Harvard Law School, Feb. 15, 1913," reprinted in *Speeches of Oliver Wendell Holmes* (Boston: Little, Brown, 1913).

3. Charles Warren, "New Light on the History of the Federal Judiciary Act of 1789," *Harvard Law Review* 37 (1923), pp. 49, 52, quoting "Address Before the American Bar Association, Aug. 20, 1911."

4. Paul M. Bator, "Judiciary Act of 1789," in *Encyclopedia of the American Constitution*, vol. 3 (New York: Macmillan, 1986), p. 1075.

5. 1 Cranch 137 (1803).

6. Alexis de Tocqueville, *Democracy in America*, vol. 1 (New York: Schocken Books, 1961), p. 330.

7. G. E. White, *The American Judicial Tradition*, exp. ed. (New York: Oxford University Press, 1988), p. 9.

8. Ibid.

9. Felix Frankfurter, "Chief Justices I Have Known," *Virginia Law Review* 39 (1953), pp. 883, 898.

10. Ibid.

11. *Abrams v. United States*, 250 U.S. 616, 630 (1919) (Holmes, J., dissenting).

12. Learned Hand, "How Far Is a Judge Free in Rendering a Decision?" in *The Spirit of Liberty: Papers and Addresses of Learned Hand*, ed. Irving Dilliard (New York: Vintage Books, 1960), pp. 79, 84.

13. Learned Hand, "Mr. Justice Holmes at Eighty-five," in Dilliard, *Spirit of Liberty*, pp. 18, 21.

14. James B. Thayer, "The Origin and Scope of the American Doctrine of Judicial Review," *Harvard Law Review* 7 (1893), pp. 129, 156.

15. 347 U.S. 483 (1954).

16. U.S. Constitution, amend. 14.

17. Jack Bass, *Unlikely Heroes* (New York: Simon & Schuster, 1981), p. 17.

18. Id. at p. 79.

19. Id. at p. 115.

CHAPTER 10 *Impeachment and Judicial Independence*

1. U.S. Constitution, art. 3 (modern spelling and capitalization).

2. William H. Rehnquist, *Grand Inquests: The Historic Impeachments of Justice Samuel Chase and President Andrew Jackson* (New York: William Morrow, 1992), p. 130.

3. U.S. Constitution, art. 3, sec. 1; art. 2, sec. 4.

4. Id. at p. 27 (views of Senator William Branch Giles of Virginia, as related by John Quincy Adams).
5. Id. at p. 18.
6. Id. at p. 16.
7. Id. at p. 99.
8. Id. at p. 104.
9. Id. at p. 113.
10. Id. at pp. 114, 119–120.

CHAPTER 11 *A President, a Chief Justice, and the Writ of Habeas Corpus*

1. Carl Sandburg, *Abraham Lincoln: The War Years* (New York: Harcourt, Brace & Co., 1939), p. 469.
2. Id. at p. 455.
3. Ibid.
4. U.S. Constitution, art. 1, sec. 9, cl. 2.
5. Paul Finkelman, "Civil Liberties and Civil War: The Great Emancipator as Civil Libertarian," book review, *Michigan Law Review* 91 (1993), pp. 1353, 1354.
6. Mark E. Neely, Jr., *The Fate of Liberty: Abraham Lincoln and Civil Liberties* (New York: Oxford University Press, 1991), p. xv.
7. Id. at pp. 4–6; David Herbert Donald, *Lincoln* (New York: Simon & Schuster, 1995), pp. 297–299.
8. Donald, *Lincoln*, p. 297.
9. Neely, *Fate of Liberty*, p. 5.
10. *Circuit Court of Appeals Act* (1891), after *In re Neagle*, 135 U.S. 1 (1890) (federal marshal Neagle shot David Terry to protect Justice Stephen Field).
11. *Ex Parte Merryman*, 17 F. Cas. 144, 146 (C.C.D. Md. 1861) (No. 9, 487) (Taney, C. J., in chambers).
12. 17 F. Cas. 149.
13. Abraham Lincoln, "Message to Congress in Special Session" (July 4, 1861), in *Abraham Lincoln: His Speeches and Writings*, ed. Roy P. Basler (Cleveland, New York: World Publishing Co., 1946), p. 601.
14. Abraham Lincoln, "Letter to Erastus Corning and Others" (June 12, 1863), in Basler, *Abraham Lincoln*, p. 703.
15. Neely, *Fate of Liberty*, p. xvii.
16. Id. at p. 92.
17. Id. at pp. 136–137.
18. Id.
19. Bruce Catton, *Glory Road* (Garden City, N.Y.: Doubleday, 1952), p. 223.
20. Neely, *Fate of Liberty*, p. 69.

21. Id. at p. 72.

22. Finkelman, "Civil Liberties," p. 1376.

23. Donald, *Lincoln*, p. 417 (snakes); Catton, *Glory Road*, p. 230, n. 19 (pennies); James M. McPherson, *Battle Cry of Freedom: The Civil War Era* (New York: Oxford University Press, 1988), p. 494, n. 8 (both).

24. Donald, *Lincoln*, p. 419, n. 7.

25. Id.

26. Neely, *Fate of Liberty*, p. 66.

27. Abraham Lincoln, "Letter to Matthew Birchard and Others" (June 29, 1863), in *The Collected Works of Abraham Lincoln*, vol. 6, ed. Roy P. Basler (New Brunswick, N.J.: Rutgers University Press, 1953), p. 304.

28. Catton, *Glory Road*, p. 232.

29. Id.

30. Id.

31. Lincoln, "Letter to Erastus Corning," p. 704.

32. Neely, *Fate of Liberty*, p. 68.

33. Lincoln, "Letter to Erastus Corning," p. 705.

34. Abraham Lincoln, "Speech at Edwardsville, Illinois" (Sept. 11, 1858), in Basler, *Abraham Lincoln*, p. 473.

CHAPTER 12 *The Rights of the Individual and the Legacy of Holmes*

1. Oliver Wendell Holmes, "John Marshall," in *Collected Legal Papers* (New York: Harcourt, Brace & Co., 1920, reprinted 1952), p. 269.

2. The other was Justice Brandeis. *Terminiello v. Chicago*, 337 U.S. 1, 29 (Jackson, J., dissenting).

3. Felix Frankfurter, "Mr. Justice Holmes and the Constitution," *Harvard Law Review* 41 (1927), pp. 121, 124.

4. Oliver Wendell Holmes, "The Path of the Law" (1897), in *Collected Legal Papers*, pp. 171–172.

5. Oliver Wendell Holmes, "Natural Law" (1918), in *Collected Legal Papers*, pp. 312, 314.

6. Mark DeWolfe Howe, ed., *Holmes-Laski Letters*, vol. 1 (Cambridge, Mass.: Harvard University Press, 1953), p. 21.

7. *Lochner v. New York*, 198 U.S. 45, 75–76 (1905) (Holmes, J., dissenting).

8. *Adkins v. Children's Hospital*, 261 U.S. 525 (1923).

9. *Coppage v. Kansas*, 236 U.S. 1 (1915).

10. *Lochner v. New York*, 65.

11. Ibid.

12. 219 U.S. 219, 247 (1911) (Holmes, J., dissenting).

13. *Bartels v. Iowa*, 262 U.S. 404, 412 (1923) (Holmes, J., dissenting); *Meyer v. Nebraska*, 262 U.S. 390 (1923).

14. 274 U.S. 200, 207 (1927). The bleak view of the world embodied in Holmes's opinion was also evident when Learned Hand asked Holmes whether he regretted his childlessness. After some reflection, Holmes replied: "This is not the kind of world I want to bring anyone else into." Liva Baker, *The Justice from Beacon Hill: The Life and Times of Oliver Wendell Holmes* (New York: HarperCollins, 1991), p. 228.

15. See H. L. Pohlman, *Justice Oliver Wendell Holmes: Free Speech and the Living Constitution* (New York: New York University Press, 1991), pp. 1–2, 15, n. 1 (summarizing and listing examples of such criticism).

16. *Patterson v. Colorado*, 205 U.S. 454, 462 (1907) (emphasis in original).

17. For more detail on this transformation, see David S. Bogen, "The Free Speech Metamorphosis of Mr. Justice Holmes," *Hofstra Law Review* 11 (1982), p. 97.

18. For a detailed account of *Schenck*, see Jeremy Cohen, *Congress Shall Make No Law: Oliver Wendell Holmes, the First Amendment, and Judicial Decision-Making* (Ames: Iowa State University Press, 1989).

19. 249 U.S. 47, 51 (1919).

20. Id. at p. 52.

21. Ibid.

22. Baker, *Justice from Beacon Hill*, pp. 537–538.

23. 250 U.S. 616, 630 (1919).

24. On the evolution of Holmes's views and their influence, see generally Gerald Gunther, *Constitutional Law*, 13th ed. (Westbury, N.Y.: Foundation Press, 1997), pp. 1034–1076.

25. *Gitlow v. New York*, 268 U.S. 652 (1925) (Holmes, J., dissenting); *Whitney v. California*, 274 U.S. 357 (1927) (Brandeis, J., concurring, joined by Holmes). Holmes joined Court majorities in *Stromberg v. California*, 283 U.S. 359 (1931), which struck down a statute prohibiting the display of a red flag, and *Near v. Minnesota*, 283 U.S. 697 (1931), which struck down a statute authorizing the suppression of newspapers before publication.

26. *Dennis v. United States*, 341 U.S. 494 (1951); *Scales v. United States*, 367 U.S. 203 (1961).

27. *Brandenburg v. Ohio*, 395 U.S. 444, 449 (1969).

28. In 1867 Congress extended the writ to state prisoners held in violation of the Constitution. The current version of that statute is codified at 28 U.S.C. sec. 2254. Before 1867 the writ was available only where jurisdiction had been lacking in the court in which the prisoner had been convicted. See, e.g., *Ex Parte Watkins*, 28 U.S. 193, 202 (1830).

29. 237 U.S. 309 (1915).

30. See Hugo Adam Bedau and Michael L. Radelet, "Miscarriages of Justice in Potentially Capital Cases," *Stanford Law Review* 40 (1987), pp. 21, 115. The governor of Georgia commuted Frank's sentence to life imprisonment, but Frank was killed by a mob two months later. He was pardoned posthumously in 1986.

31. Id. at p. 347 (Holmes, J., dissenting).

32. Id. at pp. 348–349.

33. Id. at p. 349.

34. *Moore v. Dempsey*, 261 U.S. 86, 91 (1923).

35. See, e.g., *Brown v. Allen*, 344 U.S. 443, 464 (1953); *Wainwright v. Sykes*, 433 U.S. 72, 79 (1977); *McCleskey v. Zant*, 499 U.S. 467, 478 (1991).

36. See Samuel J. Konefsky, *The Legacy of Holmes and Brandeis* (New York: Macmillan, 1956), p. 262.

37. Benjamin N. Cardozo, "Mr. Justice Holmes," *Harvard Law Review* 44 (1931), pp. 682, 687.

38. Thomas C. Grey, "Holmes and Legal Pragmatism," *Stanford Law Review* 41 (1989), pp. 787, 850.

CHAPTER 13 *William Howard Taft and the Importance of Unanimity*

1. Donald F. Anderson, "Building National Consensus: The Career of William Howard Taft," *University of Cincinnati Law Review* 68 (2000), pp. 323, 328.

2. Allen E. Ragan, *Chief Justice Taft* (Columbus: The Ohio State Archaeological and Historical Society, 1938), p. 164.

3. Id. at p. 336.

4. Kenneth Starr, "William Howard Taft: The Chief Justice as Judicial Architect," *University of Cincinnati Law Review* 60 (1992), pp. 963–965.

5. Id. at p. 965.

6. Id.

7. Robert Post, "The Supreme Court Opinion as Institutional Practice: Dissent, Legal Scholarship and Decisionmaking in the Taft Court," *Minnesota Law Review* 85 (2001), pp. 1267–1277.

8. Id. at p. 968.

9. Id.

10. Percival E. Jackson, *Dissent in the Supreme Court: A Chronology* (Buffalo, N.Y.: W. S. Hein, 1969), p. 21.

11. Id.

12. Id. at p. 22.

13. *Bank of United States v. Dandridge*, 25 U.S. (12 Wheat.) 64, 90 (1827) (Marshall, C. J., dissenting).

14. Jackson, *Dissent*, p. 23.

15. Post, "Supreme Court Opinion," p. 1283.

16. Id. at p. 1311.

17. Id.

18. Alpheus Thomas Mason, *William Howard Taft: Chief Justice* (New York: Simon & Schuster, 1964), p. 223.

19. Alpheus Thomas Mason, *The Supreme Court from Taft to Warren* (Baton Rouge: Louisiana State University Press, 1958), p. 50.

20. 261 U.S. 525, 562 (1923) (Taft, C. J., dissenting).

21. Post, "Supreme Court Opinion," p. 1284.

22. Mason, *William Howard Taft*, p. 219.

23. See, e.g., *Whitney v. California*, 274 U.S. 357 (1927); *United States v. Schwimmer*, 279 U.S. 644 (1929).

24. Post, "Supreme Court Opinion," p. 1326.

25. Jackson, *Dissent*, p. 18.

26. Mason, *William Howard Taft*, p. 201.

27. Id. at p. 219.

28. Id. at p. 223, citing David J. Danelski, "The Influence of the Chief Justice in the Decisional Process of the Supreme Court," paper, Sept. 1963, p. 20, n. 122.

29. Id. at p. 171.

30. Id. at p. 199.

31. Id. at p. 212.

32. Post, "Supreme Court Opinion," pp. 1332–1333.

33. Id. at p. 1301.

34. Mason, *William Howard Taft*, p. 202.

35. Id. at p. 204 (discussing *Sanitary Dist. of Chicago v. United States*, 266 U.S. 405 [1925]).

36. Post, "Supreme Court Opinion," pp. 1340–1341.

37. Anthony Lewis, "In Memoriam: William J. Brennan, Jr.," *Harvard Law Review* 111 (1997), pp. 29, 32.

38. Charles Evans Hughes, *The Supreme Court of the United States: Its Foundations, Methods and Achievements: An Interpretation* (New York: Columbia University Press, 1928), pp. 67–68.

39. Post, "Supreme Court Opinion," p. 1356.

40. 198 U.S. 45, 76 (1905).

41. 163 U.S. 537, 551 (1896).

42. 349 U.S. 294 (1955).

43. Karl Llewellyn, *The Common Law Tradition: Deciding Appeals* (Boston: Little, Brown, 1960), p. 26.

44. William J. Brennan, Jr., "In Defense of Dissents," *Hastings Law Journal* 37 (1986), p. 427.

45. Hughes, *Supreme Court*, pp. 67–68, n. 38.

CHAPTER 14 *Charles Evans Hughes and President Roosevelt's Court-Expansion Plan*

1. "Message from the President of the United States Transmitting a Recommendation to Reorganize the Judicial Branch of the Federal Government" (Feb. 5, 1937), in *Senate Report* 75–711, at pp. 25–26 (1937).

2. Burton K. Wheeler and Paul F. Healy, *Yankee from the West: The Candid, Turbulent Life Story of the Yankee-Born U.S. Senator from Montana Burton K. Wheeler* (Garden City, N.Y.: Doubleday, 1962), p. 339.

3. Herbock, "Precedent for the President" (cartoon), reprinted in Leonard Baker, *Back to Back: The Duel Between FDR and the Supreme Court* (New York: Macmillan, 1967).

4. Elderman, "To Furnish the Supreme Court Practical Assistance" (cartoon), reprinted in Baker, *Back to Back.*

5. "Message from the President," p. 25.

6. Ibid., p. 26.

7. Ibid., p. 27.

8. "Statement of Homer Cummings," in *Senate Report* 75–711, p. 4.

9. Wheeler and Healy, *Yankee,* p. 328.

10. "Statement of Burton K. Wheeler," in *Senate Report* 75–711, p. 485.

11. Id. at p. 488.

12. Id. at p. 491.

13. Wheeler and Healy, *Yankee,* p. 333.

14. Ibid.

15. Id. at p. 339.

CHAPTER 15 *Thurgood Marshall: The Influence of a Raconteur*

* An earlier version of this was published as Sandra Day O'Connor, "Thurgood Marshall: The Influence of a Raconteur," *Stanford Law Review* 44 (1992), p. 1217.

1. 347 U.S. 483 (1954).

CHAPTER 16 *Warren E. Burger*

* An earlier version of this was published as Sandra Day O'Connor, "A Tribute to Warren E. Burger," *William Mitchell Law Review* 22 (1996), p. 7.

1. "Statement of Warren E. Burger Before the Senate Committee on the Judiciary" (June 3, 1969), reprinted in *Supreme Court of the United States: Hearings and Reports on Successful and Unsuccessful Nomination of Supreme Court Justices by the Senate Judiciary Committee, 1916–1975,* vol. 7, eds. Roy M. Mersky and J. Myron Jacobstein (Buffalo, N.Y.: W. S. Hein, 1977).

2. Warren E. Burger, "The State of Judiciary—1970," *American Bar Association Journal* 56 (1970), pp. 929–932.

3. Warren E. Burger, "The Legal Profession Is a Monopoly," address before the American Inns of Court, June 1, 1990.

4. Warren E. Burger, "Lawrence H. Cooke: A Tireless Judicial Administrator," *Fordham Law Review* 53 (1984), p. 147.

5. See Warren E. Burger, "The Special Skills of Advocacy," remarks given at Fordham University Law School, Nov. 26, 1973, in Warren E. Burger, *Delivery of Justice: Proposals for Changes to Improve the Administration of Justice* (St. Paul, Minn.: College of William & Mary Press, 1990), pp. 187, 190–193.

6. Warren E. Burger, "The Future of Legal Education," remarks delivered to the American Bar Association, Aug. 10, 1969, in *Burger, Delivery of Justice*, pp. 166, 169.

7. Id. at p. 168.

8. *Reed v. Reed*, 404 U.S. 71 (1971).

9. *United States v. Nixon*, 418 U.S. 683 (1974).

10. *INS v. Chadha*, 462 U.S. 919 (1983).

11. Warren E. Burger, foreword to Catherine D. Bowen, *Miracle at Philadelphia: The Story of the Constitutional Convention* (Boston: Little, Brown, 1966), p. x.

CHAPTER 17 *Lewis F. Powell, Jr.*

* An earlier version of this was published as Sandra Day O'Connor, "A Tribute to Lewis F. Powell, Jr.," *Washington and Lee Law Review* 56 (1999), p. 4.

1. See John Bartlett, *Familiar Quotations* (Boston: Little, Brown, 1982), p. 509.

2. John C. Jeffries, Jr., *Justice Lewis F. Powell, Jr. and the Era of Judicial Balance* (New York: C. Scribner's Sons, 1994), p. 562.

CHAPTER 18 *Women in Society: The American Experience*

* An earlier version of this was published as Sandra Day O'Connor, "The Legal Status of Women: The Journey Toward Equality," *Journal of Law and Religion* 15 (2000), p. 29.

1. *Bradwell v. Illinois*, 16 Wall. 130 (1872).

2. Joan Hoff, *Law, Gender, and Injustice: A Legal History of U.S. Women* (New York: New York University Press, 1991), p. 62.

3. Deborah L. Rhode, *Justice and Gender: Sex Discrimination and the Law* (Cambridge, Mass.: Harvard University Press, 1989), p. 20.

4. Ibid., p. 9.

5. Hoff, *Law, Gender*, p. 37.

6. Alfred, Lord Tennyson, *Locksley Hall* (Boston: Ticknor and Fields, 1869).

7. Hoff, *Law, Gender*, p. 39.

8. Belva Lockwood, "My Efforts to Become a Lawyer," reprinted in *Women in the American Economy: A Documentary History, 1675–1929*, eds. W. Elliot Brownlee and Mary M. Brownlee (New Haven, Conn.: Yale University Press, 1976), pp. 297–298.

9. See *In re Lockwood*, 154 U.S. 116 (1894).

10. *Bradwell's Case*, 55 Ill. 535 (1869).

11. *Bradwell v. Illinois*, 16 Wall. 130 (1872).

12. Rhode, *Justice and Gender*, p. 24.

13. Hoff, *Law, Gender*, p. 119.

14. Ibid., p. 128.

15. 78 Iowa 177 (1889).

16. Rhode, *Justice and Gender*, p. 27.

17. *Bradley v. State*, 1 Miss. 156 (1824).

18. Hoff, *Law, Gender*, p. 133.

19. See Kristin Choo, "Moving into the Driver's Seat," *American Bar Association Journal* (2001), p. 84.

20. *Minor v. Happersett*, 88 U.S. 162 (1875).

21. Ibid., 176.

22. *Muller v. Oregon*, 208 U.S. 412 (1908).

23. *Goesaert v. Cleary*, 335 U.S. 464 (1948).

24. *Hoyt v. Florida*, 368 U.S. 57 (1961), overruled by *Taylor v. Louisiana*, 419 U.S. 522 (1975).

25. Rhode, *Justice and Gender*, p. 53.

26. Ibid., p. 54.

27. 404 U.S. 71 (1971).

28. Id.

29. *Frontiero v. Richardson*, 411 U.S. 677, 684 (1973) (plurality).

30. *Stanton v. Stanton*, 421 U.S. 7, 14–15 (1975).

31. *Craig v. Boren*, 429 U.S. 190 (1976).

32. *California v. Goldfarb*, 430 U.S. 199 (1977).

33. *Craig v. Boren*, 190.

34. *Orr v. Orr*, 440 U.S. 268 (1979).

35. *California v. Westcott*, 443 U.S. 76 (1979).

36. *Kirchberg v. Feenstra*, 450 U.S. 455 (1981).

37. 518 U.S. 515 (1996).

38. *Hishon v. King & Spaulding*, 467 U.S. 69 (1984).

39. *Meritor Savings Bank, FSB v. Vinson*, 477 U.S. 57 (1986).

40. *California Fed. S. & L. Ass'n. v. Guerra*, 479 U.S. 272, 289 (1987).

CHAPTER 19 *The Women's Suffrage Movement and Its Aftermath*

* An earlier version of this was published as Sandra Day O'Connor, "The History of the Women's Suffrage Movement," *Vanderbilt Law Review* 49 (1996), p. 657.

1. See generally Olivia Coolidge, *Women's Rights: The Suffrage Movement in America, 1848–1920* (New York: Dutton, 1966); and Eleanor Flexner, *Century of Struggle: The Woman's Rights Movement in the United States* (Cambridge, Mass.: Belknap Press of Harvard University, 1975).

2. Elizabeth Cady Stanton, *Eighty Years and More* (1898), pp. 147–148 (quoted in Flexner, *Century of Struggle*, pp. 73–74).

3. Quoted in Flexner, *Century of Struggle*, p. 77.

4. *Congressional Globe*, 39th Cong., 1st sess., May 10, 1866, 2539 (emphasis added); Benjamin B. Kendrick, *Journal of the Joint Committee of Fifteen on Reconstruction: 39th Congress, 1865–1867* (New York: Columbia University, 1914), p. 116.

5. Elizabeth Frost and Kathryn Cullen DuPont, *Women's Suffrage in America: An Eyewitness History* (New York: Facts on File, 1992), p. 172.

6. *Minor v. Happersett*, 88 U.S. 162 (1875).

7. Joan Hoff, *Law, Gender, and Injustice: A Legal History of U.S. Women* (New York: New York University Press, 1991), p. 157.

8. Coolidge, *Women's Rights*, p. 63.

9. *Congressional Record*, 51st Cong., 1st sess., June 26, 1890, 21 (statement of Senator John H. Reagan).

10. Carrie Chapman Catt and Nettie Rogers Shuler, *Woman Suffrage and Politics: The Inner Story of the Suffrage Movement* (Seattle: University of Washington Press, 1969), p. 177.

11. Coolidge, *Women's Rights*, p. 99.

12. Grover Cleveland, "Would Woman Suffrage Be Unwise?" *Ladies' Home Journal*, Oct. 1905, p. 7.

13. A. Elizabeth Taylor, "Tennessee: The Thirty-sixth State," in *Votes for Women! The Woman Suffrage Movement in Tennessee, the South, and the Nation*, ed. Marjorie Spruill Wheeler (Knoxville: University of Tennessee Press, 1995), pp. 53, 64–66.

14. M. Margaret Conway, *Political Participation in the United States*, 2d ed. (Washington, D.C.: Congressional Quarterly Press, 1991), p. 9.

15. Susan Ware, *Beyond Suffrage: Women in the New Deal* (Wilmington, Del.: Scholarly Resources, 1981), pp. 56, 120.

16. George H. Gallup, *The Gallup Poll: Public Opinion, 1935–1971* (New York: Random House, 1972), p. 39.

17. United Nations, *The World's Women 1995: Trends and Statistics* (1995), p. 129.

18. See David Margolick, "Women's Milestone: Majority on Minnesota Court," *New York Times*, Feb. 22, 1991, p. B16.

19. See, e.g., *California Fed. S. & L. Ass'n. v. Guerra*, 479 U.S. 22, 289 (1987) (upholding California's pregnancy disability leave statute).

20. American Bar Association, Commission for Women in the Profession, "A Snapshot of Women in the Law in the Year 2000"; Center for American Women and Politics, "Fact Sheet: Women in the U.S. Congress 2000," "Fact Sheet: Women in State Legislatures 2000," "Fact Sheet: Women in Elective Office 2000," "Fact Sheet: Statewide Elective Executive Women 2000"; Dorothy French, "Facts About Women and the Law," DCBA brief online, *http://www.dcba.org/brief/octissue/1999/art 81099.htm* (visited Oct. 10, 2000).

21. Republic of South Africa, *House of Assembly Debates (Hansard)*, vol. 15, col. 6243, May 18, 1965, quoted in Helen Suzman, *In No Uncertain Terms* (New York: Knopf, 1993), p. 83. Cf. id. at 102 (another National party M.P., reacting to Suzman's criticism of an extension of the reviled pass laws: "When the Hon. Member gets up in the House, she reminds me of a cricket in a thorn tree when it is very dry in the bushveld. His chirping makes you deaf but the tune remains the same, year in and year out.").

CHAPTER 20 *Women in Judging*

1. Elizabeth K. Maurer, "The Sphere of Carrie Burnham Kilgore," *Temple Law Review* 65 (1992), pp. 827, 833, quoting letter from Carrie B. Kilgore to Margaret Klingelsmith (1902).

2. Ibid., p. 849.

3. Ibid.

4. Karen Berger Morello, "Bar Admission Was Rough for 19th Century Women," *New York Law Journal* 189 (May 13, 1983), p. 19.

5. Virginia Elwood-Akers, "Clara Shortridge Foltz, California's First Woman Lawyer," *Pacific Historian* 28 (1984), pp. 23, 25.

6. Faye Dambrot and Barbara Vassel, "Women Lawyers: The Employment Status of Their Mothers and the Role Models They Select," *Psychological Reports* 52 (1983), pp. 27, 30.

7. *Judicature*, Dec./Jan. 1982, p. 292, quoting "Women on Texas Supreme Court Bench," *Law Student* 2 (Apr. 1, 1925), p. 3.

8. "Burnita Matthews, 93, Dies, First Woman Federal Trial Judge," *Washington Post*, Apr. 27, 1988.

9. Learned Hand, *The Bill of Rights* (Cambridge, Mass.: Harvard University Press, 1958), p. 77.

10. Learned Hand, *The Spirit of Liberty* (New York: Knopf, 1952), p. 41.

11. Suzanna Sherry, "Civic Virtue and the Feminine Voice in Constitutional Adjudication," *Virginia Law Review* 72 (1986), p. 543.

12. Judith Resnik, "On the Bias: Feminist Reconsiderations of the Aspirations of Our Judges," *Southern California Law Review* 61 (1988), pp. 1877, 1912.

13. *In re Application of Mrs. C. B. Kilgore, Weekly Notes of Cases* 14 (Phila. Ct. of Common Pleas 1884), pp. 255, 256–257.

14. "United States Supreme Court Justice Ruth Bader Ginsburg Address: Remarks for California Women Lawyers, Sept. 22, 1994," *Pepperdine Law Review* 22 (1994), pp. 4–5.

15. Judge Patricia Wald, "Remarks at the National Association of Women Judges Conference," Scottsdale, Ariz., Oct. 1, 1994.

16. See David Margolick, "Women's Milestone: Majority on Minnesota Court," *New York Times*, Feb. 22, 1991, p. B16.

17. Ellen Goodman, "When Mars Eclipses Venus," *Boston Globe*, Mar. 12, 1995, p. 73.

CHAPTER 21 *Women in Power*

1. John Gruhl, Cassia Spohn, and Susan Welch, "Women as Policymakers: The Case of Trial Judges," *American Journal of Political Science* 25 (1981), p. 308.

2. Frieda Gehlen, "Women Members of Congress: A Distinctive Role," in *A Portrait of Marginality: The Political Behavior of American Women*, eds. Marianne Githens and Jewel Prestage (New York: D. McKay Co., 1977).

3. Gruhl, Spohn, and Welch, "Policymakers."

4. Kristin Choo, "Moving into the Driver's Seat," *American Bar Association Journal*, June 2001, p. 84.

5. Elizabeth Holtzman and Shirley Williams, "Women in the Political World: Observations," *Daedalus*, Fall 1987, p. 25.

6. "100 Most Powerful Women," *Washingtonian Magazine*, Sept. 1989, p. 132.

7. Stephen Breyer, "Commencement Address," Stanford University, June 18, 1997, available at *http://www.stanford.edu/dept/news/report/news/june18/breyer1.htm*.

CHAPTER 22 *Organization and Structure of the American Judicial System*

1. U.S. Constitution, art. 1, sec. 3.

2. U.S. Constitution, art. 6, cl. 2.

CHAPTER 23 *Juries: Problems and Solutions*

* An earlier version of this was published as Sandra Day O'Connor, "Juries: They May Be Broken, but We Can Fix Them," *Federal Law* 44 (1997), p. 20.

1. Mark Twain, *Roughing It* (New York: Library of America, 1984), p. 782.

2. U.S. Constitution, amend. 6.

3. Most of the historical material here is taken from Valerie P. Hans and Neil Vidmar, *Judging the Jury* (New York: Plenum Press, 1986), and Albert W. Alschuler and Andrew G. Deiss, "A Brief History of the Criminal Jury in the United States," *University of Chicago Law Review* 61 (1994), p. 867.

4. 124 Eng. Rep. 1006 (1670); 6 *Howell's State Trials* 999 (1670).

5. See Alschuler and Deiss, "Brief History," p. 884, citing Leon F. Litwack, *North of Slavery: The Negro in the Free States* (Chicago: University of Chicago Press, 1961), p. 94.

6. Massachusetts *Statutes* 234, sec. 1A; see also *Commissioner v. Morgan*, 339 N.E. 2d 723 (1975).

7. *Hoyt v. Florida*, 368 U.S. 57 (1961).

8. *Taylor v. Louisiana*, 419 U.S. 522 (1975).

9. See Stephen J. Adler, *The Jury: Trial and Error in the American Courtroom* (New York: Time Books, 1994), p. 54.

10. See Joel Achenbach, "Jury Selection Could Be Key for Simpson; Consultants Helping Both Sides Seek Edge," *Washington Post*, Sept. 26, 1994, p. A1.

11. Michael Fleeman, "Prospective Simpson Jurors Queried About Racial Views, Knife Collections," Associated Press, Sept. 30, 1994.

12. See generally Jeffrey B. Abramson, *We, the Jury: The Jury System and the Ideal of Democracy* (New York: Basic Books, 1994), ch. 4, and the studies cited there on p. 281, n. 10.

13. See Anthony Lewis, "Abroad at Home: Mocking Justice," *New York Times*, Dec. 12, 1994, p. A19. ("The way juries are selected in this country, in high-profile cases especially, is outrageously expensive and damaging to respect for law.")

14. Twain, *Roughing It*, p. 782.

15. See Rori Sherman, "Gripes Are Changing Jury Duty," *National Law Journal*, Aug. 2, 1993, p. 14.

16. Alexis de Tocqueville, *Democracy in America*, vol. 1 (New York: Schocken Books, 1961), pp. 336–337.

17. See B. Michael Dann, "'Learning Lessons' and 'Speaking Rights': Creating Educated and Democratic Juries," *Indiana Law Journal* 68 (1993), pp. 1246–1247.

18. Jan Hoffman, "New York Casts for Solutions to Gaping Holes in Juror Net," *New York Times*, Sept. 26, 1993, sec. 1, pp. 1, 44.

19. Tocqueville, *Democracy in America*, p. 339.

20. Hans and Vidmar, *Judging the Jury*, p. 48.

21. Criminal Justice Act, 1988, c. 33, sec. 118(1) (Eng.).

22. See Hans and Vidmar, *Judging the Jury*, p. 48.

23. See, e.g., Jeffrey Rosen, "Jurymandering: A Case Against Peremptory Challenges," *New Republic*, Nov. 30, 1992, p. 15; Lewis, "Abroad"; H. Lee Sarokin and Thomas Munsterman, "Recent Innovations in Jury Trial Procedures," in *Verdict: Assessing the Civil Jury System*, ed. Robert E. Litan (Washington, D.C.: Brookings Institution, 1993); *Batson v. Kentucky*, 476 U.S. 79, 102 (1986) (Marshall, J., concurring).

24. Twain, *Roughing It*, p. 783.

25. *Johnson v. Louisiana*, 406 U.S. 356 (1972) (9–3 acceptable); *Burch v. Louisiana*, 441 U.S. 130 (1979) (5–1 not acceptable).

26. See Oregon Constitution, art. I, sec. 11 (10 of 12 permissible, except for murder); Louisiana Constitution, art. I, sec. 17 (10 of 12 permissible, except for capital crimes).

27. *Criminal Justice Act of 1967*, ch. 80, sec. 13 (1); see Abramson, *We, the Jury*, p. 180.

28. See, e.g., Abramson, *We, the Jury*, ch. 5.

CHAPTER 24 *Professionalism*

* An earlier version of this was published as Sandra Day O'Connor, "Professionalism," *Oregon Law Review* 78 (1999), p. 385, and Sandra Day O'Connor, "Professionalism," *Washington University Law Quarterly* 76 (1998), p. 5.

1. David Margolick, "Law: At the Bar," *New York Times*, Aug. 17, 1990, p. B5.

2. Nancy McCarthy, "Pessimism for the Future: Given a Second Chance, Half of the State's Attorneys Would Not Become Lawyers," *California State Bar Journal*, Nov. 1994, p. 1.

3. Michael Asimow, "Bad Lawyers in the Movies," *Nova Law Review* 24 (2000), pp. 533, 577.

4. Quoted in Douglas W. Hillman, "Professionalism—A Plea for Action!" *Michigan Business Journal* 69 (1990), pp. 894, 895.

5. *Nix v. Whiteside*, 475 U.S. 157 (1986).

6. This concept, although not this language, can be found in Georg Wilhelm Friedrich Hegel, *Philosophy of Right*, trans. T. M. Knox (Oxford: Clarendon Press, 1953), paras. 260–262.

7. Sam Benson, "Why I Quit Practicing Law," *Newsweek*, Nov. 4, 1991, p. 10.

8. Katherine Schwett, "Law Too Tension-filled, Survey of Lawyers Show," *Chicago Daily Law Bulletin*, May 21, 1990, p. 1.

9. Ginny Carroll and David A. Kaplan, "How's Your Lawyers' Left Jab?" *Newsweek*, Feb. 26, 1991, p. 70.

10. See John W. Frost II, "The Topic Is Civility—You Got a Problem with That?" *Florida Business Journal*, Jan. 1997, p. 6.

11. William Shakespeare, *The Taming of the Shrew*, act I, sc. 2.

12. Oliver Wendell Homes, "William Crowinshield Endicott" (Nov. 24, 1900), in *The Occasional Speeches of Oliver Wendell Holmes*, ed. Mark DeWolfe Howe (Cambridge, Mass.: Belknap Press of Harvard University, 1962), p. 127.

13. Frost, "Civility."

14. See John Koslov, "Courtly Behavior: Observing Decorum Is Not Just Good Manners—It's Successful Advocacy," *California Law* 54 (July 1990), pp. 54, 56; see also Gary Taylor, "Rambo or Dumbo?" *National Law Journal*, May 7, 1990, p. 7 (questioning the efficacy of an attorney's aggressive tactics).

15. See *Shapero v. Kentucky Bar Assn.*, 486 U.S. 466, 488–489 (1988) (O'Connor, J., dissenting) (emphasis added).

16. Legal Services Corp., *Serving the Civil Legal Needs of Low-Income Americans: A Special Report to Congress*, Apr. 30, 2000, p. 12.

17. Oliver Wendell Holmes, "The Path of the Law," *Harvard Law Review* 10 (1897), pp. 457, 478.

CHAPTER 25 *Broadening Our Horizons*

* An earlier version of this was published as Sandra Day O'Connor, "Broadening Our Horizons," *Federal Law* 45 (1998), p. 20.

1. 304 U.S. 64 (1938).

2. 9 Ex. 341, 156 Eng. Rep. 145 (1854).

CHAPTER 26 *Shield of Freedom: The American Constitution and Its Court*

1. Abraham Lincoln, "Speech at Kalamazoo, Michigan" (Aug. 27, 1856), in *The Collected Works of Abraham Lincoln*, vol. 2, ed. Roy P. Basler (New Brunswick, N.J.: Rutgers University Press, 1953), p. 366.

2. John Milton, "Samson Agonistes," in *The Complete Poems of John Milton* (New York: P. F. Collier, 1909), p. 419.

3. *Marbury v. Madison*, 1 Cranch 137 (1803).

4. Id. at p. 177.

5. Alexis de Tocqueville, *Democracy in America*, vol. 1 (New York: Schocken Books, 1961), p. 106.

6. U.S. Constitution, art. 3, sec. 1.

7. U.S. Census Bureau, *Statistical Abstract of the United States* (Washington, D.C.: Government Printing Office, 2000), p. 13 (showing 27.3 percent of total population over age fifty in 1999).

8. Cf. id. at 7, 416.

9. U.S. Census Bureau, *Statistical Abstract of the United States* (Washington, D.C.: Government Printing Office, 2000), p. 13; Jonathan Glater, "Women Are Close to Being Majority of Law Students," *New York Times*, Mar. 26, 2001, p. A1.

10. *Bush v. Gore*, 531 U.S. 98 (2000).

11. 347 U.S. 483 (1954).

12. Federal Rule of Civil Procedure 23.

13. T. S. Eliot, *Shakespeare and the Stoicism of Seneca* (London: Published for the Shakespeare Association by H. Milford, Oxford University Press, 1927), p. 8.

14. Alfredo Corchado, "Winner Promises Reform," *Dallas Morning News*, July 3, 2000, p. 1A.

15. *Proceedings and Debates of the Virginia State Convention of 1829–30* (1830), p. 616.

CHAPTER 27 *The Life of the Law: Principles of Logic and Experience from the United States*

1. Charles de Montesquieu, *The Spirit of Laws,* trans. T. Nugent (Cincinnati: R. Clarke & Co.; 1st French ed. Geneva, 1748).

2. Dwight D. Eisenhower, "Attributed Remark," quoted in Henry J. Abraham, *Justices and Presidents: A Political History of Appointments to the Supreme Court* (New York: Oxford University Press, 1974), p. 246.

3. Lawyers Committee for Human Rights, "Lawyer to Lawyer Network," Nov. 1993, p. 78.

4. Centre for the Independence of Judges and Lawyers, *Attacks on Justice: The Harassment and Persecution of Judges and Lawyers,* ed. Mona Rishmawi (Chêne-Bougeries/Geneva, Switzerland: Centre for the Independence of Judges and Lawyers of the International Commission of Jurists, 1993), pp. 163–164.

5. 347 U.S. 483 (1954).

6. Thomas Jefferson, "A Bill for Establishing Religious Freedom" (1779), in *Papers of Thomas Jefferson,* vol. 2, ed. Julian P. Boyd (Princeton, N.J.: Princeton University Press, 1950), p. 546.

7. "Out of the Frying Pan, Into Fire," *Economist,* Apr. 2, 1994, p. 49.

8. Amnesty International, *Romania: Broken Commitments to Human Rights* (New York, May 1995), p. 8.

9. 1 *Annals of Congress* (1834), 437.

10. See generally Warren E. Burger, "The Interdependence of Judicial and Journalistic Independence," *Georgetown Law Journal* 63 (1975), p. 1195.

11. J. Skelly Wright, "Fair Trial—Free Press," in *Federal Rules Decisions* 38, pp. 435, 436 (remarks to annual meeting of the Bar Association of the Seventh Federal Circuit, Chicago, Ill., May 11, 1965).

12. Oliver Wendell Holmes, *The Common Law,* ed. Mark DeWolfe Howe (Boston: Little, Brown, 1963).

CHAPTER 28 *Through the Looking Glass and into the Crystal Ball*

1. James Madison, "Amendments to the Constitution," in *The Papers of James Madison,* vol. 12, eds. Robert A. Rutland et al. (Charlottesville, Va.: University Press of Virginia, 1973), pp. 196, 207 (speech to the House of Representatives, June 8, 1789).

2. Irving Brant, *The Bill of Rights: Its Origin and Meaning* (Indianapolis: Bobbs-Merrill, 1965), p. 337, quoting Senator Jacob M. Howard.

3. Joan Biskupic and Elder Witt, *The Supreme Court and Individual Rights* (Washington, D.C.: Congressional Quarterly, 1996), p. 1.

4. Melvin I. Urofsky, *The Continuity of Change: The Supreme Court and Individual Liberties 1953–1986* (Belmont, Calif.: Wadsworth Publishing Co., 1991), p. 24.

5. See Mary Ann Glendon, *Rights Talk: The Impoverishment of Political Discourse* (New York: Free Press, 1991), p. 4.

6. *New York Times Co. v. Sullivan,* 376 U.S. 254 (1964).

7. *Baker v. Carr,* 369 U.S. 186 (1962).

8. *Gray v. Sanders,* 372 U.S. 368 (1963).

9. *Mapp v. Ohio,* 367 U.S. 643 (1961).

10. *Gideon v. Wainwright,* 372 U.S. 335 (1963).

11. *Malloy v. Hogan,* 378 U.S. 1 (1964).

12. *Pointer v. Texas,* 380 U.S. 400 (1965).

13. *Klopfer v. North Carolina,* 386 U.S. 213 (1967).

14. *Duncan v. Louisiana,* 391 U.S. 145 (1968).

15. *Benton v. Maryland,* 395 U.S. 784 (1969).

16. 410 U.S. 113 (1973).

17. See, e.g., *Reed v. Reed,* 404 U.S. 71 (1971).

18. 347 U.S. 483 (1954).

19. 163 U.S. 537 (1896).

20. *Korematsu v. United States,* 323 U.S. 214 (1944).

21. See *Adarand Constructors, Inc. v. Pena,* 515 U.S. 200, 224 (1995).

22. See Glendon, *Rights Talk,* p. 16.

23. Thomas Jefferson, "Inaugural Address," in *The Life and Selected Writings of Thomas Jefferson* (New York: Modern Library, 1944), p. 323.

24. Michael Kantor, *The President's Trade Policy Agenda: Review and Outlook* (Washington, D.C.: Office of U.S. Trade Rep., 1996), p. 1.

25. David A. Gantz, "Introduction to the World Trading System and Trade Laws Protecting U.S. Business," *Whittier Law Review* 18 (1997), pp. 289, 290.

26. See Jonathan I. Charney, "Third Party Dispute Settlement and International Law," *Columbia Journal of Transnational Law* 36 (1997), pp. 65, 69.

27. *Breard v. Greene,* 523 U.S. 371 (1998) (*per curiam*).

28. John Kenneth Galbraith, *A Journey Through Economic Time* (Boston: Houghton Mifflin, 1994), p. 242.

EPILOGUE

1. Amy Wallace and David Ferrell, "Verdicts Greeted with Outrage and Disbelief Reaction," *Los Angeles Times,* Apr. 30, 1992, p. A1 (describing public reaction to acquittal in Rodney King police-brutality case).

Bibliography

Henry J. Abraham, *The Judicial Process: An Introductory Analysis of the Courts of the United States, England and France,* 7th ed., 74 (New York: Oxford University Press, 1998).

————, *Justices and Presidents: A Political History of Appointments to the Supreme Court,* 246 (New York: Oxford University Press, 1974).

————, *Justices and Presidents: A Political History of Appointments to the Supreme Court,* 3rd ed., 70 (New York: Oxford University Press, 1992).

Jeffrey B. Abramson, *We, the Jury: The Jury System and the Ideal of Democracy,* ch. 4 (New York: BasicBooks, 1994).

Achenbach, *Jury Selection Could Be Key for Simpson: Consultants Helping Both Sides Seek Edge, Washington Post,* Sept. 26, 1994, at a1.

John Adams, *A Defence of the Constitutions of Government of the United States of America Against the Attack of M. Turgot, in His Letter to Dr. Price, Dated the Twenty-second Day of March, 1778, in The Works of John Adams,* 404 (Boston: Little, Brown & Co., 1851).

Stephen J. Adler, *The Jury: Trial and Error in the American Courtroom,* 54 (New York: Times Books, 1994).

Albert W. Alschuler and Andrew G. Deiss, "A Brief History of the Criminal Jury in the United States," 61 *U. Chi. L. Rev.* 867 (1994).

American Bar Association, *The Commission for Women in the Profession,* "A Snapshot of Women in the Law in the Year 2000"; Center for American Women and Politics, *Fact Sheet: Women in the U.S. Congress 2000;* Center for American Women and Politics, *Fact Sheet: Women in State Legislatures 2000;* Center for American Women and Politics, *Fact Sheet: Women in Elective Office 2000;* Center for American Women and Politics, *Fact Sheet: Statewide Elective Executive Women 2000;* French, Dorothy, "Facts About Women and the Law," DCBA brief online, *http://www.dcba.org/brief/octissue/1999/art 81099.htm* (visited Oct. 10, 2000).

American Bar Association, *Perceptions of the U.S. Justice System*, 23 (1999).

Amnesty International, *Romania: Broken Commitments to Human Rights*, 8 (May 1995).

Donald F. Anderson, "Building National Consensus: The Career of William Howard Taft," 68 *U. Cin. L. Rev.* 323, 328 (2000).

Michael Asimow, *Bad Lawyers in the Movies*, 24, *Nova L. Rev.* 533, 577 (2000).

Leonard Baker, *Back to Back: The Duel Between FDR and the Supreme Court* (New York: Macmillan, 1967).

———, *John Marshall: A Life in Law*, 745 (New York: Macmillan, 1974).

Liva Baker, *The Justice from Beacon Hill: The Life and Times of Oliver Wendell Holmes*, 228 (New York: HarperCollins, 1991).

John Bartlett, *Familiar Quotations*, 509 (Boston: Little, Brown & Co., 1982).

Paul M. Bator, "Judiciary Act of 1789," in *Encyclopedia of the American Constitution*, 1075 (New York: Macmillan, 1986).

Hugo Adam Bedau and Michael L. Radelet, "Miscarriages of Justice in Potentially Capital Cases," 40, *Stan. L. Rev.* 21, 115 (1987).

San Benson, "Why I Quit Practicing Law," *Newsweek*, Nov. 4, 1991, 10.

Joan Biskupic and Elder Witt, *Guide to the U.S. Supreme Court*, 846–847, 849 (Washington, D.C.: Congressional Quarterly, 1997).

———, *The Supreme Court and Individual Rights*, 1 (Washington, D.C.: Congressional Quarterly, 1996).

David S. Bogen, "The Free Speech Metamorphosis of Mr. Justice Holmes," 11 *Hofstra L. Rev.* 97 (1982).

Irving Brant, *The Bill of Rights: Its Origin and Meaning* (quoting Senator Jacob M. Howard), 337 (Indianapolis, IN: Bobbs-Merrill, 1965).

William J. Brennan, Jr., "In Defense of Dissents," 37, *Hastings L. J.* 427 (1986).

Stephen Breyer, "Commencement Address at Stanford University" (June 18, 1997), available at *http://www.stanford.edu/dept/news/report/news/june18/breyer1.htm*.

Richard D. Brown, "Shays' Rebellion and the Ratification of the Constitution in Massachusetts," in Beeman, Botein, and Carter, supra note 1, at 113, 123 (1987).

Warren E. Burger, *Delivery of Justice*, 187, 190–93 (1990).

———, Foreword to Catherine D. Bowen, *Miracle at Philadelphia*, x (Boston: Little, Brown & Co., 1966).

———, "The Interdependence of Judicial and Journalistic Independence," 63 *Geo. L. J.* 1195 (1975).

———, "Lawrence H. Cooke: A Tireless Judicial Administrator," 53, *Fordham L. Rev.* 147 (1984).

———, "The Legal Profession Is a Monopoly," address before the American Inns of Court (June 1, 1990).

———, "The State of Judiciary—1970," 56 *A.B.A.J.* 929, 932 (1970).

"Burnita Matthews, 93, Dies, First Woman Federal Trial Judge," *Washington Post* (obituaries), Apr. 27, 1988.

Harold H. Burton, "The Cornerstone of Constitutional Law: The Extraordinary Case of Marbury v. Madison," 36, *A.B.A.J.* 805 (Oct. 1950).

Benjamin N. Cardozo, "Mr. Justice Holmes," 44 *Harv. L. Rev.* 682, 687 (1931).

Ginny Carroll and David A. Kaplan, "How's Your Lawyer's Left Jab?," *Newsweek*, Feb. 26, 1991.

Carrie Chapman Catt and Nettie Rogers Shuler, *Woman Suffrage and Politics; The Inner Story of the Suffrage Movement*, 177 (Seattle: University of Washington Press, 1969).

Bruce Catton, *The Army of the Potomac: Glory Road*, 223 (Garden City, NY: Doubleday, 1952).

Centre for the Independence of Judges and Lawyers, *Attacks on Justice: The Harassment and Persecution of Judges and Lawyers*, 163–164 (Mona Rishmawi, ed., Geneva, 1993).

Jonathan I. Charney, "Third Party Dispute Settlement and International Law," 36, *Colum. J. Transnat'l. L.* 65, 69 (1997).

Kristin Choo, "Moving into the Driver's Seat," *A.B.A.J.*, June 2001, at 84.

Winston S. Churchill, *The Birth of Britain*, 257 (London: Cassell & Co., 1956).

Grover Cleveland, "Would Woman Suffrage Be Unwise?" *Ladies' Home Journal*, 7 (Oct. 1905).

Jeremy Cohen, *Congress Shall Make No Law: Oliver Wendell Holmes, the First Amendment, and Judicial Decision-Making* (Ames, IA: Iowa State University Press, 1989).

M. Margaret Conway, *Political Participation in the United States*, 2nd ed., 9 (Washington, D.C.: CQ Press, 1991).

Olivia Coolidge, *Women's Rights: The Suffrage Movement in America, 1848–1920* (New York: Dutton, 1966).

Alfredo Corchado, "Winner Promises Reform," *Dallas Morning News,* July 3, 2000, at 1A.

Faye Dambrot and Barbara Vassel, "Women Lawyers: The Employment Status of Their Mothers and the Role Models They Select," 52, *Psych. Rep.* 27, 30 (1983).

B. Michael Dann, " 'Learning Lessons' and 'Speaking Rights': Creating Educated and Democratic Juries," 68 *Ind. L. J.* 1229, 1246–1247 (1993).

David Herbert Donald, *Lincoln,* 297–99 (New York: Simon & Schuster, 1995).

Edward Dumbauld, *The Bill of Rights and What It Means Today,* 3 (Norman, OK: University of Oklahoma Press, 1957).

T. S. Eliot, *Shakespeare and the Stoicism of Seneca,* 8 (London: Published for the Shakespeare Association by H. Milford, Oxford University Press, 1927).

J. Elliot, *The Debates in the Several State Conventions on the Adoption of the Federal Constitution,* 8 (Philadelphia: Lippincott, 1876).

Virginia Elwood-Akers, *Clara Shortridge Foltz, California's First Woman Lawyer,* 28 Pacific Historian 23, 25 (1984).

Lee Epstein, *et al.,* "The Supreme Court Compendium," 88–93 (table 2-9) (Washington, D.C.: *Congressional Quarterly,* 2nd ed., 1996).

Paul Finkelman, "Civil Liberties and Civil War: The Great Emancipator as Civil Libertarian," 91, *Mich. L. Rev.* 1353, 1354 (1993).

John Fiske, *The Critical Period in American History, 1783–1789,* 4th ed., 339 (Boston: Houghton-Mifflin, 1889).

Michael Fleeman, "Prospective Simpson Jurors Queried About Racial Views, Knife Collections," Associated Press, Sept. 30, 1994.

Eleanor Flexner, *Century of Struggle: The Woman's Rights Movement in the United States* (Cambridge, MA: Belknap Press of Harvard University Press, 1975).

John P. Frank, "Judicial Appointments: Controversy and Accomplishment," in *Supreme Court Historical Society Yearbook 1977,* at 85.

Felix Frankfurter, "Chief Justices I Have Known," 39, *Va. L. Rev.* 883, 898 (1953).

———, "Mr. Justice Holmes and the Constitution," 41, *Harv. L. Rev.* 121, 124 (1927).

Felix Frankfurter and James M. Landis, *The Business of the Supreme Court,* 4 (New York: Macmillan, 1927).

Lawrence M Friedman, *A History of American Law,* 2nd ed., 557–563 (New York: Simon & Schuster, 1985).

Elizabeth Frost and Kathryn Cullen DuPont, *Women's Suffrage in America: An Eyewitness History*, 172 (New York: Facts on File, 1992).

John W. Frost II, "The Topic is Civility—You Got a Problem with That?" 71, *Fla. B. J.*, Jan. 1997.

John Kenneth Galbraith, *A Journey Through Economic Time*, 242 (Boston: Houghton-Mifflin, 1994).

George H. Gallup, *The Gallup Poll: Public Opinion, 1935–1971*, 39 (New York: Random House, 1972).

David A. Gantz, "Introduction to the World Trading System and Trade Laws Protecting U.S. Business," 18, *Whittier L. Rev.* 289, 290 (1997).

Frieda Gehlen, "Women Members of Congress: A Distinctive Role," in Marianne Githens and Jewel Prestage, eds., *A Portrait of Marginality: The Political Behavior of American Women* (New York: D. McKay Co., 1977).

Jonathan Glater, "Women Are Close to Being Majority of Law Students," *New York Times*, Mar. 26, 2001, at A1.

Mary Ann Glendon, *Rights Talk: The Impoverishment of Political Discourse*, 4 (New York: Free Press, 1991).

Amy Goldstein, "Bush Curtails ABA Role in Selecting U.S. Judges," *Washington Post*, Mar. 23, 2001, at A1.

Ellen Goodman, "When Mars Eclipses Venus," *Boston Globe*, Mar. 12, 1995, at 73.

Thomas C. Grey, "Holmes and Legal Pragmatism," 41 *Stan. L. Rev.* 787, 850 (1989).

John Gruhl, Cassia Spohn, and Susan Welch, "Women as Policymakers: The Case of Trial Judges," 25 *Am. J. Polit. Sci.* 308 (1981).

Gerald Gunther, *Constitutional Law*, 13th ed., 1034–1076 (Westbury, NY: Foundation Press, 1997).

Learned Hand, *The Bill of Rights*, 77 (New York: Atheneum, 1958).

———, "How Far Is a Judge Free in Rendering a Decision?" in *The Spirit of Liberty*, 79, 84 (1959).

———, "Mr. Justice Holmes at Eighty-Five," in *The Spirit of Liberty*, 18, 21 (1959).

———, *The Spirit of Liberty*, 41 (New York: Knopf, 1952).

———, *The Spirit of Liberty*, 190 (New York: Knopf, 1960).

Valerie P. Hans and Neil Vidmar, *Judging the Jury* (New York: Plenum Press, 1986).

Hegel, *Philosophy of Right*, T. M. Knox, trans., 260–62 (Oxford: Clarendon Press, 1952).

Arthur D. Hellman, "The Supreme Court, the National Law, and the Selection of Cases for the Plenary Docket," 44, *U. Pitt. L. Rev.* 521, 598 (1983).

Douglas W. Hillman, "Professionalism—A Plea for Action!" 69, *Mich. B. J.*, Sept. 1990.

Joan Hoff, *Law, Gender, and Injustice: A Legal History of U. S. Women*, 62 (New York: New York University Press, 1991).

———, *Law, Gender, and Injustice: A Legal History of U.S. Women*, 157 (New York: New York University Press, 1991).

Oliver Wendell Holmes, *The Common Law*, 5, Mark DeWolfe Howe, ed. (1881) (Cambridge, MA: Belknap Press of Harvard University Press, 1963).

———, "John Marshall," in *Collected Legal Papers* 269 (1920, reprinted New York: P. Smith, 1952).

———, "The Path of the Law," 10, *Harv. L. Rev.* 457, 478 (1897).

Holmes-Laski Letters, 21, Mark DeWolfe Howe, ed. (Cambridge, MA: Harvard University Press, 1953).

J. C. Holt, *Magna Carta*, 2nd ed. (as translated from the original Latin text), 461 (Cambridge: Cambridge University Press, 1992)

Elizabeth Holtzman and Shirley Williams, "Women in the Political World: Observations," *Daedalus*, Fall 1987, at 25.

Charles Evans Hughes, *The Supreme Court of the United States: Its Foundations, Methods and Achievements: An Interpretation*, 67–68 (New York: Columbia University Press, 1928).

"In Re Application of Mrs. C. B. Kilgore," 14, *Weekly Notes of Cases* 255, 256–257 (Phila. Ct. of Common Pleas 1884).

Percival E. Jackson, *Dissent in the Supreme Court: A Chronology*, 21 (Norman, OK: University of Oklahoma Press, 1969).

J. Myron Jacobstein and Roy M. Mersky, *The Rejected: Sketches of the 26 Men Nominated for the Supreme Court but not Confirmed by the Senate*, 174–175 (Milpitas, CA: Toucan Valley Publications, 1993).

Thomas Jefferson, "A Bill for Establishing Religious Freedom, 1779," *Papers of Thomas Jefferson*, 2:546 (Julian P. Boyd, ed., 1950).

Thomas Jefferson, "Inaugural Address," *The Life and Selected Writings of Thomas Jefferson*, Adrienne Koch and William Peden, eds., 323 (New York: Modern Library, 1944).

John C. Jeffries, Jr., *Justice Lewis F. Powell, Jr. and the Era of Judicial Balance*, 562 (New York: C. Scribner's Sons, 1994).

Craig Joyce, "The Rise of the Supreme Court Reporter: An Institutional Perspective on Marshall Court Ascendancy," 83, *Mich. L. Rev.* 1291, 1295 (1985).

"Justice Black's Speech," *New York Times*, Oct. 2, 1937, at 1A.

Michael Kantor, *The President's Trade Policy Agenda—Review and Outlook*, 1 (1996).

Benjamin B. Kendrick, *The Journal of the Joint Committee of Fifteen on Reconstruction: 39th Congress, 1865–1867*, 116 (New York: Columbia University Press, 1914).

Samuel J. Konefsky, *The Legacy of Holmes and Brandeis*, 262 (New York: Macmillan, 1956).

John Koslov, "Courtly Behavior: Observing Decorum Is Not Just Good Manners—It's Successful Advocacy," *Cal. Law.*, July 1990.

Philip B. Kurland and Ralph Lerner, eds., *The Founders' Constitution*, 470 (Chicago: University of Chicago Press, 1987).

Lawyers Committee for Human Rights, *Lawyer to Lawyer Network*, 78 (Nov. 1993).

Richard J. Lazarus, "Restoring What's Environmental About Environmental Law in the Supreme Court," 47, *U.C.L.A. L. Rev.* 703, 787–811, App. C (2000).

Legal Services Corporation, *Serving the Civil Legal Needs of Low-Income Americans, A Special Report to Congress—April 30, 2000*, 12.

Anthony Lewis, "Abroad at Home: Mocking Justice," *New York Times*, Dec. 12, 1994, at A19.

———, *Gideon's Trumpet*, 202 (New York: Random House, 1964).

———, "In Memoriam: William J. Brennan, Jr.," 111, *Harv. L. Rev.* 29, 32 (1997).

Thomas T. Lewis and Richard L. Wilson, eds., *Encyclopedia of the U.S. Supreme Court*, 674 (Pasadena, CA: Salem Press, 2001).

Abraham Lincoln, "Letter to Matthew Birchard and Others" (June 29, 1863), 6, *The Collected Works of Abraham Lincoln*, 304 (Roy P. Basler, ed., 1953).

———, "Message to Congress in Special Session" (July 4, 1861), in *Abraham Lincoln: His Speeches and Writings*, 601 (Roy P. Basler, ed.), (Cleveland: World Publishing Co., 1946).

Robert E. Litan, ed., *Verdict: Assessing the Civil Jury System* (Washington, D.C.: Brookings Institution, 1993).

Leon F. Litwack, *North of Slavery: The Negro in the Free States*, 94 (Chicago: University of Chicago Press, 1961).

Karl Llewellyn, *The Common Law Tradition: Deciding Appeals*, 26 (Boston: Little, Brown & Co., 1960).

Belva Lockwood, "My Efforts to Become a Lawyer," reprinted in *Women in the American Economy, A Documentary History, 1675–1929*, 297–98 (W. Elliot Brownlee and Mary M. Brownlee, eds.) (New Haven: Yale University Press, 1976).

James Madison, "Amendments to the Constitution," 12, *The Papers of James Madison* 196, 207 (Robert A. Rutland, *et al.*, eds.) (Charlottesville, VA: University Press of Virginia, 1973).

———, "House of Representatives Debates—June 8, 1789," in Bernard Schwartz II, *The Bill of Rights: A Documentary History*, 1031–1032 (New York: Chelsea House Publishers, 1971).

Jackson Turner Main, *The Anti-Federalists: Critics of the Constitution, 1781–1788*, 286 (New York: Norton, 1961).

David Margolick, "Women's Milestone: Majority on Minnesota Court," *New York Times*, Feb. 22, 1991, at B16.

Alpheus Thomas Mason, *The Supreme Court from Taft to Warren*, 50 (Baton Rouge, LA: Louisiana State University Press, 1958).

———, *William Howard Taft: Chief Justice*, 223 (New York: Simon & Schuster, 1964).

Elizabeth K. Maurer, "The Sphere of Carrie Burnham Kilgore," 65, *Temp. L. Rev.* 827, 833 (1992), quoting letter from Carrie B. Kilgore to Margaret Klingelsmith (1902).

Nancy McCarthy, "Pessimism for the Future: Given a Second Chance, Half of the State's Attorneys Would not Become Lawyers," *Cal. St. B. J.*, Nov. 1994, at 1.

James M. McPherson, *Battle Cry of Freedom: The Civil War Era*, 494 n.8 (New York: Oxford University Press, 1988).

Roy M. Mersky and J. Myron Jacobstein, eds., *Supreme Court of the United States: Hearings and Reports on Successful and Unsuccessful Nomination of Supreme Court Justices by the Senate Judiciary Committee 1916–1975*, 6 (Buffalo, NY: W. S. Hein, Comp. 1977).

John Milton, "Samson Agonistes," in *The Complete Poems of John Milton*, 419 (1909).

Charles de Montesquieu, *The Spirit of Laws*, 174 (T. Nugent, trans.) (Cincinnati: Clarke, 1873; first French ed., Geneva 1748).

Karen Berger Morello, "Bar Admission Was Rough for Nineteenth-Century Women," 189, *N.Y.L.J.* 19 (May 13, 1983).

Walter F. Murphy, *et al.*, *American Constitutional Interpretation*, 776 (Mineola, NY: Foundation Press, 1986).

National Constitution Center, *NCC News and Events: National Poll* (1999), available at *http://www.constitutioncenter.org/sections/news/8b4.asp*.

Mark E. Neely, Jr., *The Fate of Liberty: Abraham Lincoln and Civil Liberties*, xv (New York: Oxford University Press, 1991).

Sandra Day O'Connor, "Broadening Our Horizons," 45, *Fed. Law* 20 (1998).

———, "The History of the Women's Suffrage Movement," 49, *Vand. L. Rev.* 657 (1996).

———, "The Judiciary Act of 1789 and the American Judicial Tradition," 59, *U. Cin. L. Rev.* 1 (1990).

———, "Juries: They May Be Broken, But We Can Fix Them," 44, *Fed. Law.* 20 (1997).

———, "The Legal Status of Women: The Journey Toward Equality," 15, *J. L. and Religion* 29 (2000).

———, "Professionalism" 76, *Wash. U. L. Q.* 5 (1998).

———, "Professionalism," 78, *Or. L. Rev.* 385 (1999)

———, "A Tribute to Lewis F. Powell, Jr.," 56, *Wash. and Lee L. Rev.* 4 (1999).

———, "A Tribute to Warren E. Burger," 22, *Wm. Mitchell L. Rev.* 7 (1996).

"Out of the Frying Pan, into Fire," *Economist*, Apr. 2, 1994, at 49.

Chester J. Pach, Jr., and Elmo Richardson, *The Presidency of Dwight D. Eisenhower*, 153 (Lawrence, KS: University Press of Kansas, 1991).

H. L. Pohlman, *Justice Oliver Wendell Holmes: Free Speech and the Living Constitution*, 1–2, 15 (n. 1) (New York: New York University Press, 1991).

Robert Post, "The Supreme Court Opinion as Institutional Practice: Dissent, Legal Scholarship and Decisionmaking in the Taft Court," 85, *Minn. L. Rev.* 1267, 1277 (2001).

Proceedings and Debates of the Virginia State Convention of 1829–30, 616 (Richmond, VA: S. Shepard for Ritchie and Cook, 1830).

Allen E. Ragan, *Chief Justice Taft*, 164 (Columbus, OH: The Ohio State Archaeological and Historical Society, 1938).

Lyn Ragsdale, *Vital Statistics on the Presidency: Washington to Clinton*, 422–29 (Washington, D.C.: Congressional Quarterly Books, rev. ed. 1998).

The Records of the Federal Convention of 1787 (Max Farrand, ed.), 563–64, 631–34 (New Haven: Yale University Press, 1911).

William H. Rehnquist, *Grand Inquests: The Historic Impeachments of Justice Samuel Chase and President Andrew Johnson*, 104 (New York: Morrow, 1992).

Judith Resnik, "On the Bias: Feminist Reconsiderations of the Aspirations of Our Judges," 61, *S. Cal. L. Rev.* 1877, 1912 (1988).

Deborah L. Rhode, *Justice and Gender: Sex Discrimination and the Law*, 20 (Cambridge, MA: Harvard University Press, 1989).

Franklin D. Roosevelt, "Address on Constitution Day" (1937), in *The Public Papers and Addresses of Franklin D. Roosevelt*, 359 (New York: Random House, 1941).

Jeffrey Rosen, "Jurymandering: A Case Against Peremptory Challenges," *The New Republic*, Nov. 30, 1992, at 15.

Clinton Rossiter, ed., *The Federalist No. 76*, 457 ((New York: New American Library, 1961).

Wiley Rutledge, *A Declaration of Legal Faith*, 6 (Lawrence, KS: University of Kansas Press, 1947).

Carl Sandburg, *Abraham Lincoln: The War Years*, 469 (New York: Harcourt, Brace & Co., 1939).

Katherine Schweit, "Law Too Tension-filled, Survey of Lawyers Shows," *Chi. Daily L. Bull.*, May 21, 1990.

William Shakespeare, *The Taming of the Shrew*, act I, sc. 2.

Rori Sherman, "Gripes Are Changing Jury Duty," *Natl. L. J.*, Aug. 2, 1993, at 14.

Suzanna Sherry, "Civic Virtue and the Feminine Voice in Constitutional Adjudication," 72, *Va. L. Rev.* 543 (1986).

Kenneth Starr, "William Howard Taft: The Chief Justice as Judicial Architect," 60, *U. Cin. L. Rev.* 963, 965 (1992).

Wallace Stegner, *Where the Bluebird Sings to the Lemonade Springs*, 9–10 (New York: Random House, 1992).

Herbert J. Storing, *The Complete Anti-Federalist*, 3–6 (Chicago: University of Chicago Press, 1981).

Helen Suzman, *In No Uncertain Terms*, 83 (New York: Knopf, 1993).

A. Elizabeth Taylor, "Tennessee: The Thirty-sixth State," in *Votes for Women!: The Woman Suffrage Movement in Tennessee, the South, and the Nation*, 53, 64–66 (Marjorie Spruill Wheeler, ed.) (Knoxville, TN: University of Tennessee Press, 1995).

Alfred, Lord Tennyson, *Locksley Hall* (1842).

James B. Thayer, "The Origin and Scope of the American Doctrine of Judicial Review," 7, *Harv. L. Rev.* 129, 156 (1893).

Francis Newton Thorpe, ed., "Fundamental Orders of Connecticut—1638–39," in *The Federal and State Constitutions*, 519 (Washington, DC: 1909).

Alexis de Tocqueville, *Democracy in America*, 330 (New York: Schocken Books, 1961).

Mark Twain, *Roughing It*, 782 (New York: Library of America, 1984).

United Nations, *The World's Women 1995: Trends and Statistics*, 129 (New York, 1995).

Melvin I. Urofsky, *The Continuity of Change: The Supreme Court and Individual Liberties 1953–1986*, 24 (Belmont, CA: Wadsworth Pub. Co., 1991).

U.S. Census Bureau, "Statistical Abstract of the United States," 13 (2000).

Judge Patricia Wald, "Remarks at the National Association of Women Judges Conference," Scottsdale, AZ (Oct. 1, 1994).

Amy Wallace and David Ferrell, "Verdicts Greeted with Outrage and Disbelief Reaction," *Los Angeles Times*, Apr. 30, 1992, at A1.

Susan Ware, *Beyond Suffrage: Women in the New Deal*, 56, 120 (Cambridge, MA: Harvard University Press, 1981).

Charles Warren, "New Light on the History of the Federal Judiciary Act of 1789," 37, *Harv. L. Rev.* 49, 52 (1923).

———, *The Supreme Court in United States History*, 178 (Boston: Little, Brown & Co., 1923).

———, *The Supreme Court in United States History*, rev. ed., 17 (Boston: Little, Brown & Co., 1937).

George Washington, "First Inaugural Address" (1789), in *The Inaugural Addresses of the Presidents*, 24 (Renzo D. Bowers, ed.) (St. Louis: Thomas Law Book Co., 1929).

Burton K. Wheeler and Paul F. Healy, *Yankee from the West: The Candid, Turbulent Life Story of the Yankee-born U. S. Senator from Montana, Burton K. Wheeler*, 339 (Garden City, NY: Doubleday, 1962).

E. B. White, *The Wild Flag: Editorials from* The New Yorker *on Federal World Government and Other Matters*, 31 (editorial of July 3, 1944) (Boston: Houghton-Mifflin, 1946).

G. E. White, *The American Judicial Tradition*, expanded ed., 9 (New York: Oxford University Press, 1988).

Oscar Wilde, *The Picture of Dorian Gray*, 2 (Oxford: Oxford University Press, 1999).

John Winthrop, *The History of New England from 1630 to 1649*, 160 (Boston: Phelps & Farnham, 1825).

Gordon S. Wood, "Interests and Disinterestedness in the Making of the Constitution," in Richard Beeman, Steven Botein, and Edward C. Carter II, *Beyond Confederation: Origins of the Constitution and American National Identity,* 69 (Chapel Hill, NC: University of North Carolina Press, 1987).

World Almanac and Book of Facts, 486 (2001).

J. Skelly Wright, "Fair Trial—Free Press," 38, *Federal Rules Decisions,* 435, 436 (remarks to annual meeting of the Bar Association of the Seventh Federal Circuit, Chicago, IL., May 11, 1965).

Photograph Credits

Index